# Those Not-So-Sweet Boys

## 6

YOKO NOGIRI

# contents

## characters

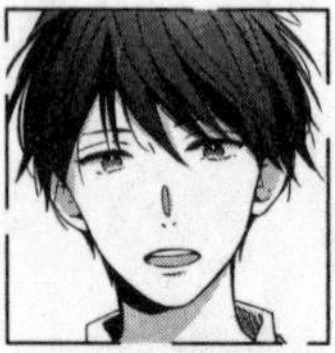

### REI ICHIJO

Heir to the Ichijo Conglomerate.
Lives alone in a fancy apartment.

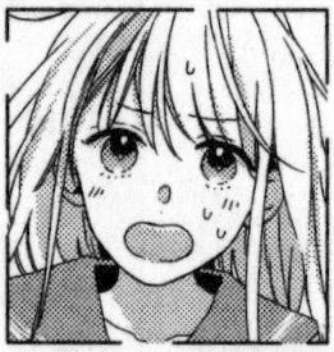

### MIDORI NANAMI

Attends high school on a scholarship to help with her family's finances.
Has Rei on her mind a lot.

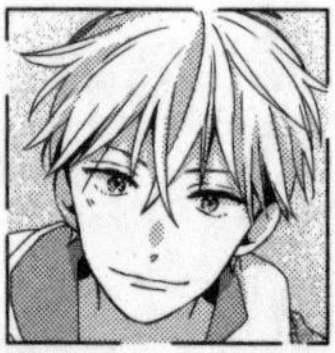

### CHIHIRO GOSHIMA

Successor to the Goshima gang.
Is used to the assumptions people make about him due to his family.

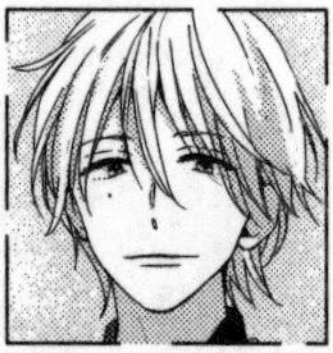

### YUKINOJO IEIRI

Son of a doctor. A good friend to Rei and Chihiro, and an overall nice person, but...

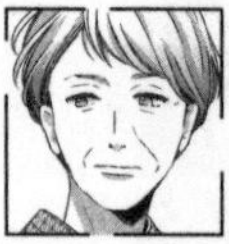

### YURIKO ICHIJO

Rei's grandmother who leads the Ichijo Conglomerate as its top executive.

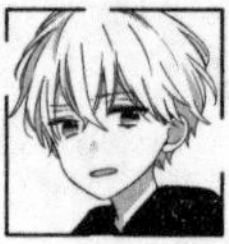

### KON NANAMI

Midori's beloved little brother who's in junior high school. A great cook, and super reliable to boot.

## story

When the school chairman catches Midori working a part-time job against school rules, she becomes a babysitter of sorts to the truants Rei, Yukinojo, and Chihiro. Her hard work pays off, they start going to school, and Midori develops a crush on Rei. After an eventful summer vacation and the school festival, Midori and Rei confess their feelings to each other and become a couple! ♥ Then, one day, Midori is tricked and "kidnapped," and she ends up joining Rei at his grandmother's birthday party! Overwhelmed by the reality that they live worlds apart, and pressured by Rei's grandmother, Midori starts to head home and is shocked to see that even Rei is now avoiding her...!

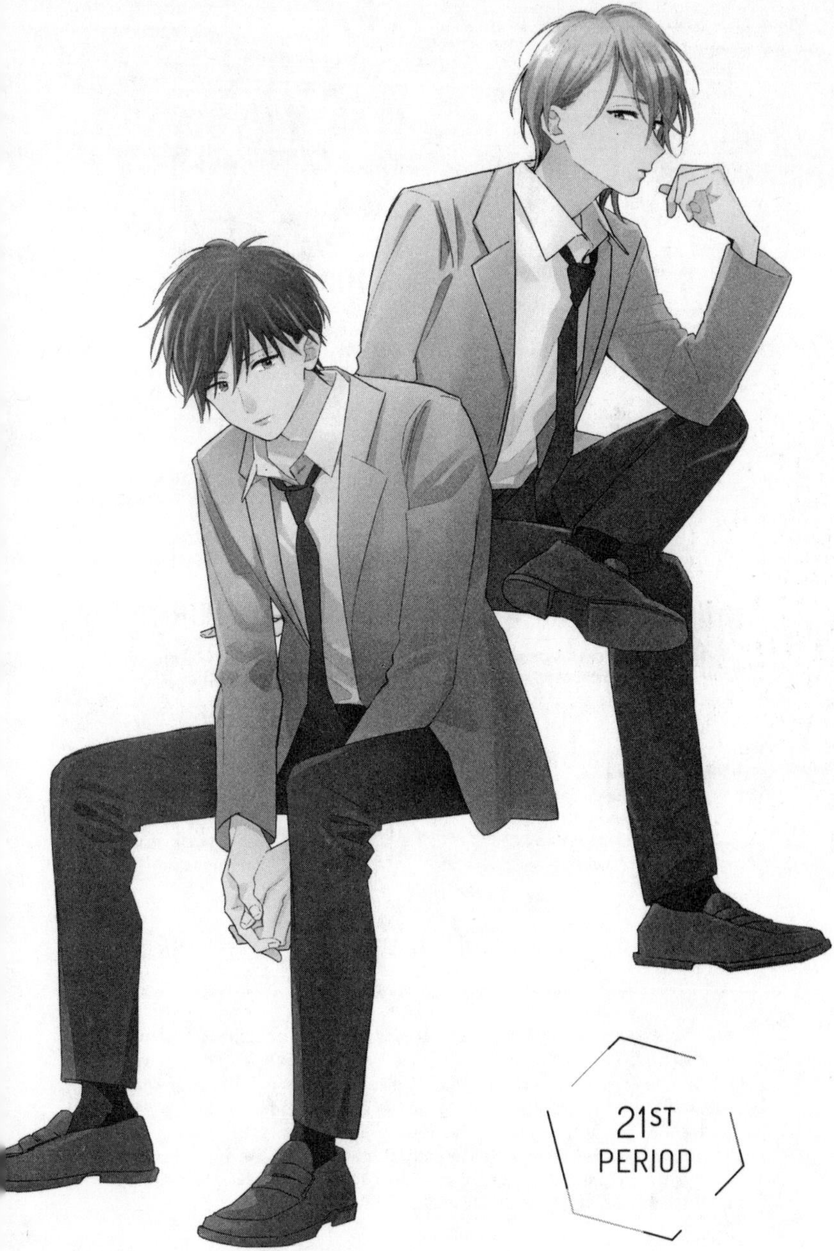

# 21ST PERIOD

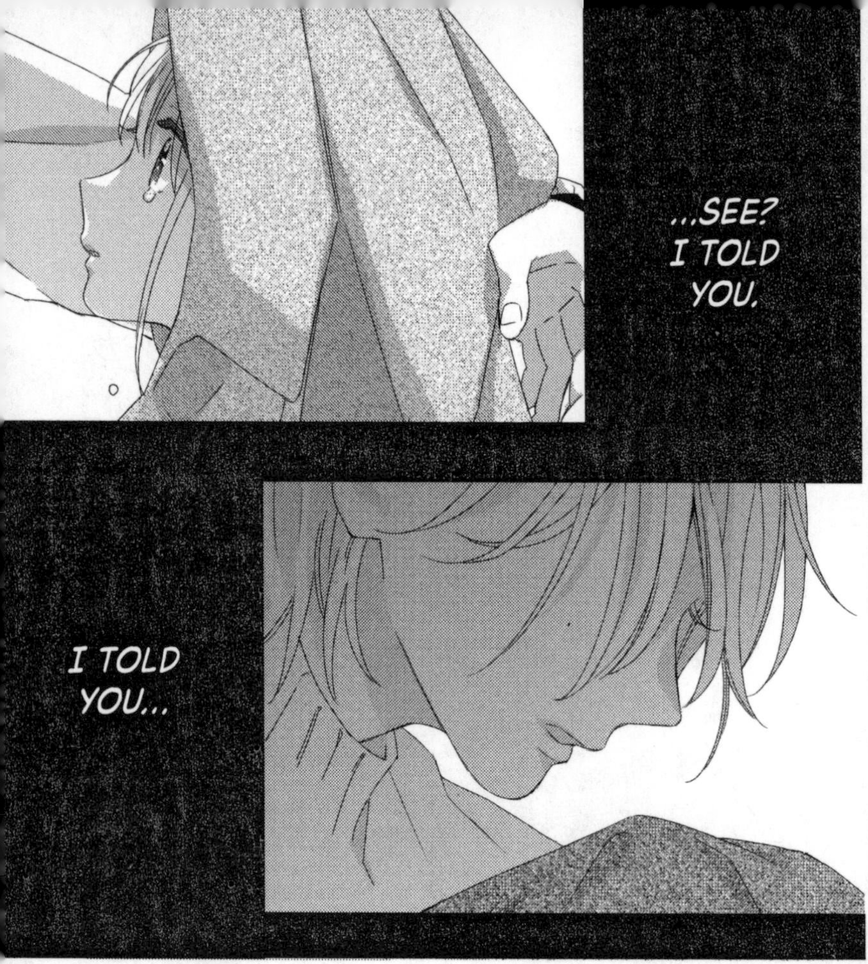
...SEE? I TOLD YOU.
I TOLD YOU...

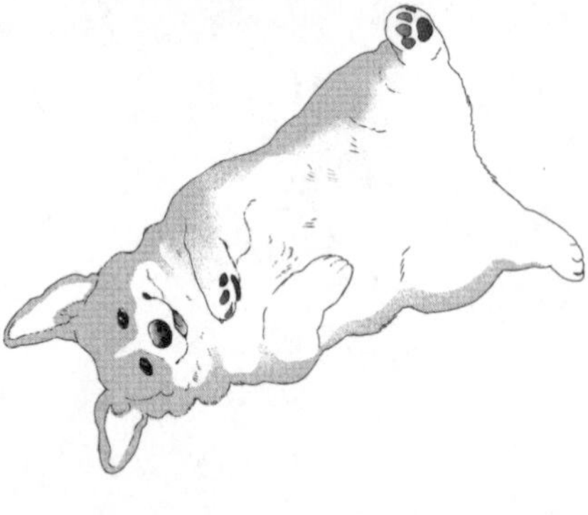

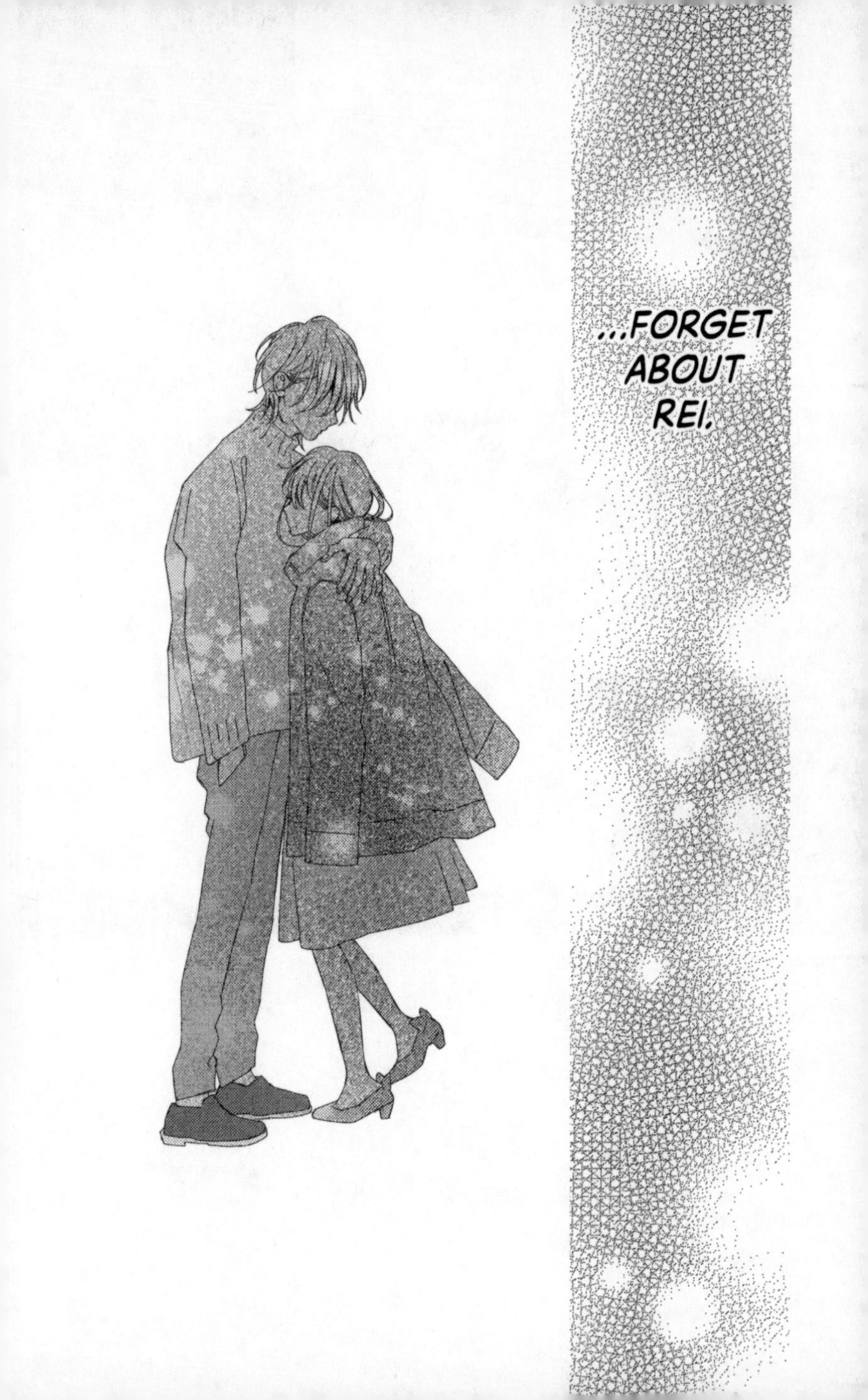
...FORGET ABOUT REI.

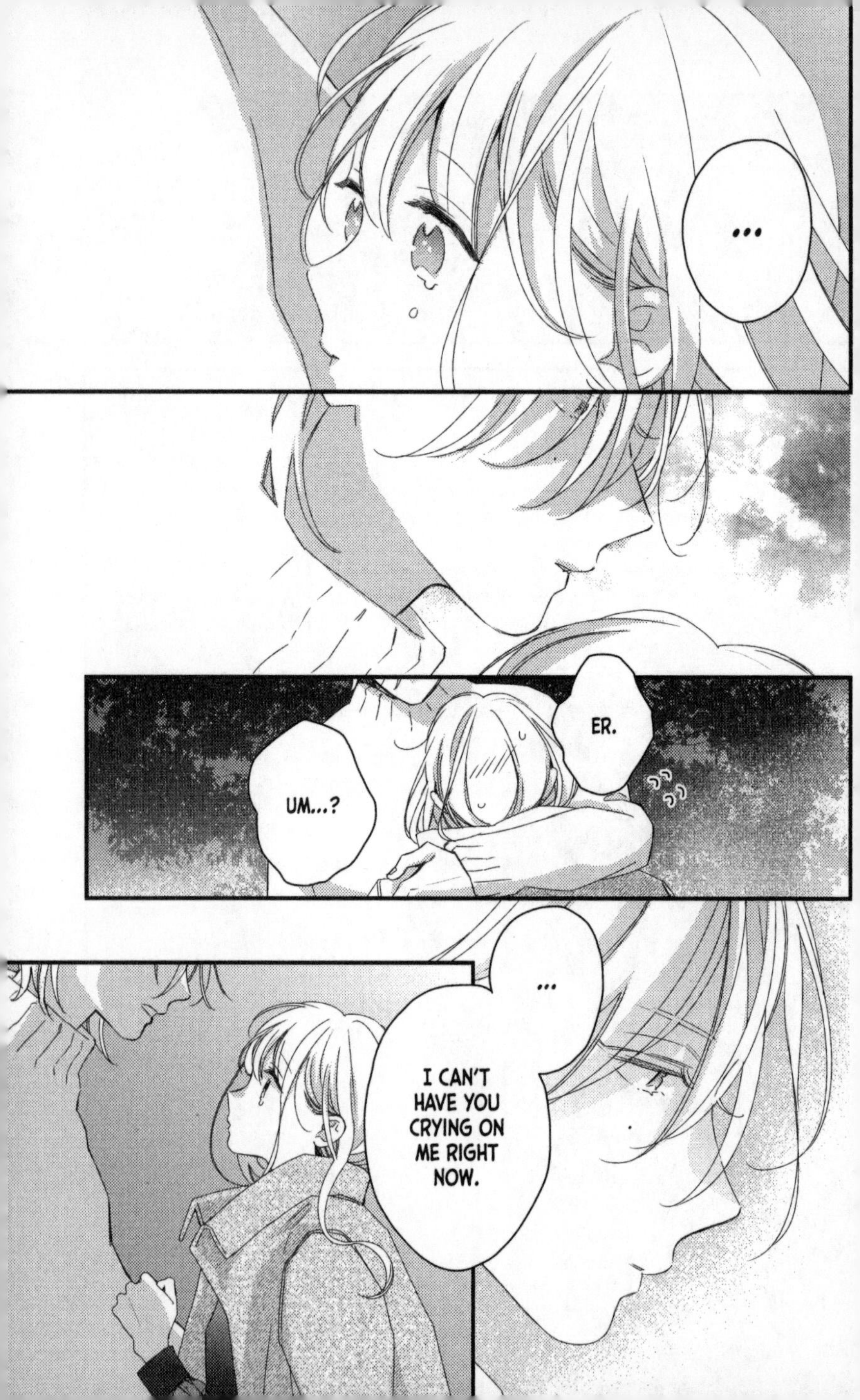
...
ER.
UM...?
...
I CAN'T HAVE YOU CRYING ON ME RIGHT NOW.

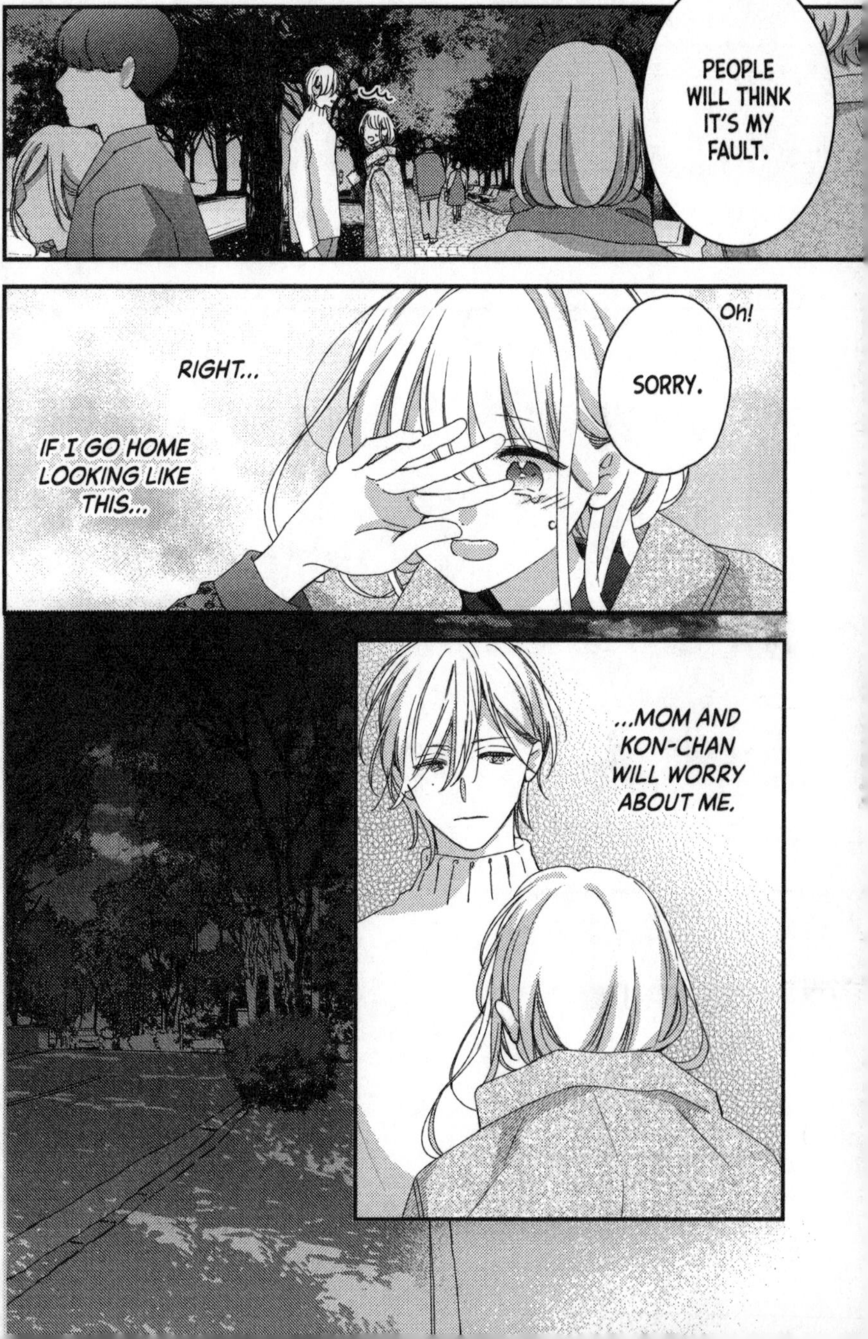
PEOPLE WILL THINK IT'S MY FAULT.
Oh!
SORRY.
RIGHT...
IF I GO HOME LOOKING LIKE THIS...
...MOM AND KON-CHAN WILL WORRY ABOUT ME.

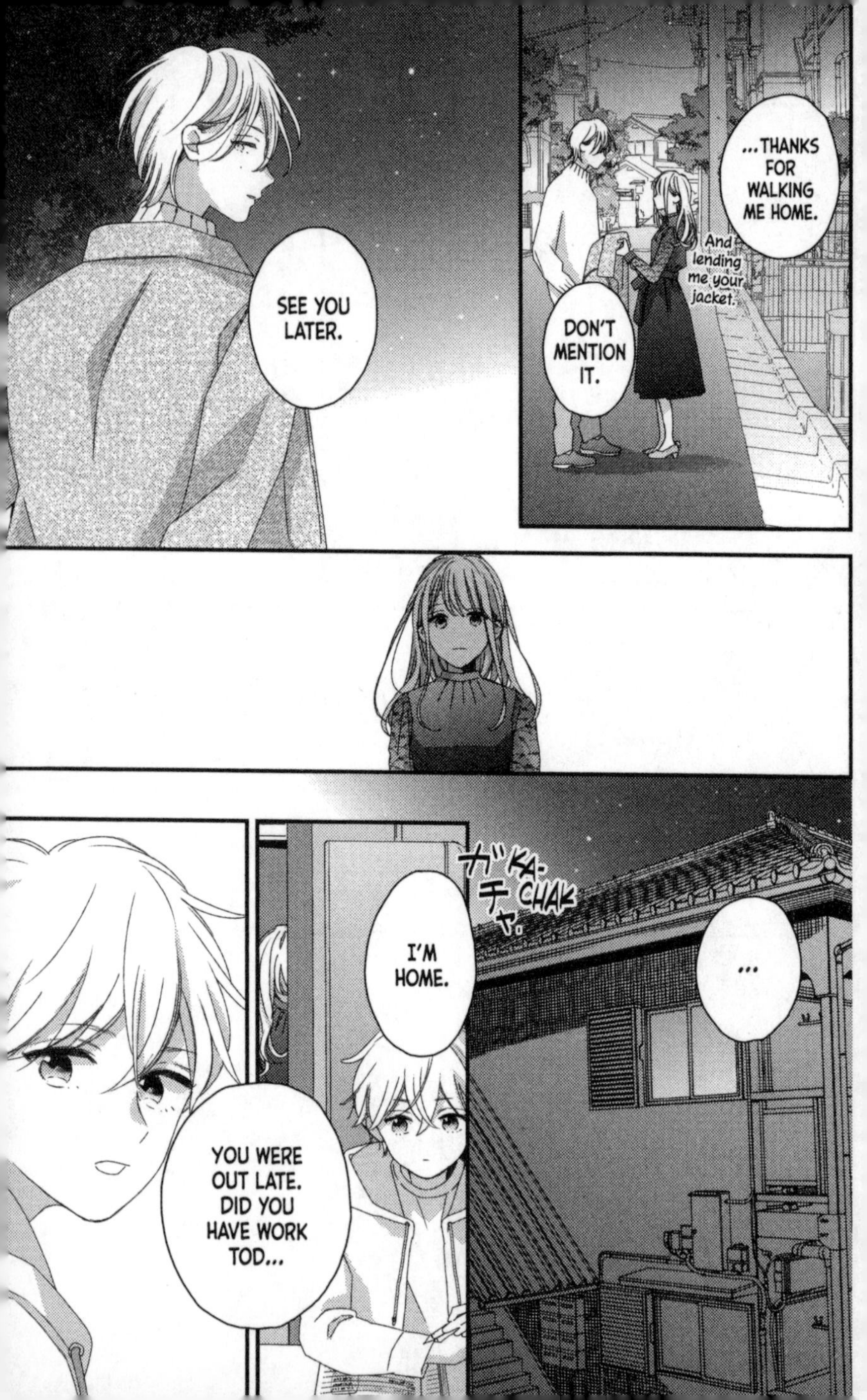
...THANKS FOR WALKING ME HOME.
And lending me your jacket.
DON'T MENTION IT.
SEE YOU LATER.
...
ガチャ。
KA-CHAK
I'M HOME.
YOU WERE OUT LATE. DID YOU HAVE WORK TOD...

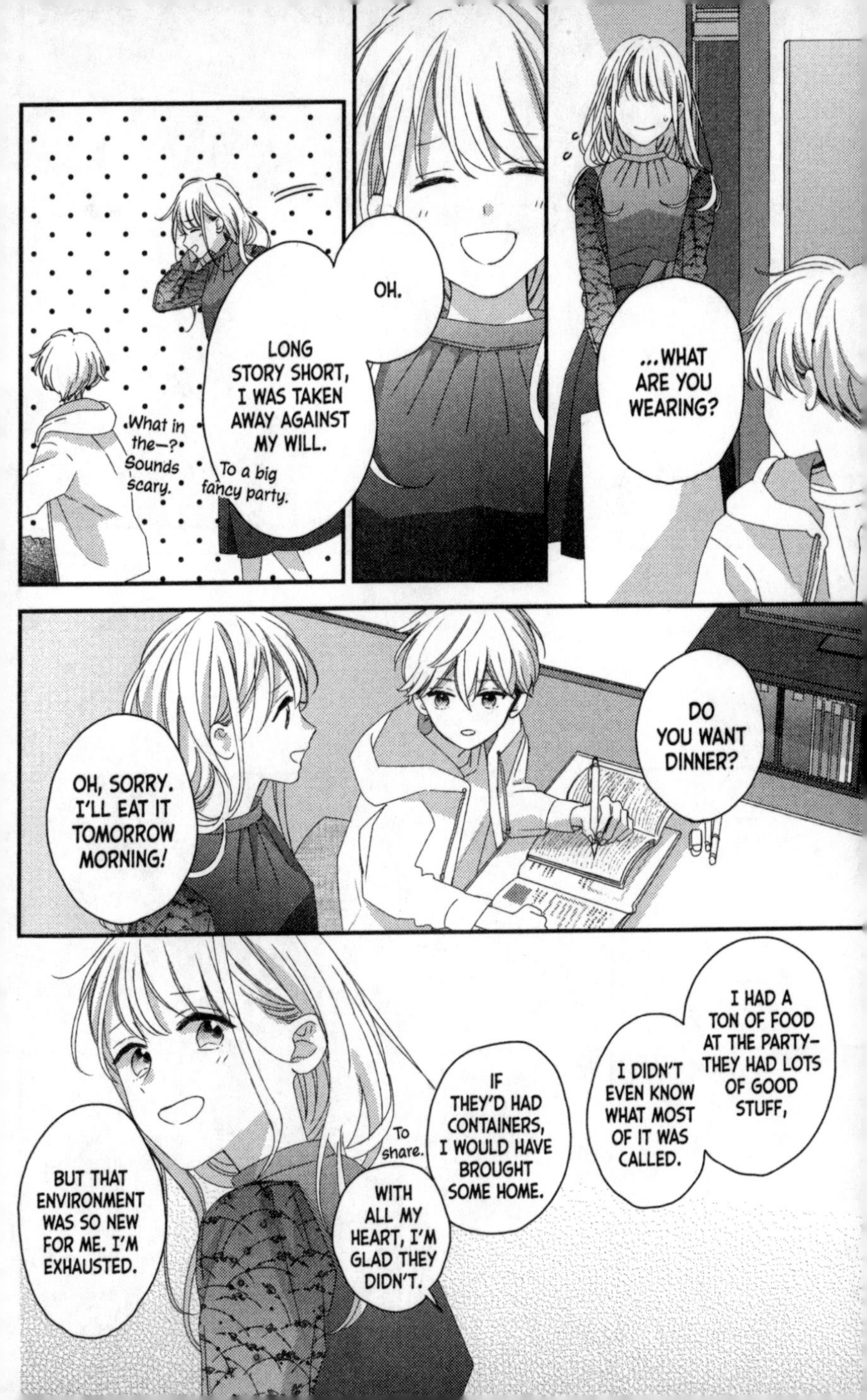
...WHAT ARE YOU WEARING?
OH.
LONG STORY SHORT, I WAS TAKEN AWAY AGAINST MY WILL.
To a big fancy party.
What in the—? Sounds scary.
DO YOU WANT DINNER?
OH, SORRY. I'LL EAT IT TOMORROW MORNING!
I HAD A TON OF FOOD AT THE PARTY—THEY HAD LOTS OF GOOD STUFF,
I DIDN'T EVEN KNOW WHAT MOST OF IT WAS CALLED.
IF THEY'D HAD CONTAINERS, I WOULD HAVE BROUGHT SOME HOME.
To share.
WITH ALL MY HEART, I'M GLAD THEY DIDN'T.
BUT THAT ENVIRONMENT WAS SO NEW FOR ME. I'M EXHAUSTED.

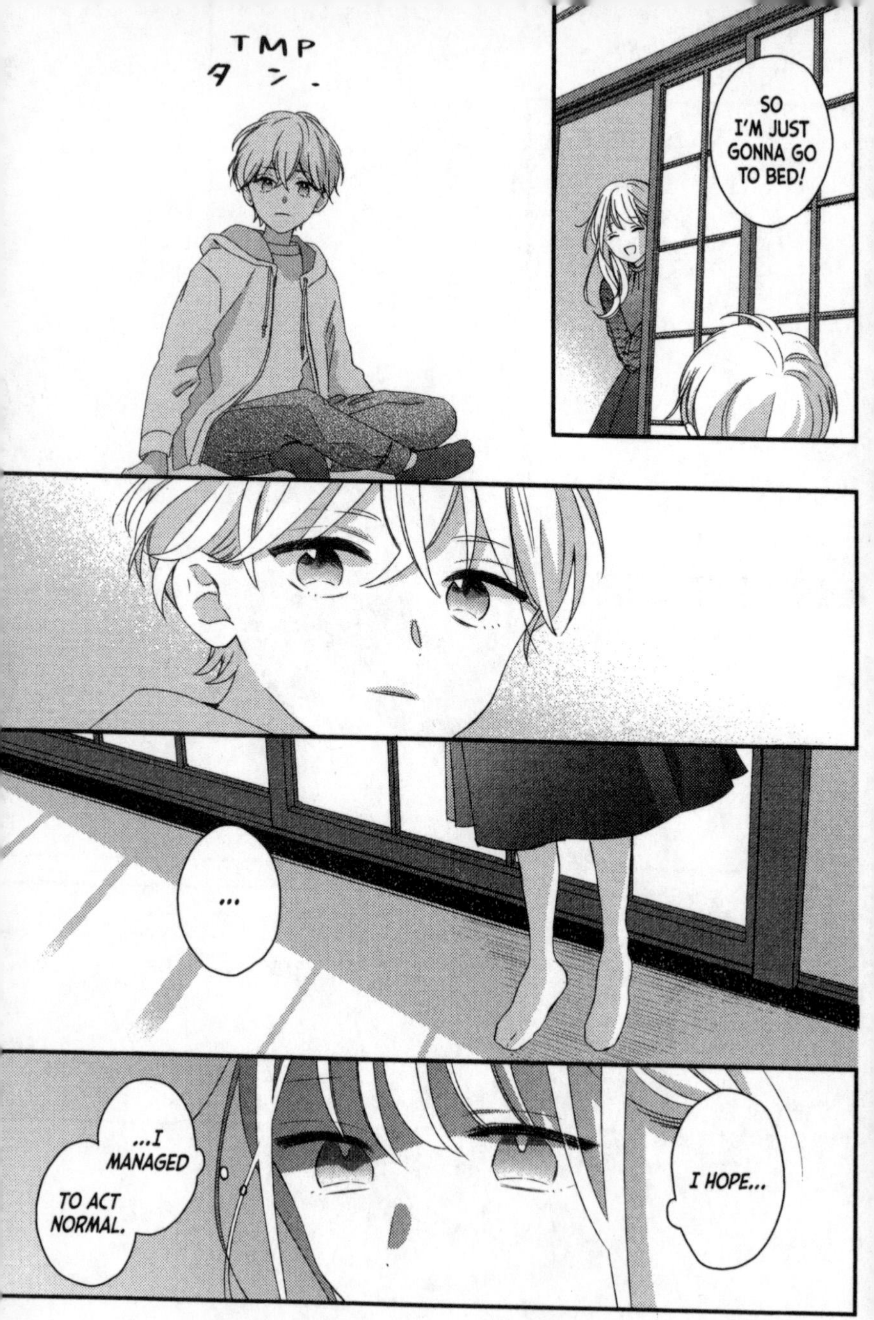
SO I'M JUST GONNA GO TO BED!
TMP
タン
...
...I MANAGED TO ACT NORMAL.
I HOPE...

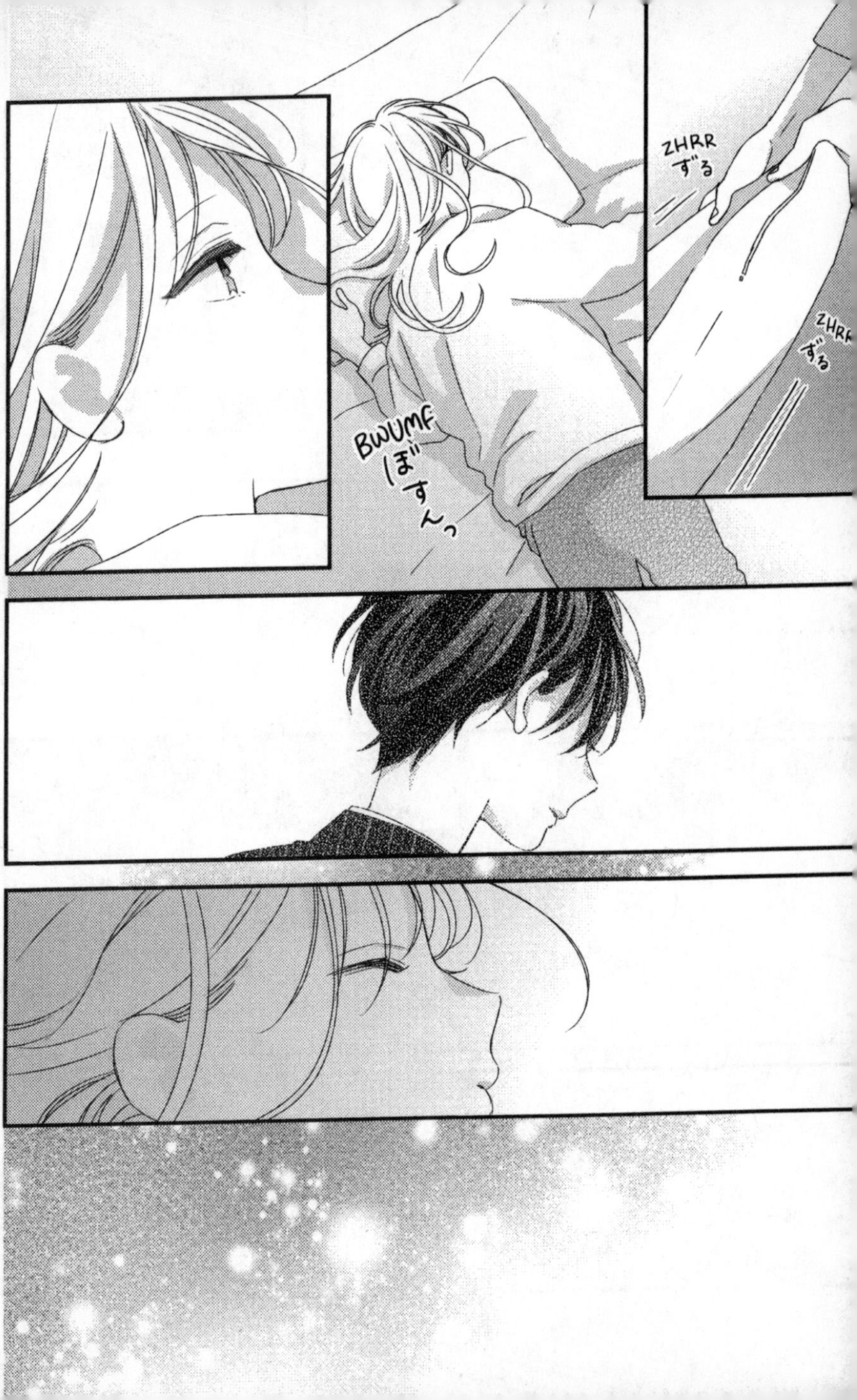
ZHRR
ずる
ZHRR
ずる
BWUMF
ぼすんっ

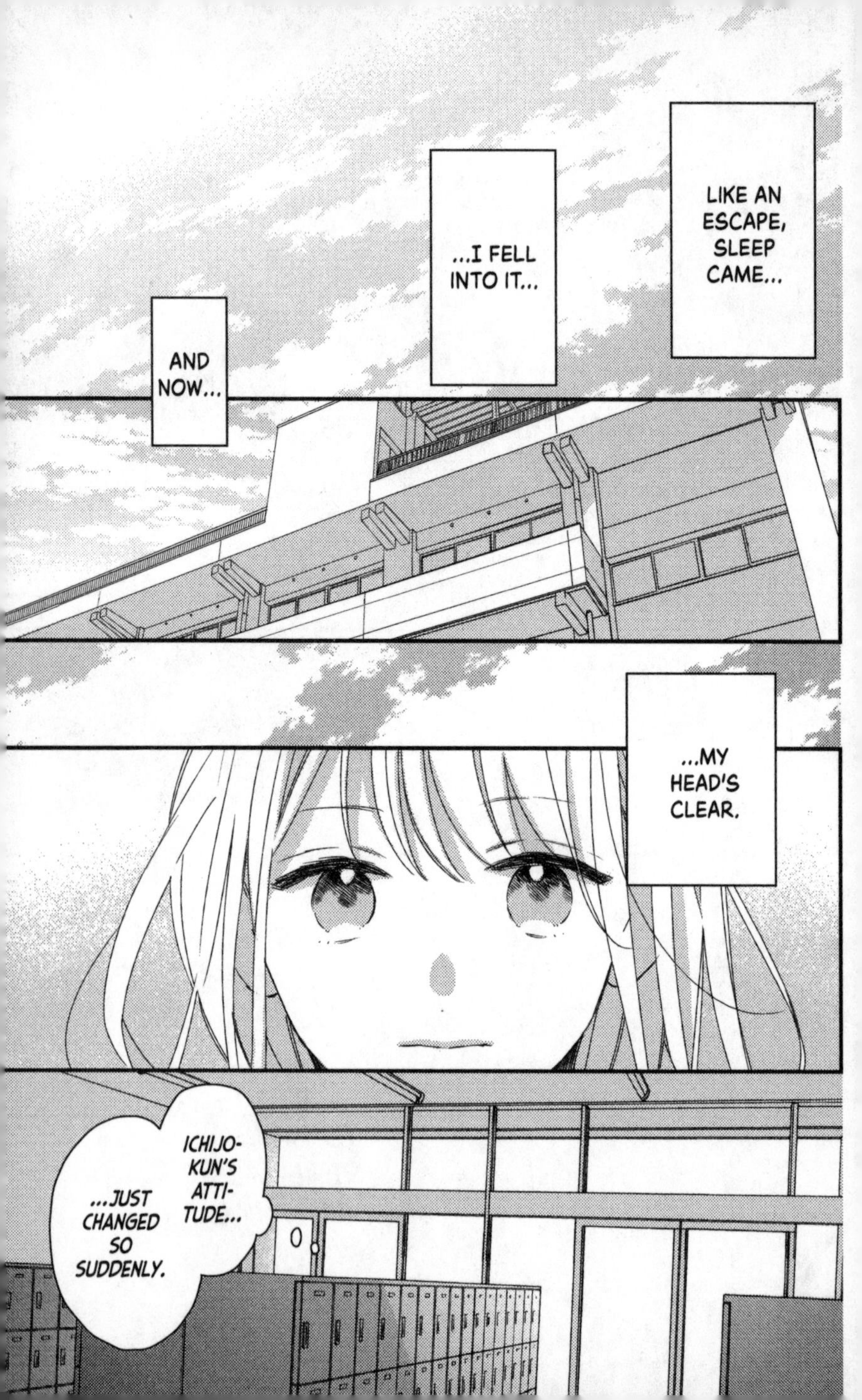
LIKE AN ESCAPE, SLEEP CAME...
...I FELL INTO IT...
AND NOW...
...MY HEAD'S CLEAR.
ICHIJO-KUN'S ATTI-TUDE...
...JUST CHANGED SO SUDDENLY.

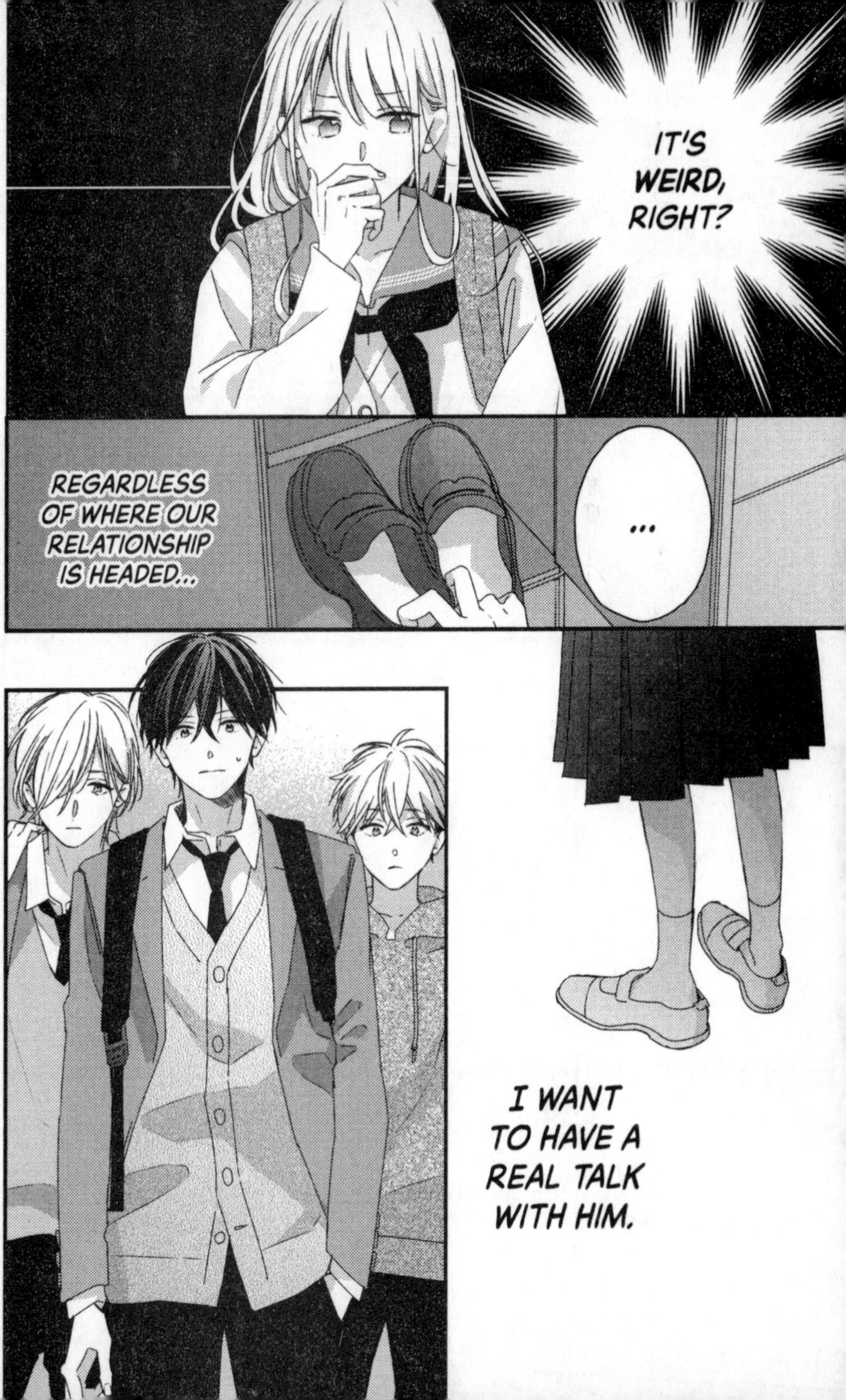
IT'S WEIRD, RIGHT?
...
REGARDLESS OF WHERE OUR RELATIONSHIP IS HEADED...
I WANT TO HAVE A REAL TALK WITH HIM.

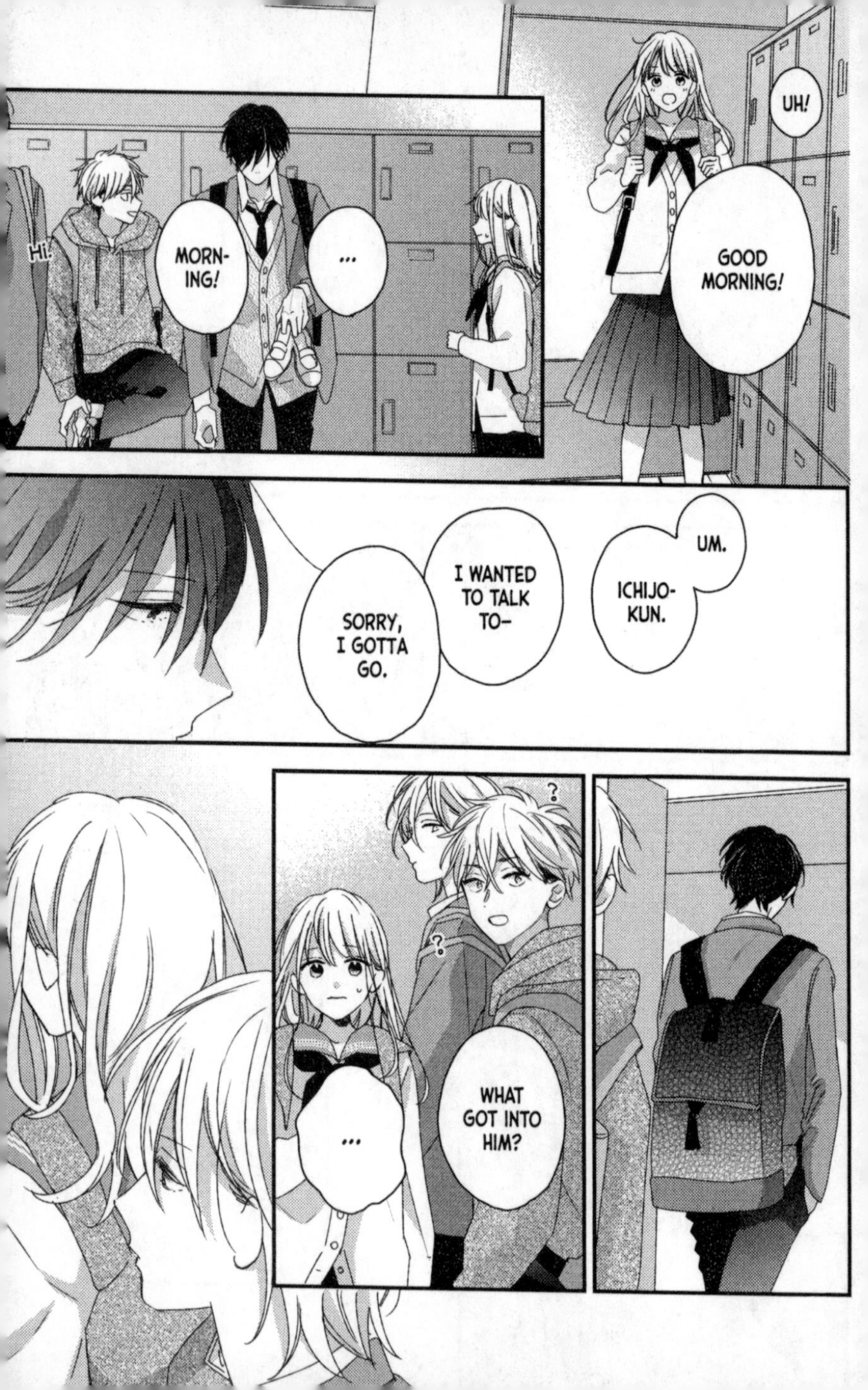
UH!
GOOD MORNING!
...
MORN-ING!
HI.
UM.
ICHIJO-KUN.
I WANTED TO TALK TO–
SORRY, I GOTTA GO.
?
?
WHAT GOT INTO HIM?
...

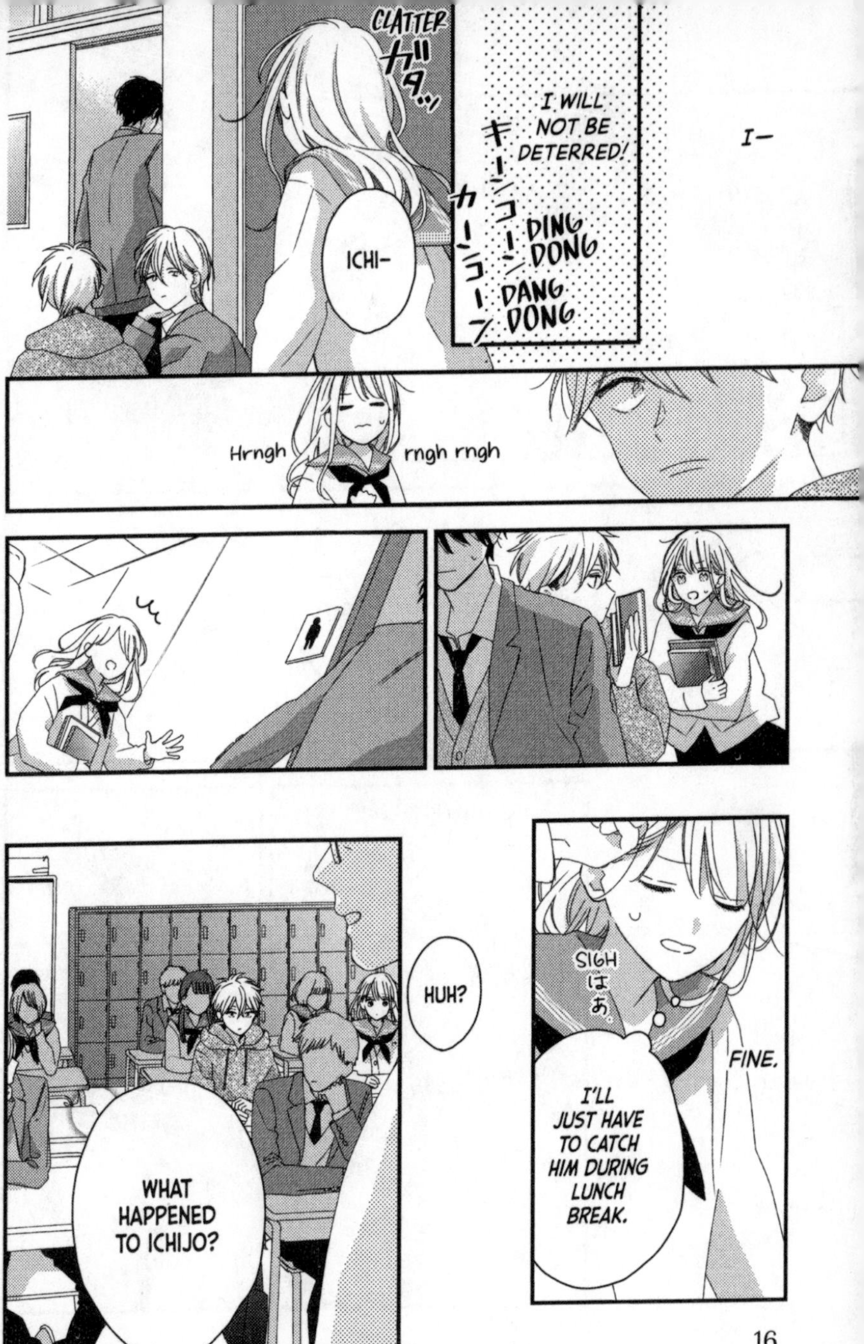
I—
I WILL NOT BE DETERRED!
キーンコーンカーンコーン
DING DONG DANG DONG
CLATTER ガタッ
ICHI-
Hrngh rngh rngh
SIGH はあ
FINE.
I'LL JUST HAVE TO CATCH HIM DURING LUNCH BREAK.
HUH?
WHAT HAPPENED TO ICHIJO?

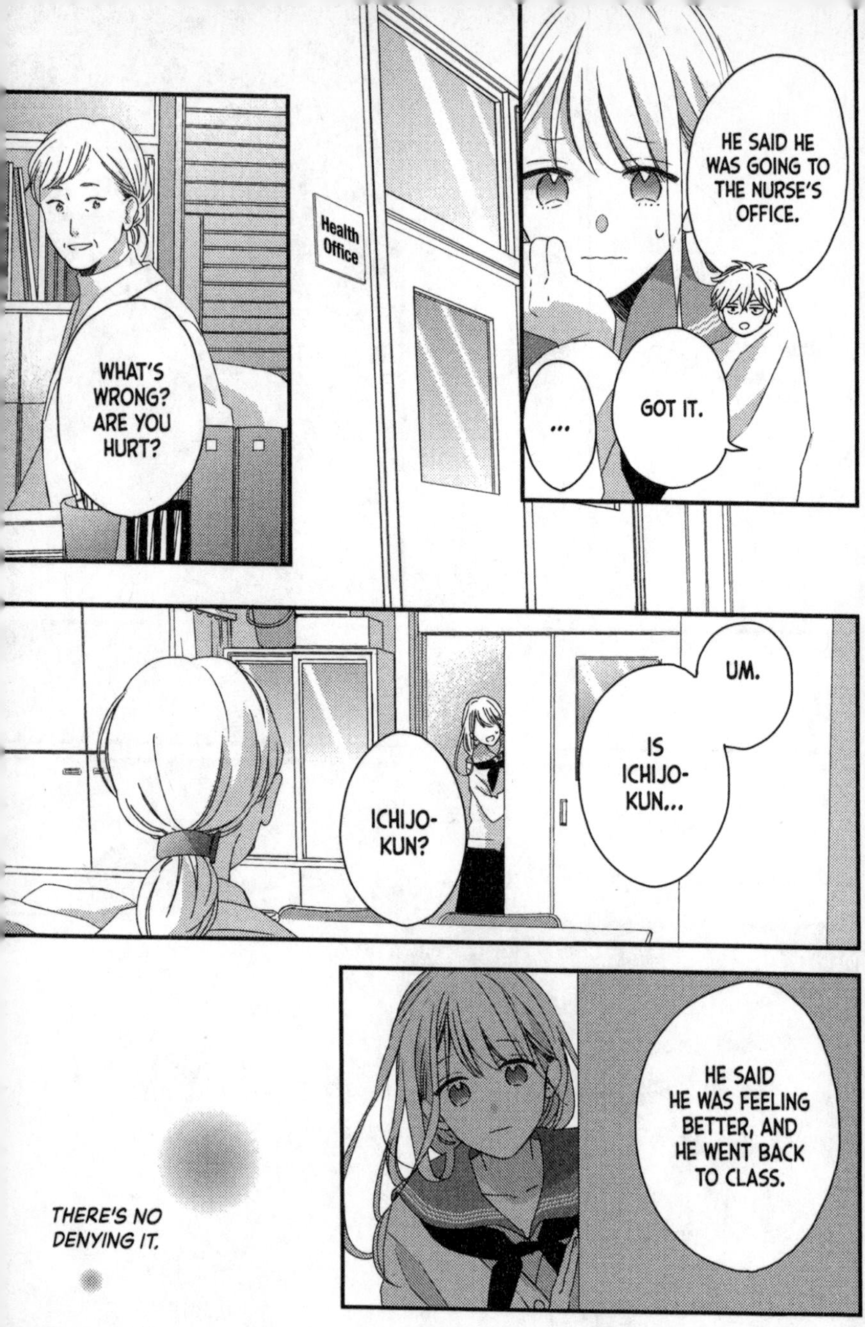
HE SAID HE WAS GOING TO THE NURSE'S OFFICE.
GOT IT.
...
Health Office
WHAT'S WRONG? ARE YOU HURT?
UM.
IS ICHIJO-KUN...
ICHIJO-KUN?
HE SAID HE WAS FEELING BETTER, AND HE WENT BACK TO CLASS.
THERE'S NO DENYING IT.

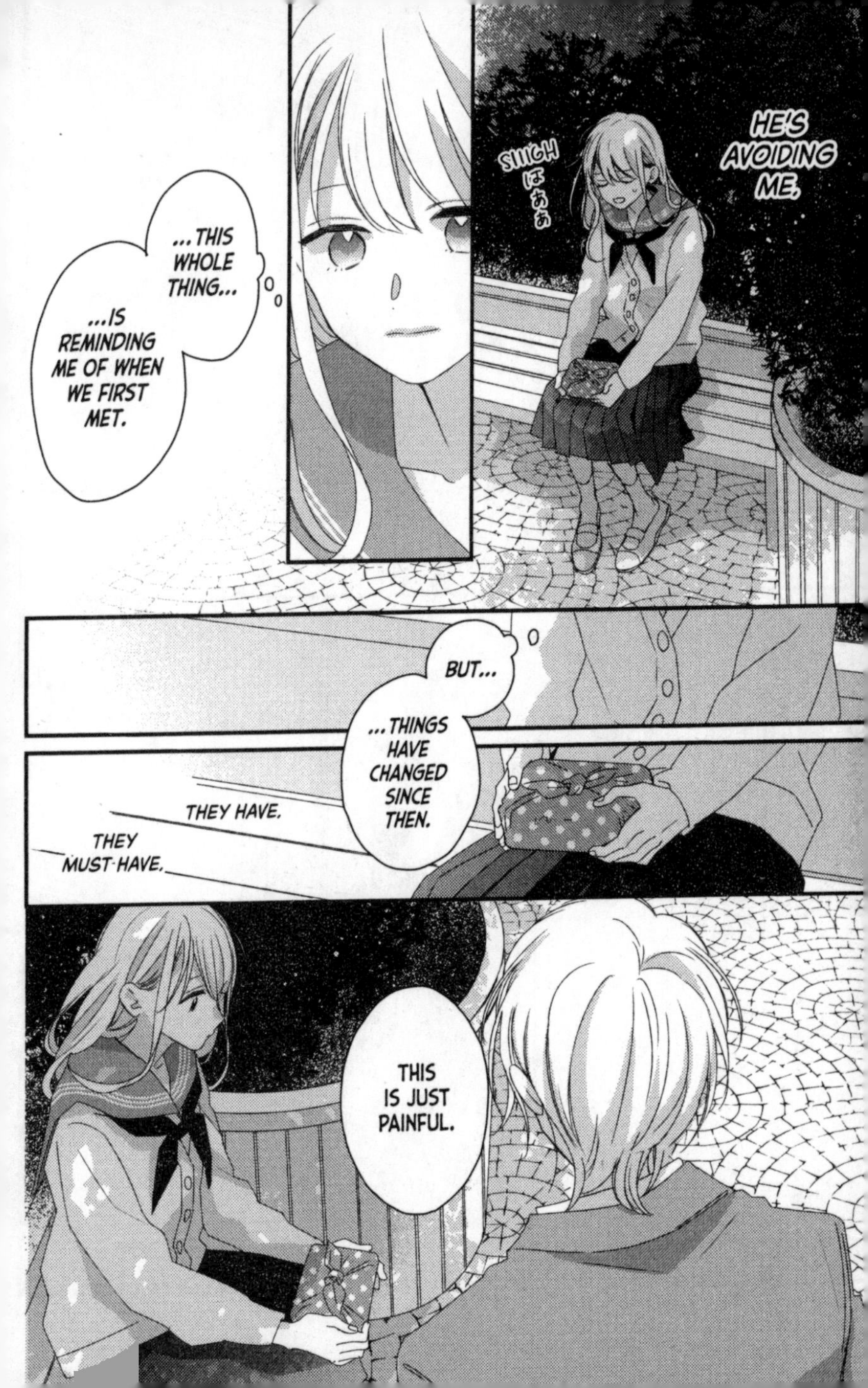
HE'S AVOIDING ME.
SIIIGH はぁぁ
...THIS WHOLE THING...
...IS REMINDING ME OF WHEN WE FIRST MET.
BUT...
...THINGS HAVE CHANGED SINCE THEN.
THEY HAVE.
THEY MUST HAVE.
THIS IS JUST PAINFUL.

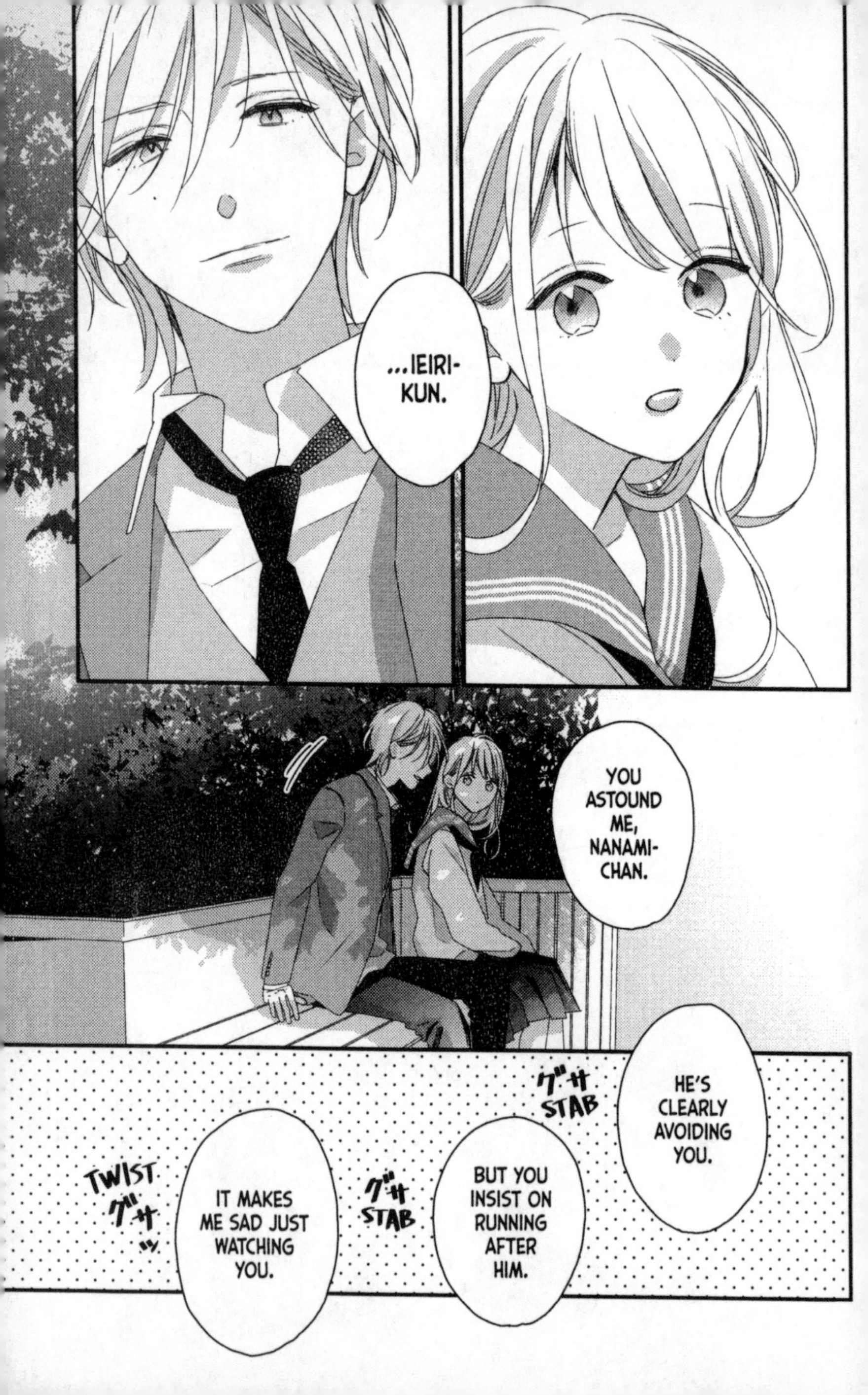
...IEIRI-KUN.
YOU ASTOUND ME, NANAMI-CHAN.
HE'S CLEARLY AVOIDING YOU.
グサ STAB
BUT YOU INSIST ON RUNNING AFTER HIM.
グサ STAB
IT MAKES ME SAD JUST WATCHING YOU.
TWIST グサッ

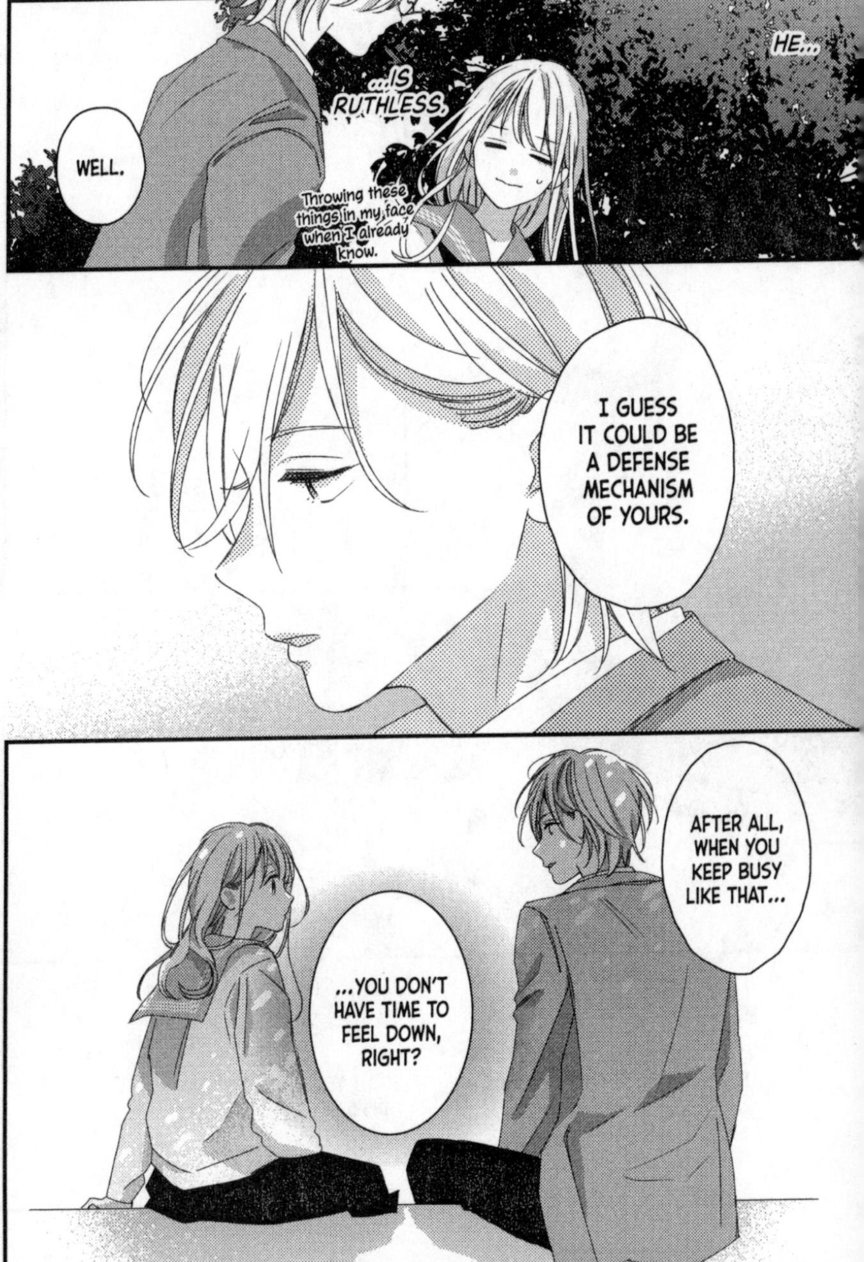
HE...
...IS RUTHLESS.
Throwing these things in my face when I already know.
WELL.
I GUESS IT COULD BE A DEFENSE MECHANISM OF YOURS.
AFTER ALL, WHEN YOU KEEP BUSY LIKE THAT...
...YOU DON'T HAVE TIME TO FEEL DOWN, RIGHT?

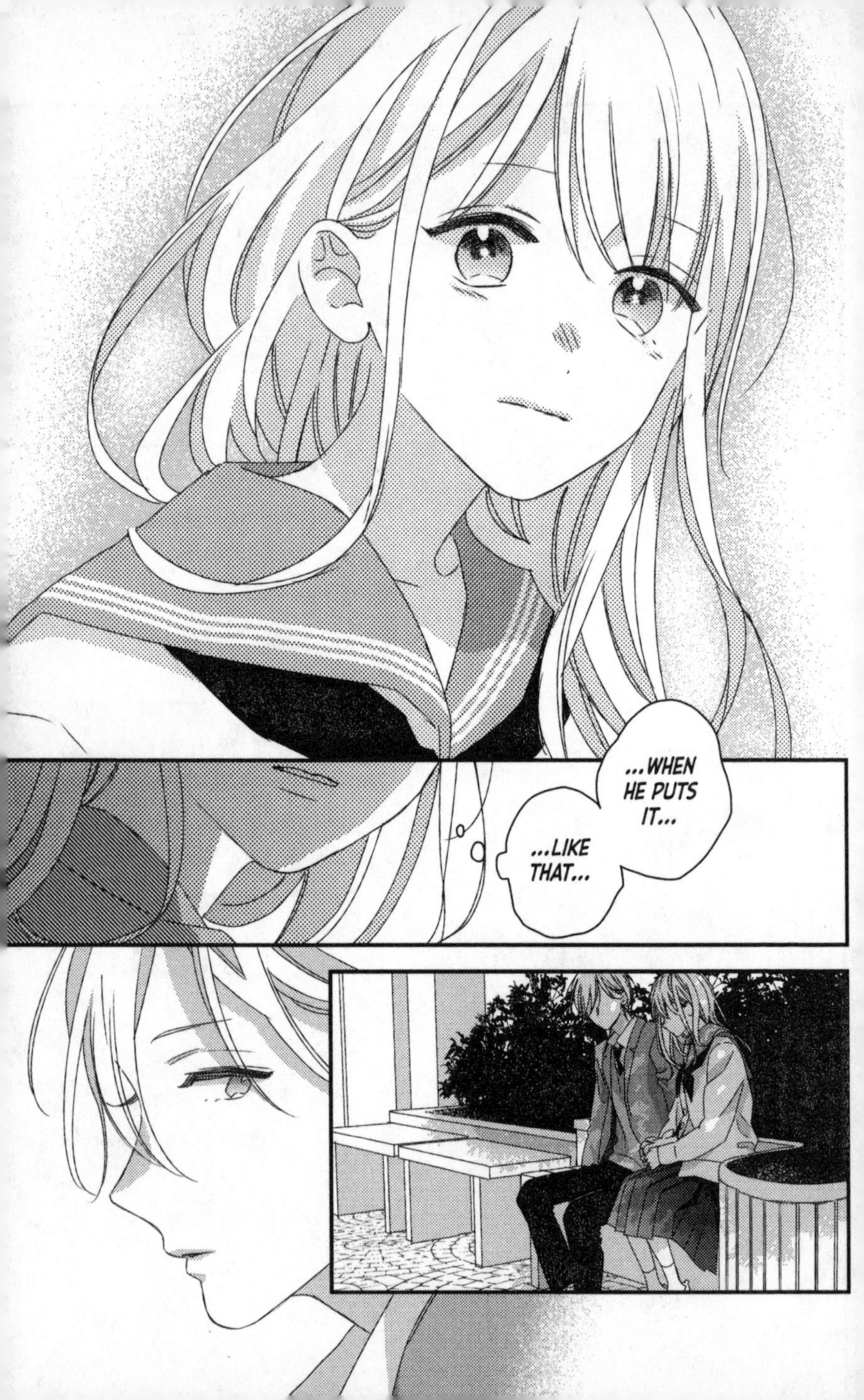
...WHEN HE PUTS IT...
...LIKE THAT...

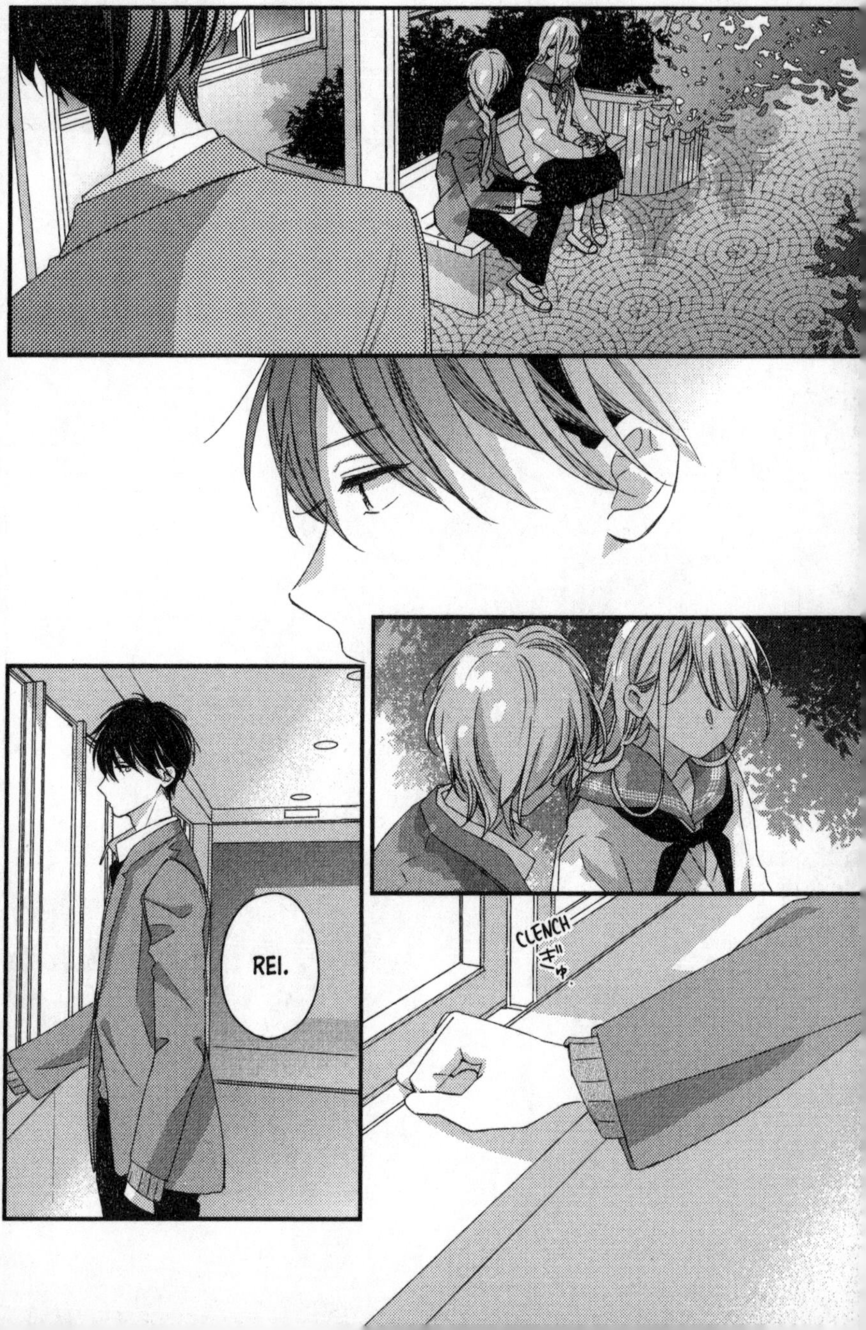
REI.
CLENCH
ぎゅ

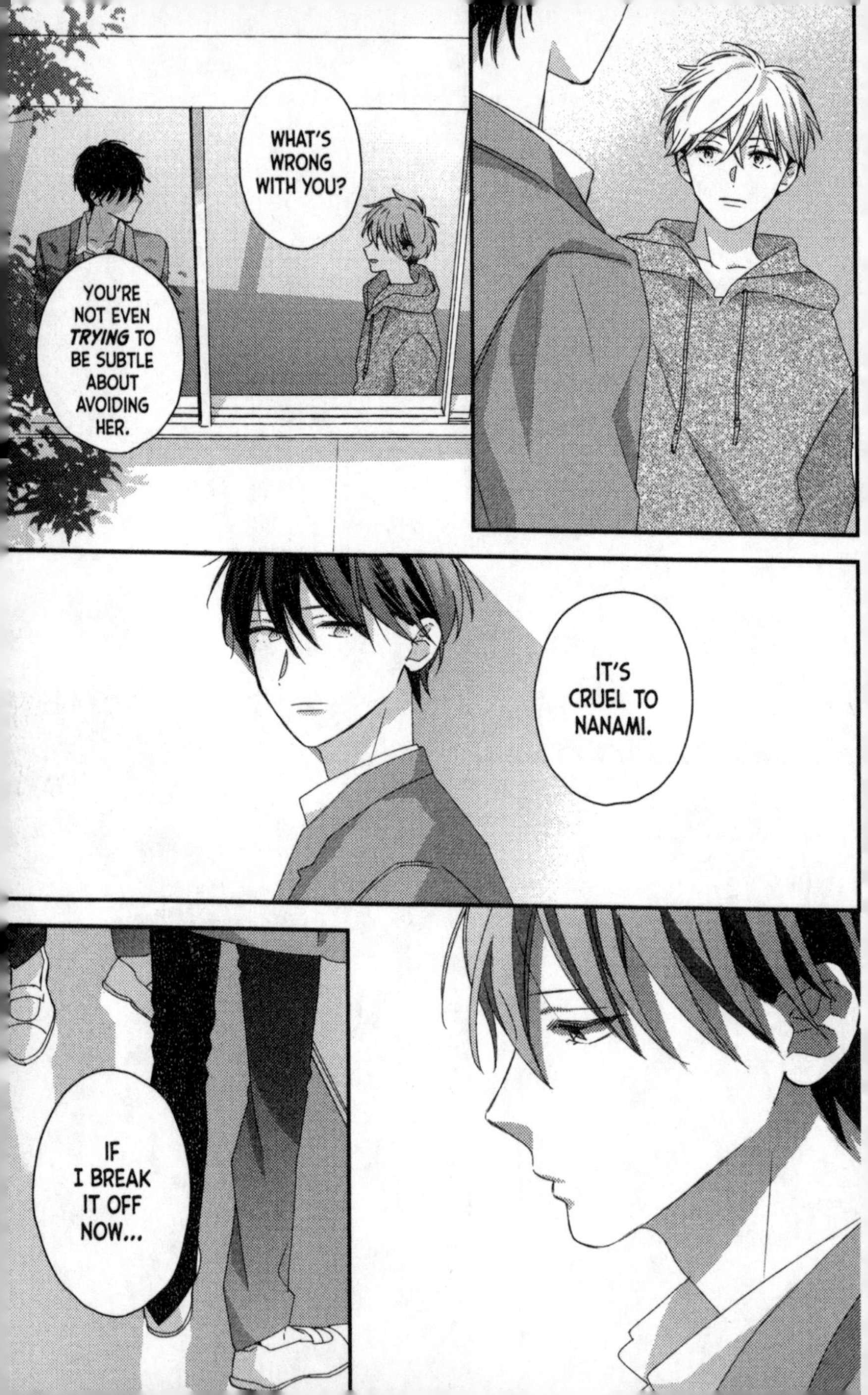
WHAT'S WRONG WITH YOU?
YOU'RE NOT EVEN *TRYING* TO BE SUBTLE ABOUT AVOIDING HER.
IT'S CRUEL TO NANAMI.
IF I BREAK IT OFF NOW...

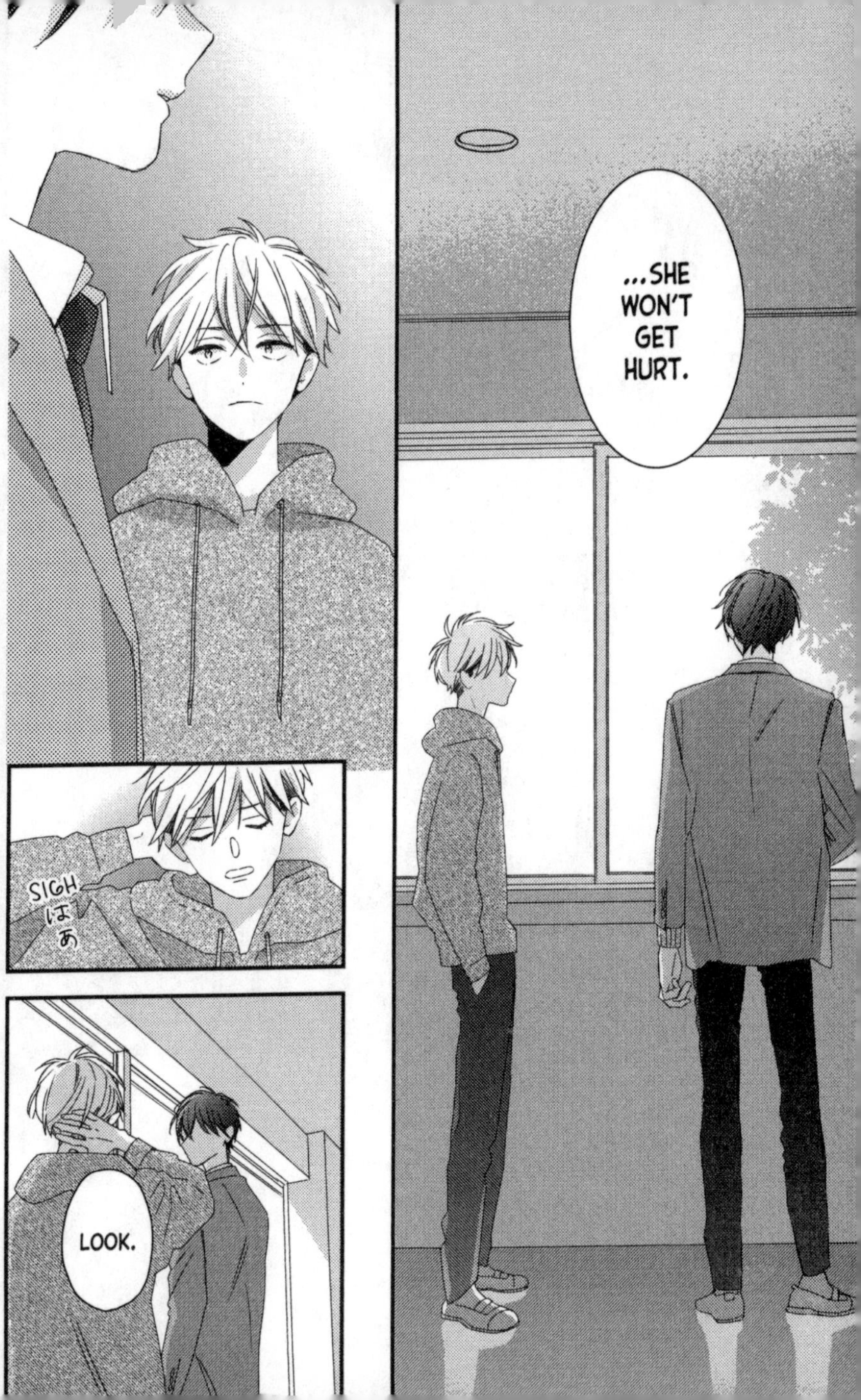
...SHE WON'T GET HURT.
SIGH はあ
LOOK.

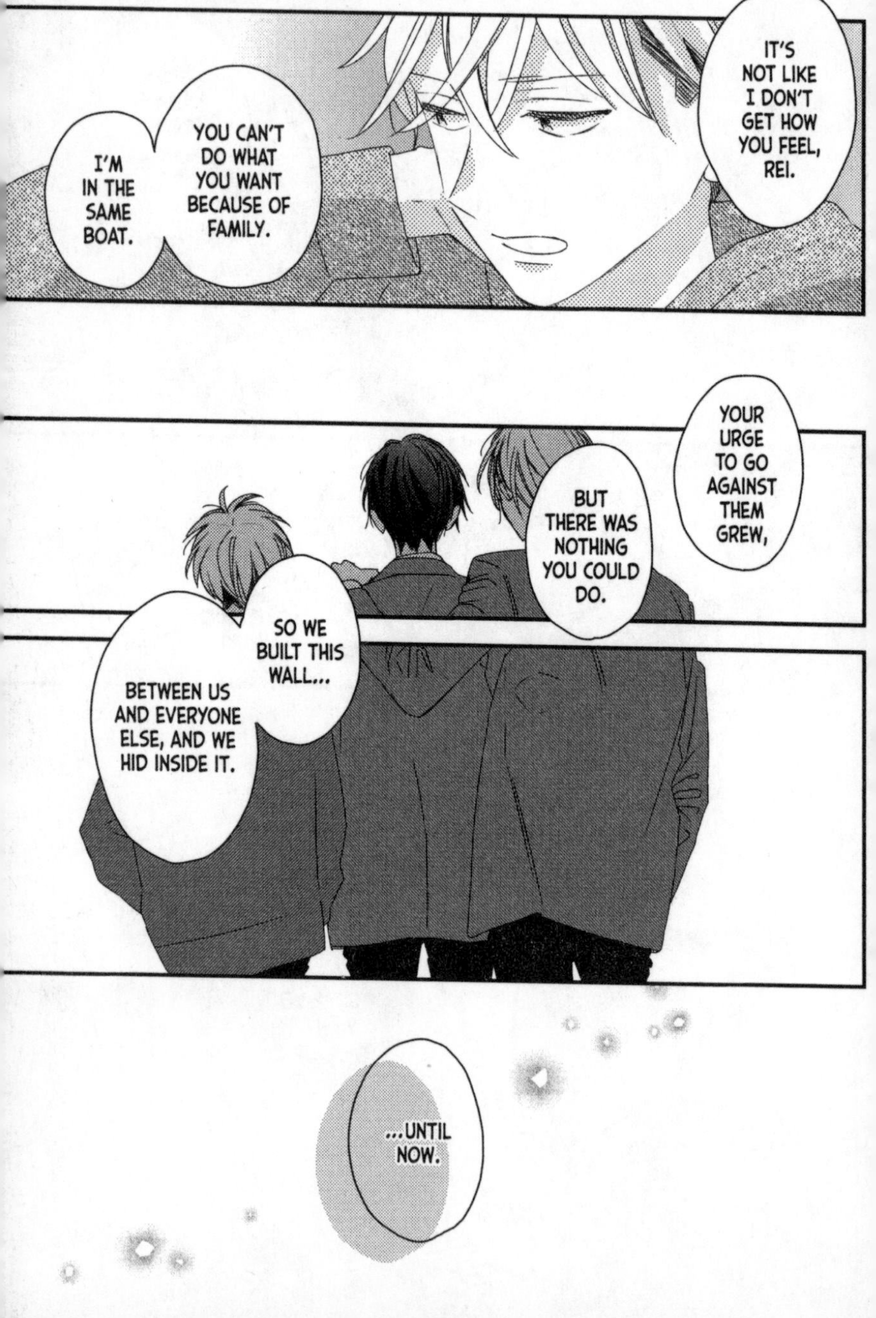
IT'S NOT LIKE I DON'T GET HOW YOU FEEL, REI.
YOU CAN'T DO WHAT YOU WANT BECAUSE OF FAMILY.
I'M IN THE SAME BOAT.
YOUR URGE TO GO AGAINST THEM GREW,
BUT THERE WAS NOTHING YOU COULD DO.
SO WE BUILT THIS WALL...
BETWEEN US AND EVERYONE ELSE, AND WE HID INSIDE IT.
...UNTIL NOW.

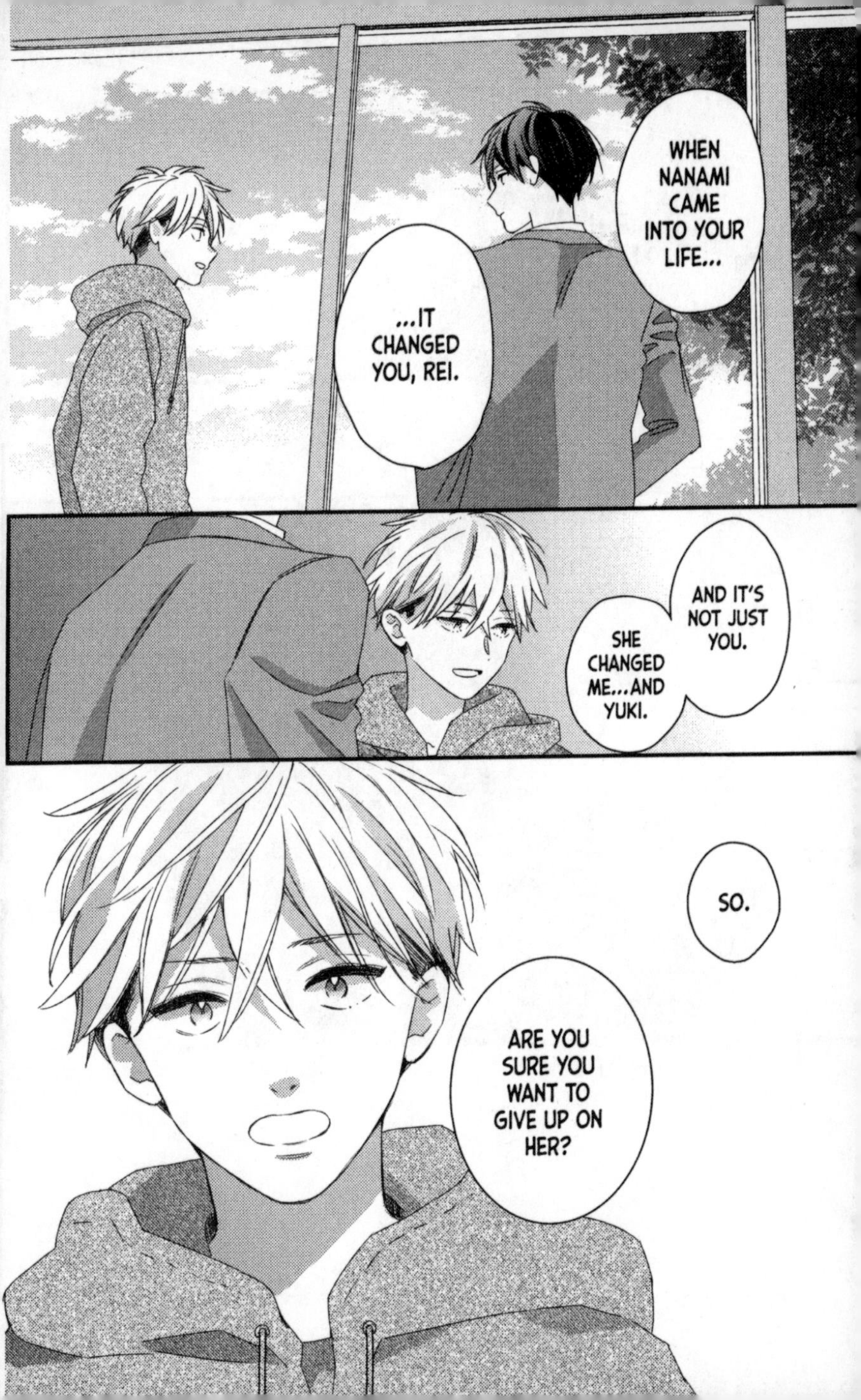
WHEN NANAMI CAME INTO YOUR LIFE...
...IT CHANGED YOU, REI.
AND IT'S NOT JUST YOU.
SHE CHANGED ME...AND YUKI.
SO.
ARE YOU SURE YOU WANT TO GIVE UP ON HER?

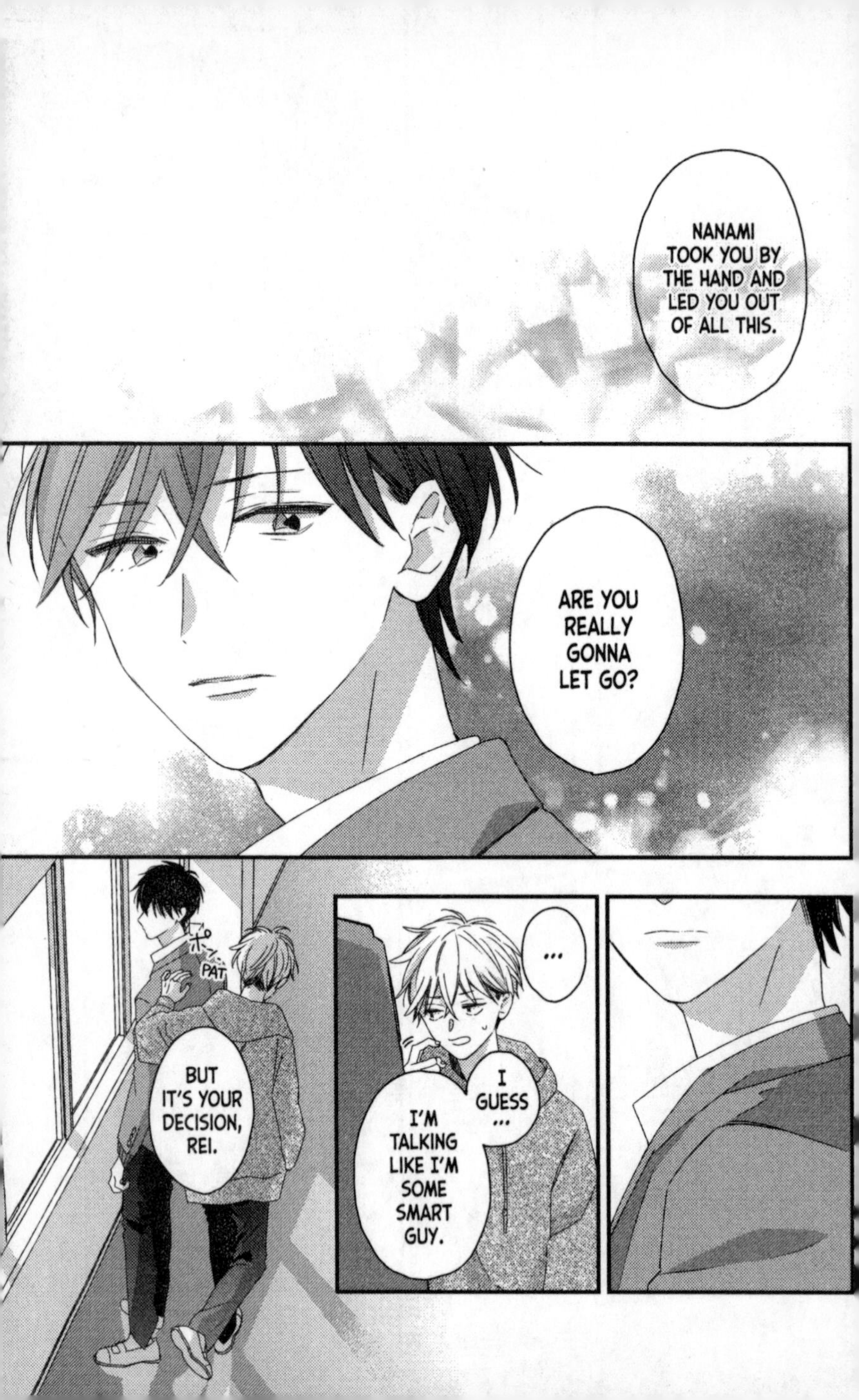
NANAMI TOOK YOU BY THE HAND AND LED YOU OUT OF ALL THIS.
ARE YOU REALLY GONNA LET GO?
...
I GUESS...
I'M TALKING LIKE I'M SOME SMART GUY.
PAT
BUT IT'S YOUR DECISION, REI.

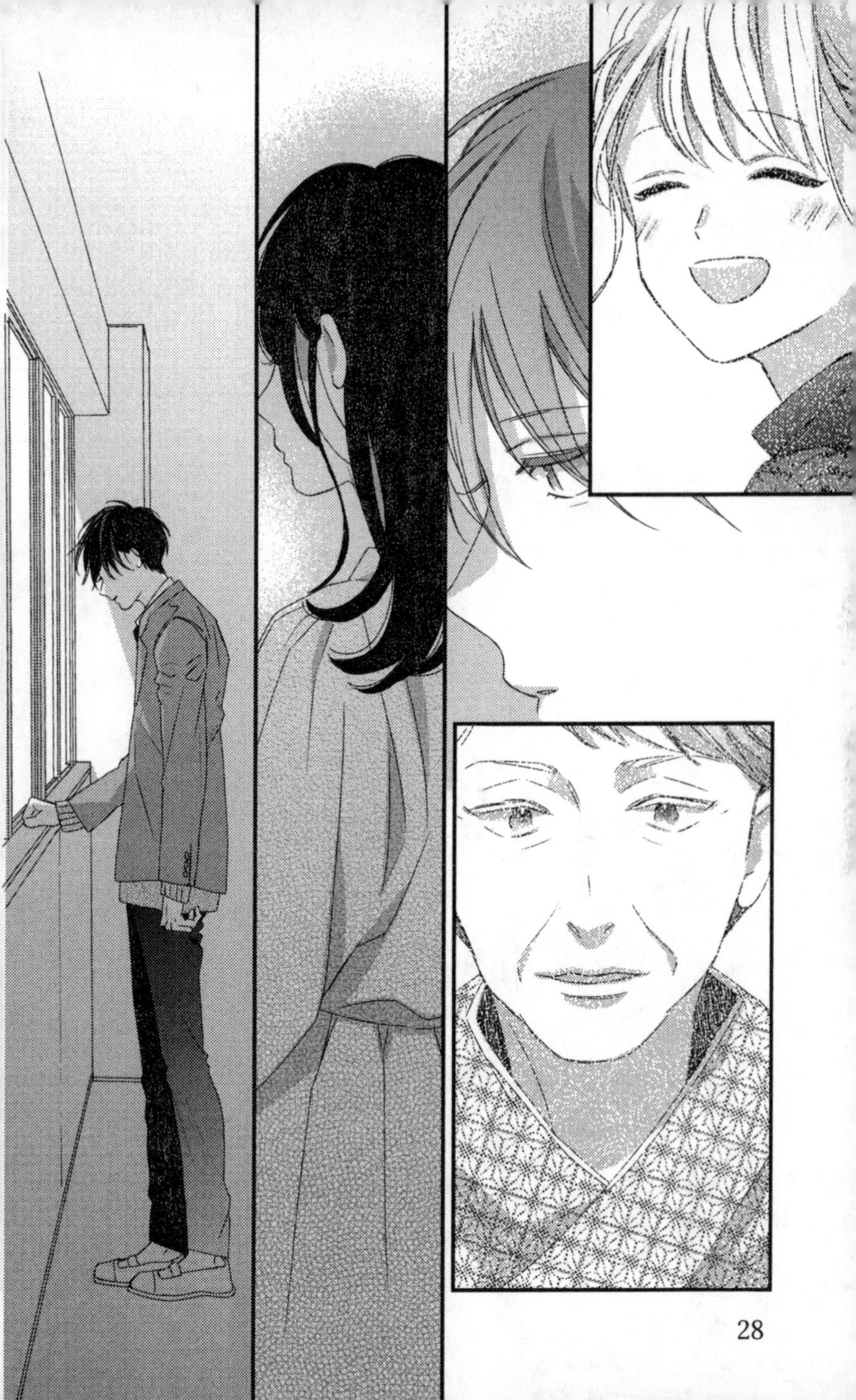

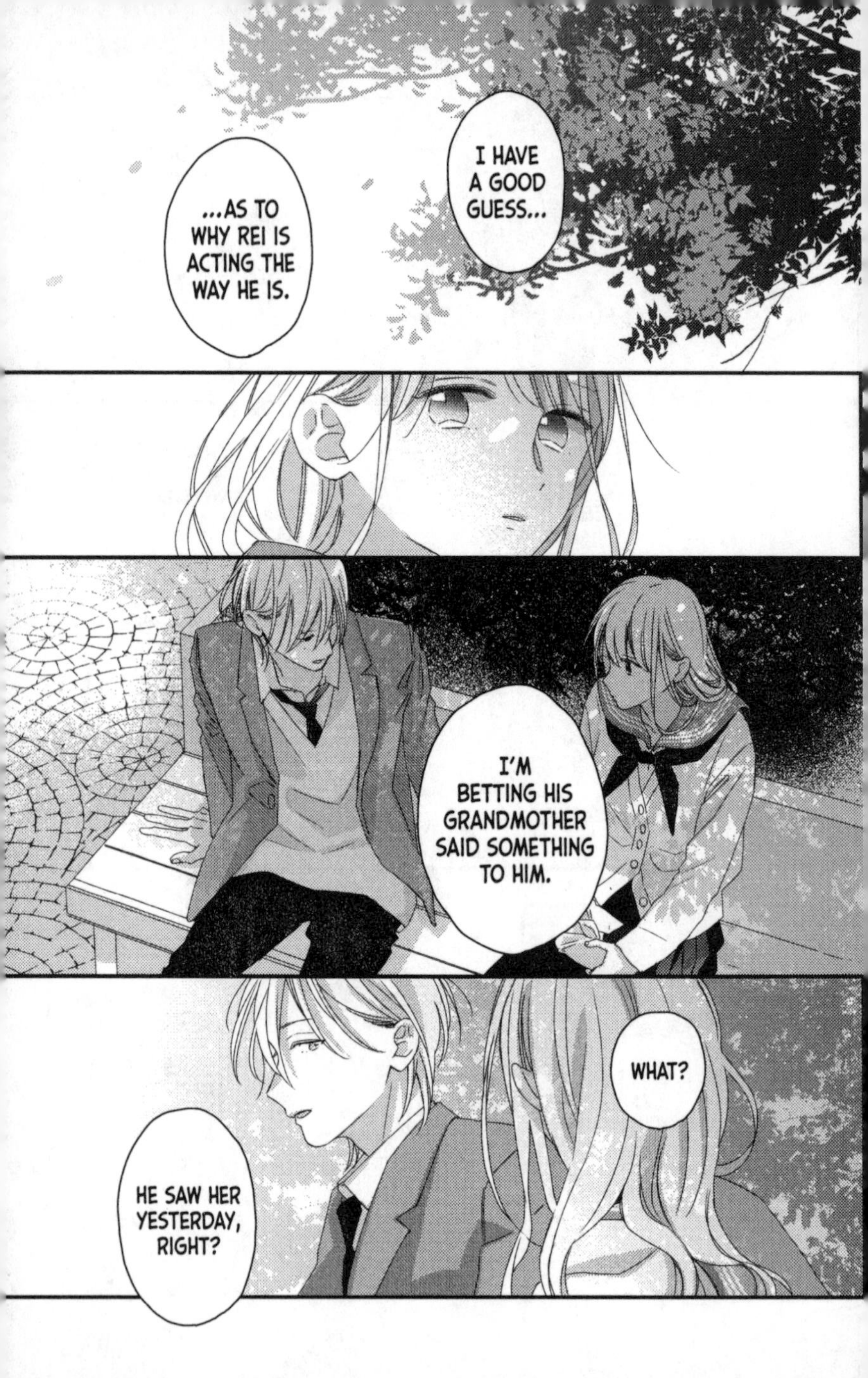
I HAVE A GOOD GUESS...
...AS TO WHY REI IS ACTING THE WAY HE IS.
I'M BETTING HIS GRANDMOTHER SAID SOMETHING TO HIM.
WHAT?
HE SAW HER YESTERDAY, RIGHT?

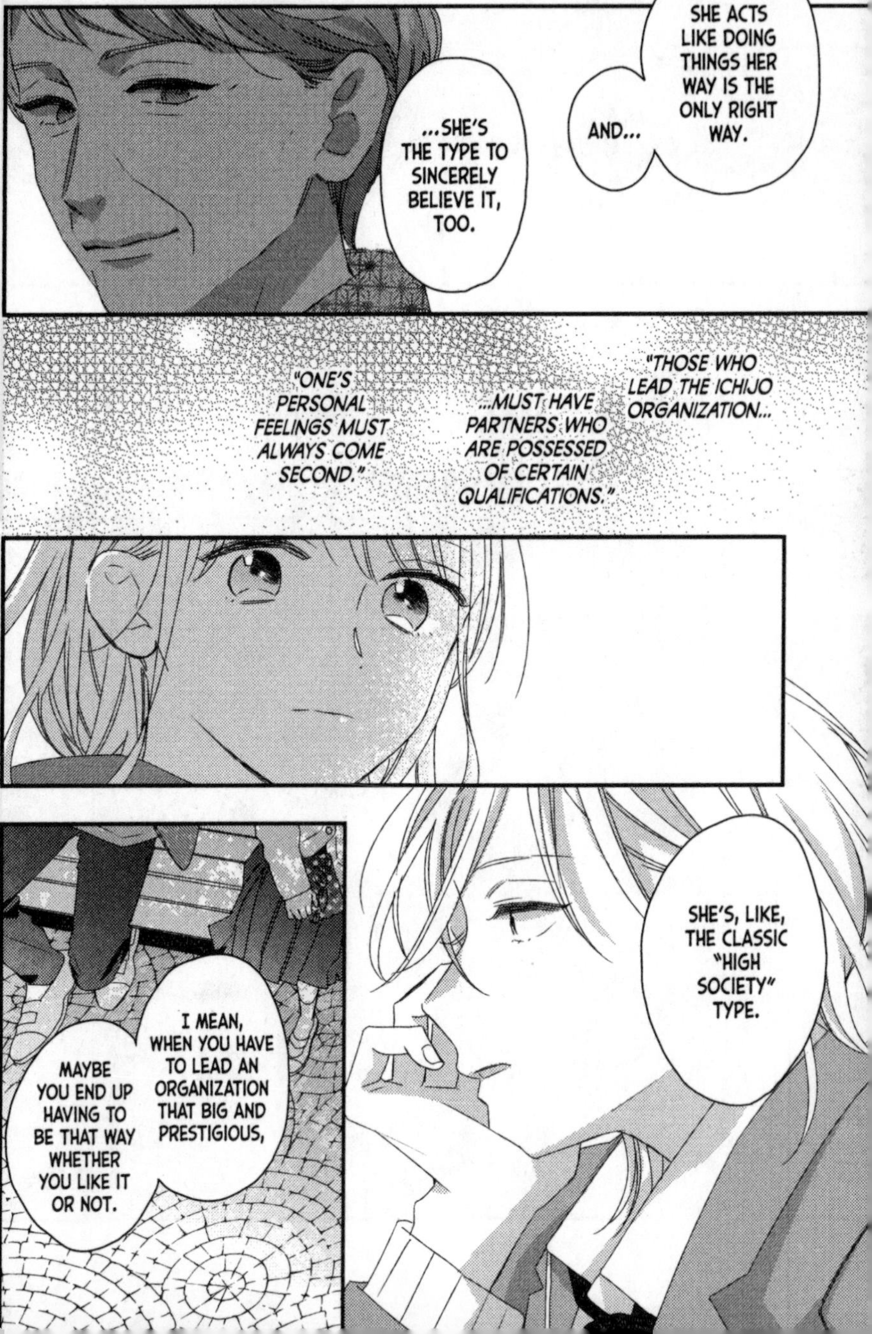
SHE ACTS LIKE DOING THINGS HER WAY IS THE ONLY RIGHT WAY.
AND...
...SHE'S THE TYPE TO SINCERELY BELIEVE IT, TOO.
"THOSE WHO LEAD THE ICHIJO ORGANIZATION...
...MUST HAVE PARTNERS WHO ARE POSSESSED OF CERTAIN QUALIFICATIONS."
"ONE'S PERSONAL FEELINGS MUST ALWAYS COME SECOND."
SHE'S, LIKE, THE CLASSIC "HIGH SOCIETY" TYPE.
I MEAN, WHEN YOU HAVE TO LEAD AN ORGANIZATION THAT BIG AND PRESTIGIOUS,
MAYBE YOU END UP HAVING TO BE THAT WAY WHETHER YOU LIKE IT OR NOT.

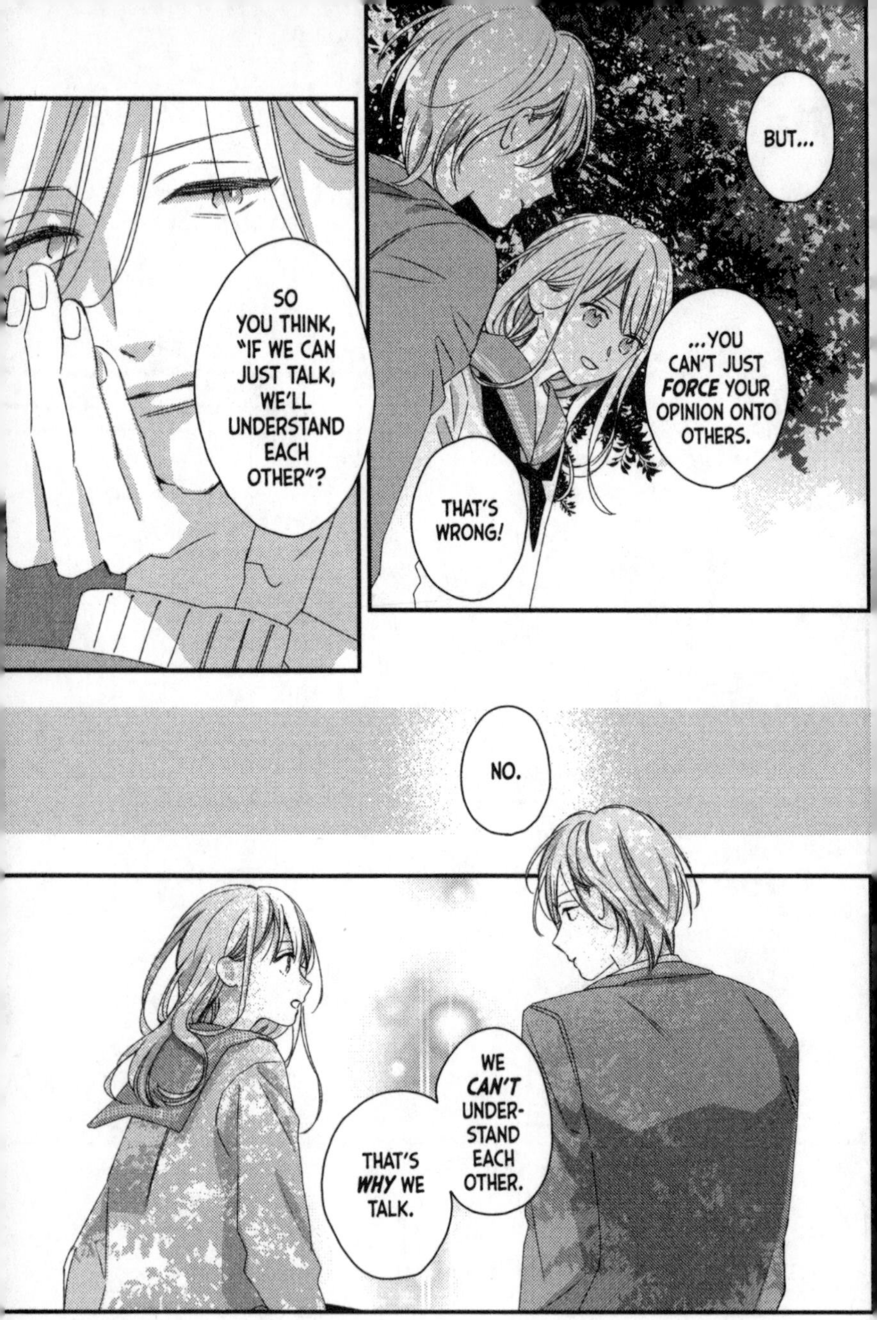
BUT...
...YOU CAN'T JUST FORCE YOUR OPINION ONTO OTHERS.
THAT'S WRONG!
SO YOU THINK, "IF WE CAN JUST TALK, WE'LL UNDERSTAND EACH OTHER"?
NO.
WE CAN'T UNDER-STAND EACH OTHER.
THAT'S WHY WE TALK.

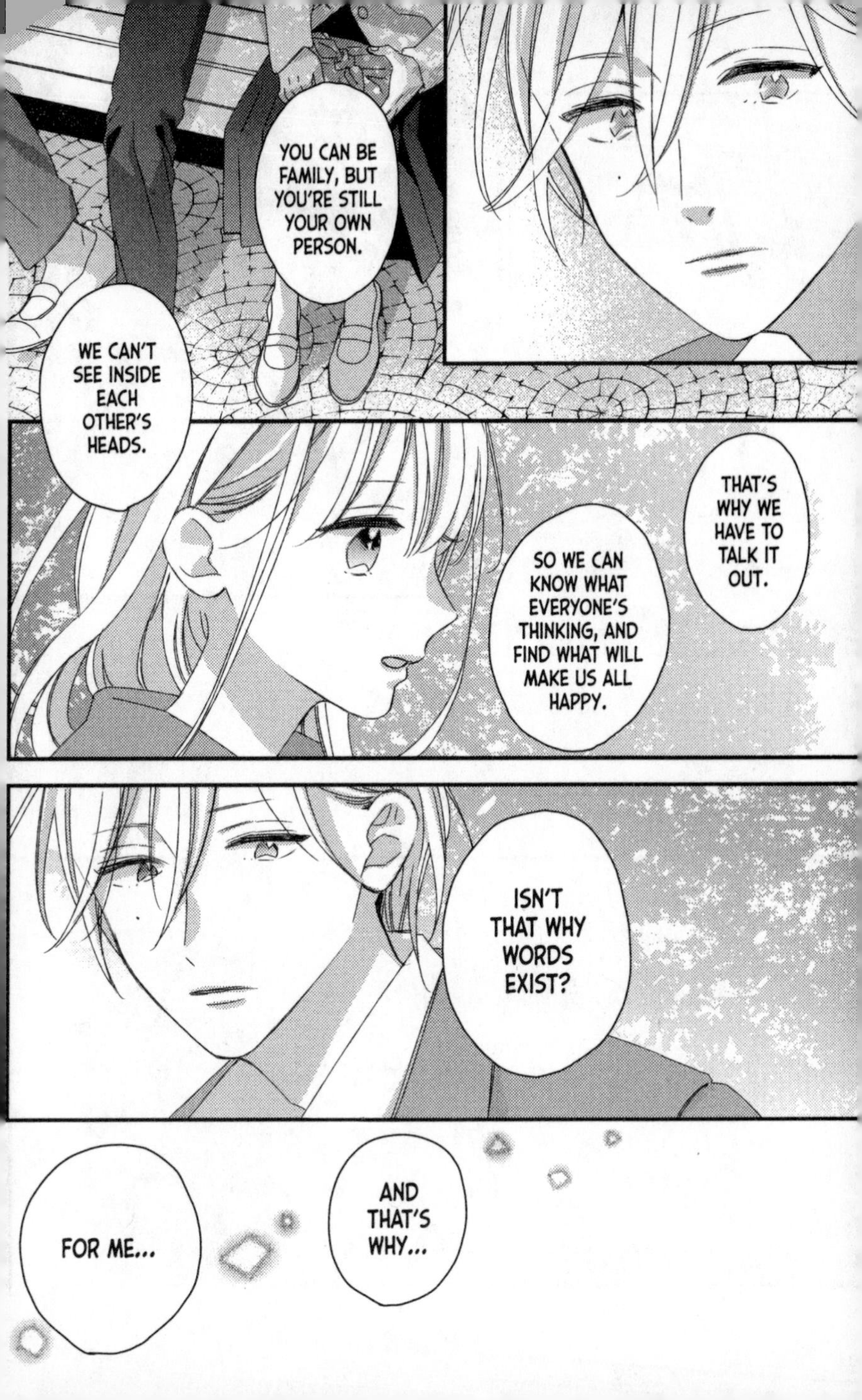
YOU CAN BE FAMILY, BUT YOU'RE STILL YOUR OWN PERSON.
WE CAN'T SEE INSIDE EACH OTHER'S HEADS.
THAT'S WHY WE HAVE TO TALK IT OUT.
SO WE CAN KNOW WHAT EVERYONE'S THINKING, AND FIND WHAT WILL MAKE US ALL HAPPY.
ISN'T THAT WHY WORDS EXIST?
AND THAT'S WHY...
FOR ME...

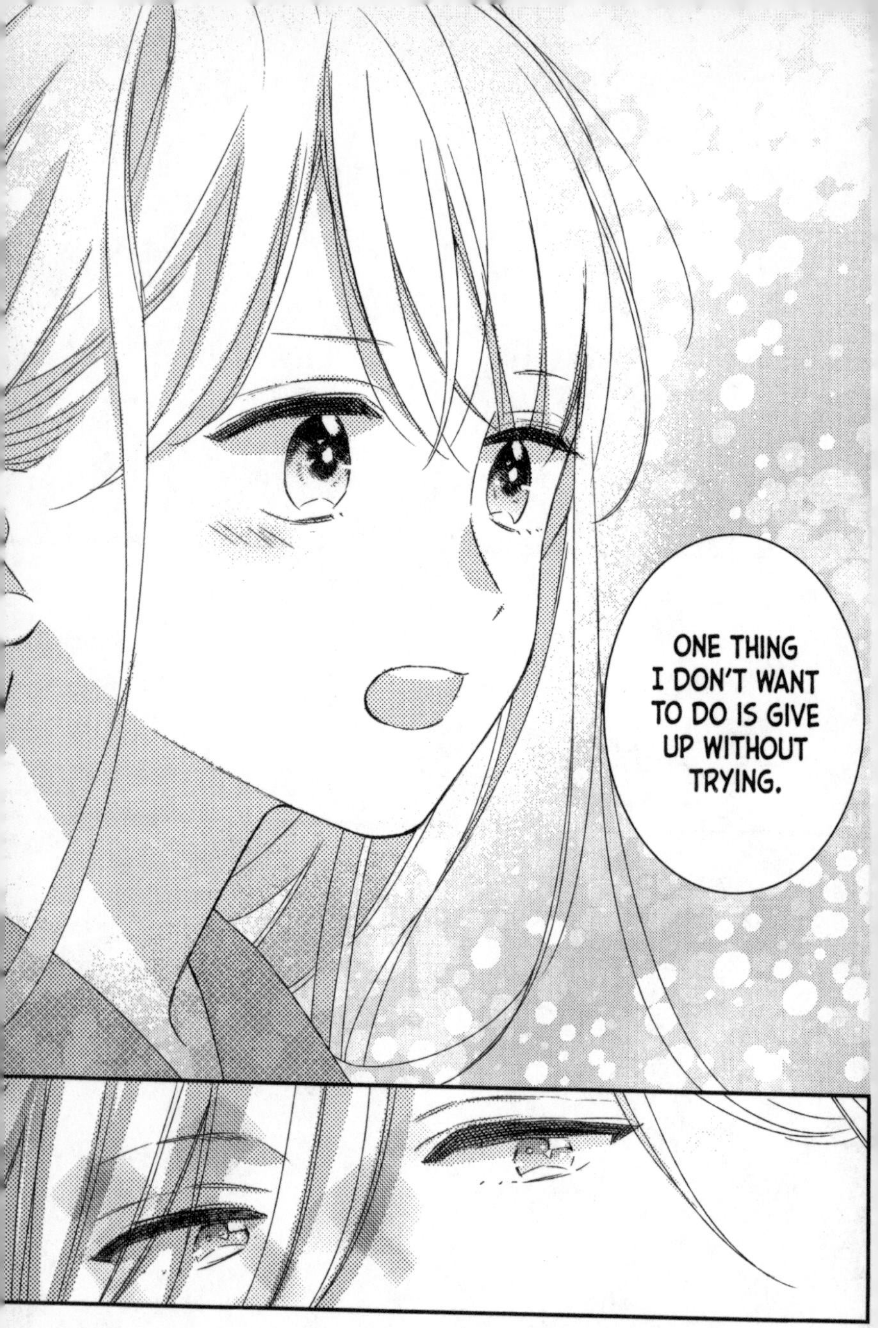
ONE THING I DON'T WANT TO DO IS GIVE UP WITHOUT TRYING.

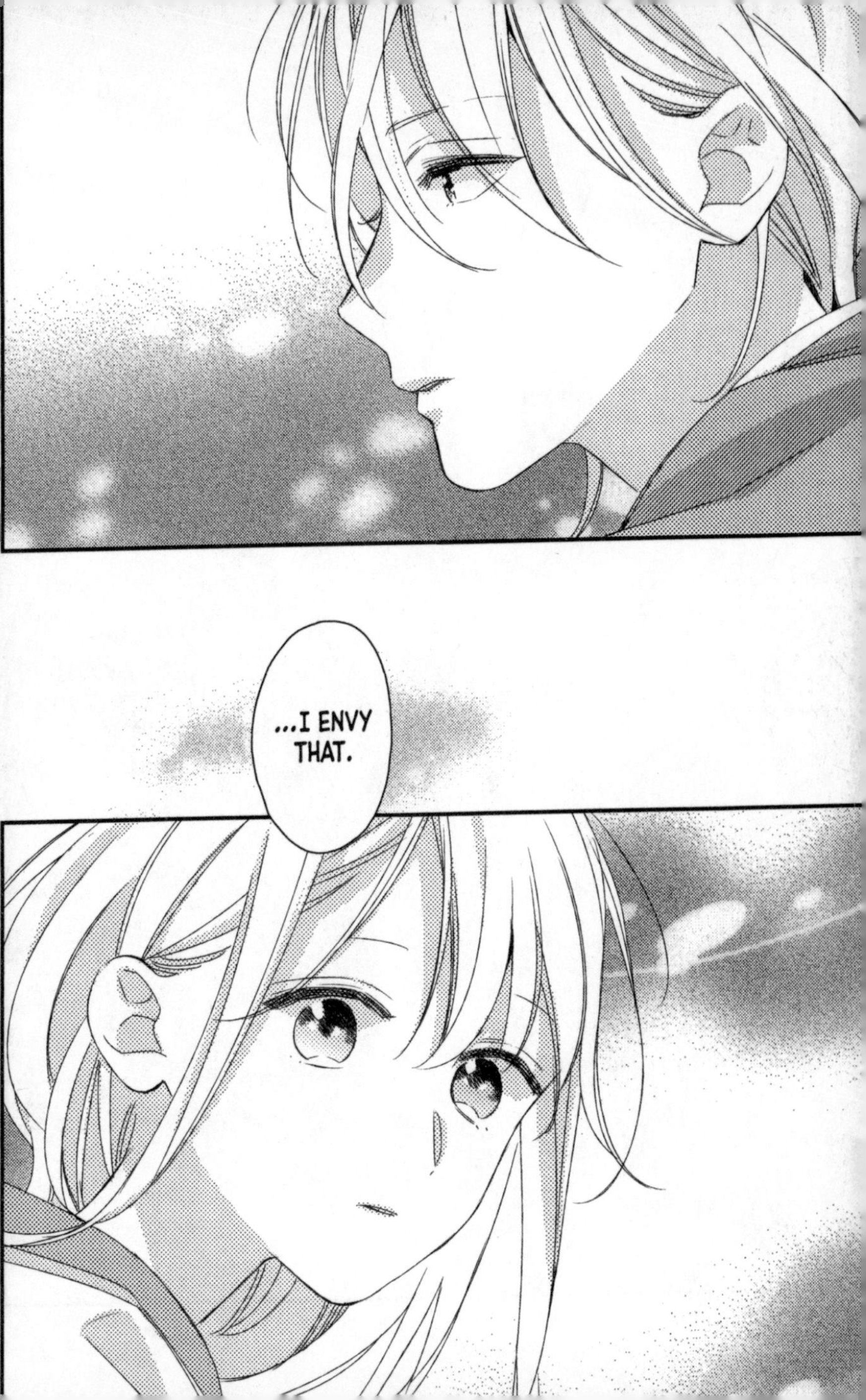
...I ENVY THAT.

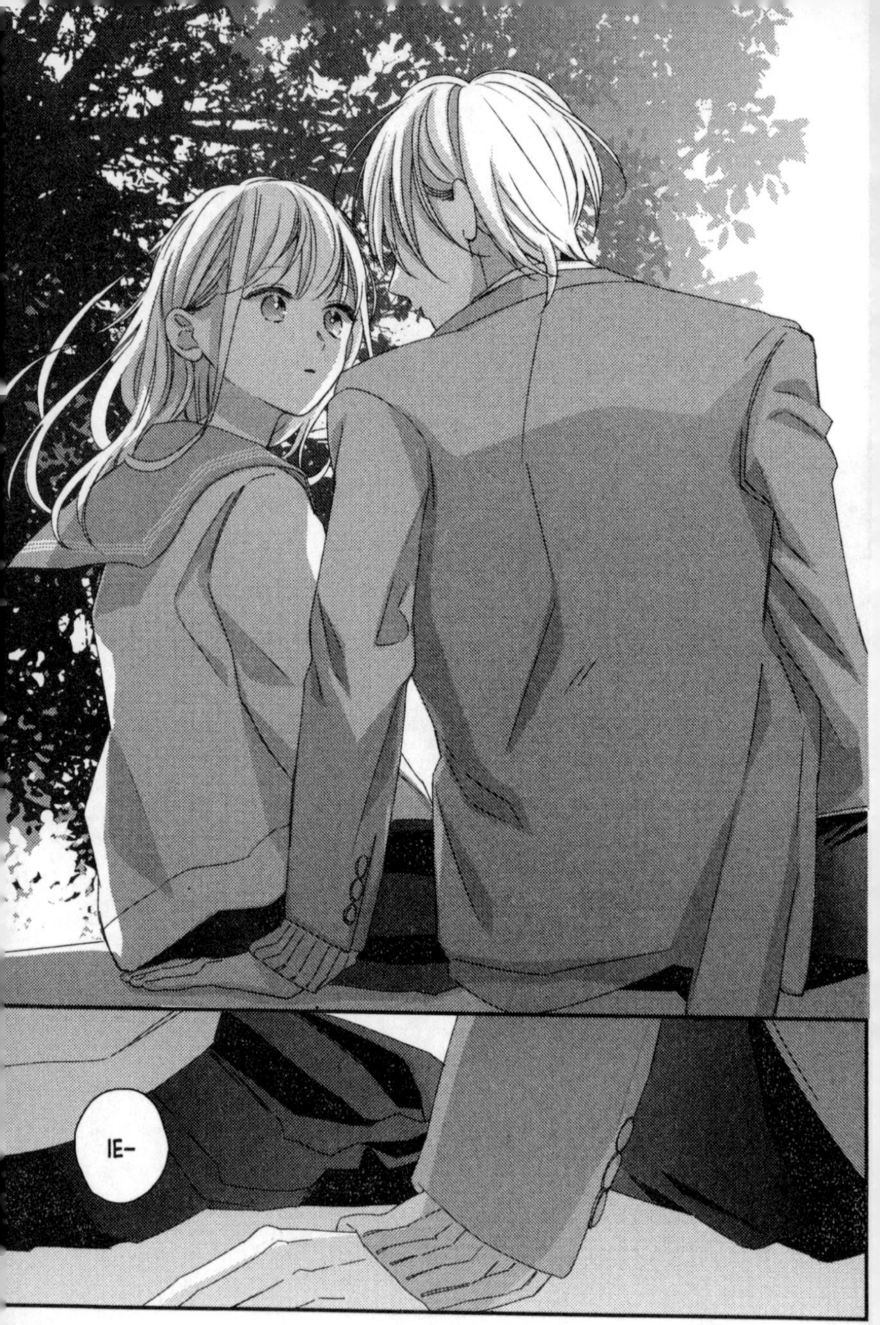
IE–

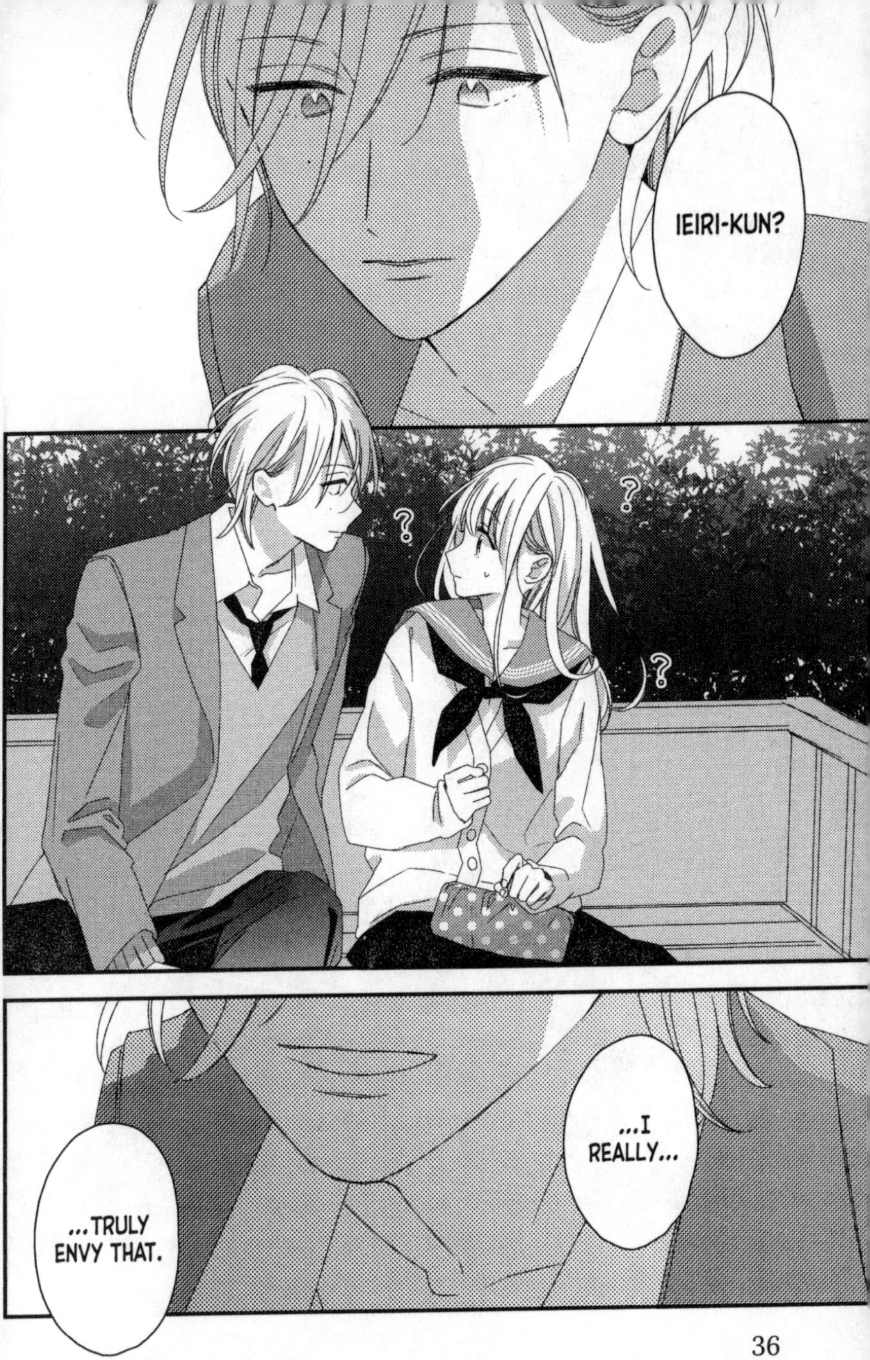
IEIRI-KUN?
...I REALLY...
...TRULY ENVY THAT.

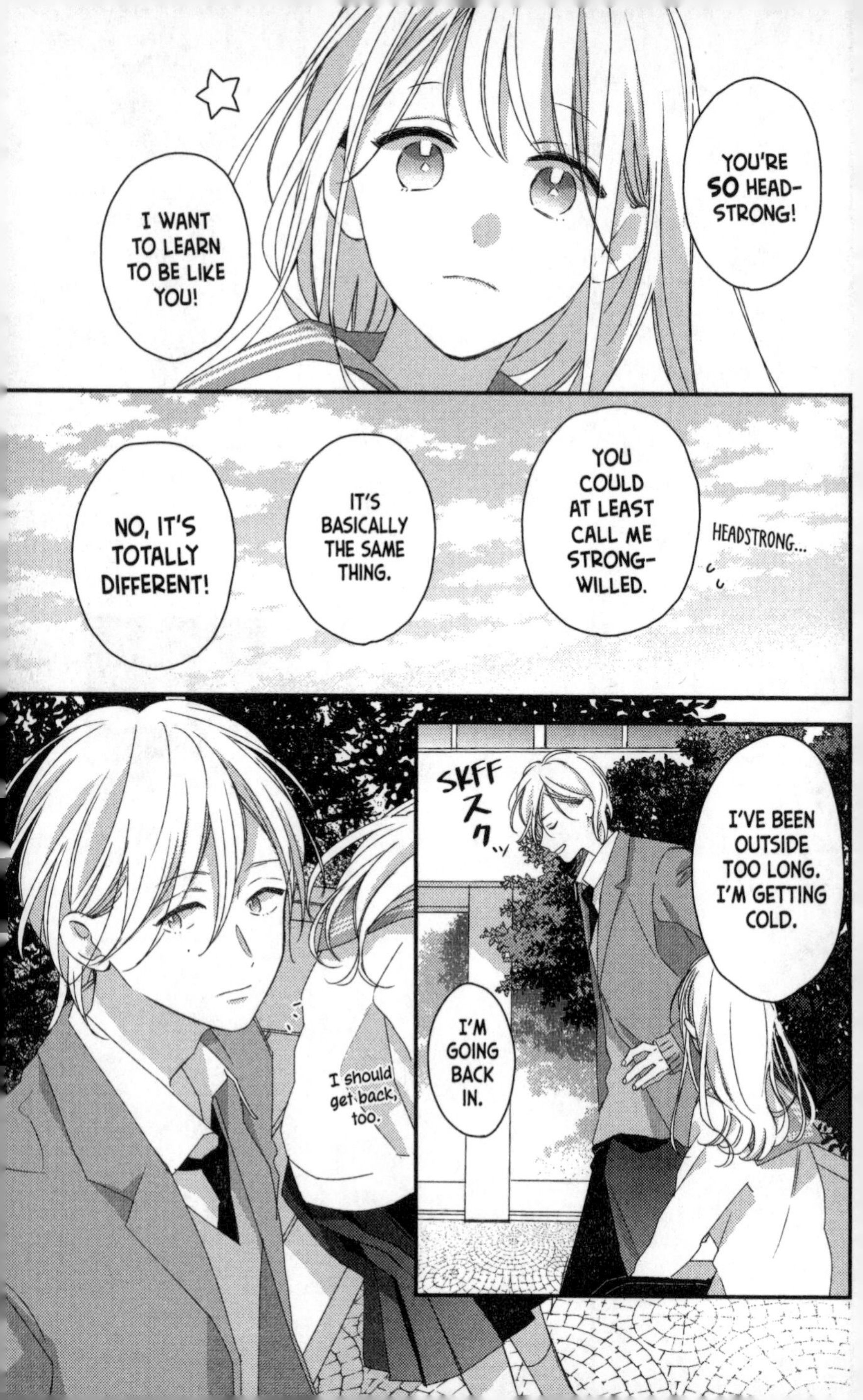
YOU'RE SO HEAD-STRONG!
I WANT TO LEARN TO BE LIKE YOU!
HEADSTRONG...
YOU COULD AT LEAST CALL ME STRONG-WILLED.
IT'S BASICALLY THE SAME THING.
NO, IT'S TOTALLY DIFFERENT!
I'VE BEEN OUTSIDE TOO LONG. I'M GETTING COLD.
SKFF
スクッ
I'M GOING BACK IN.
I should get back, too.

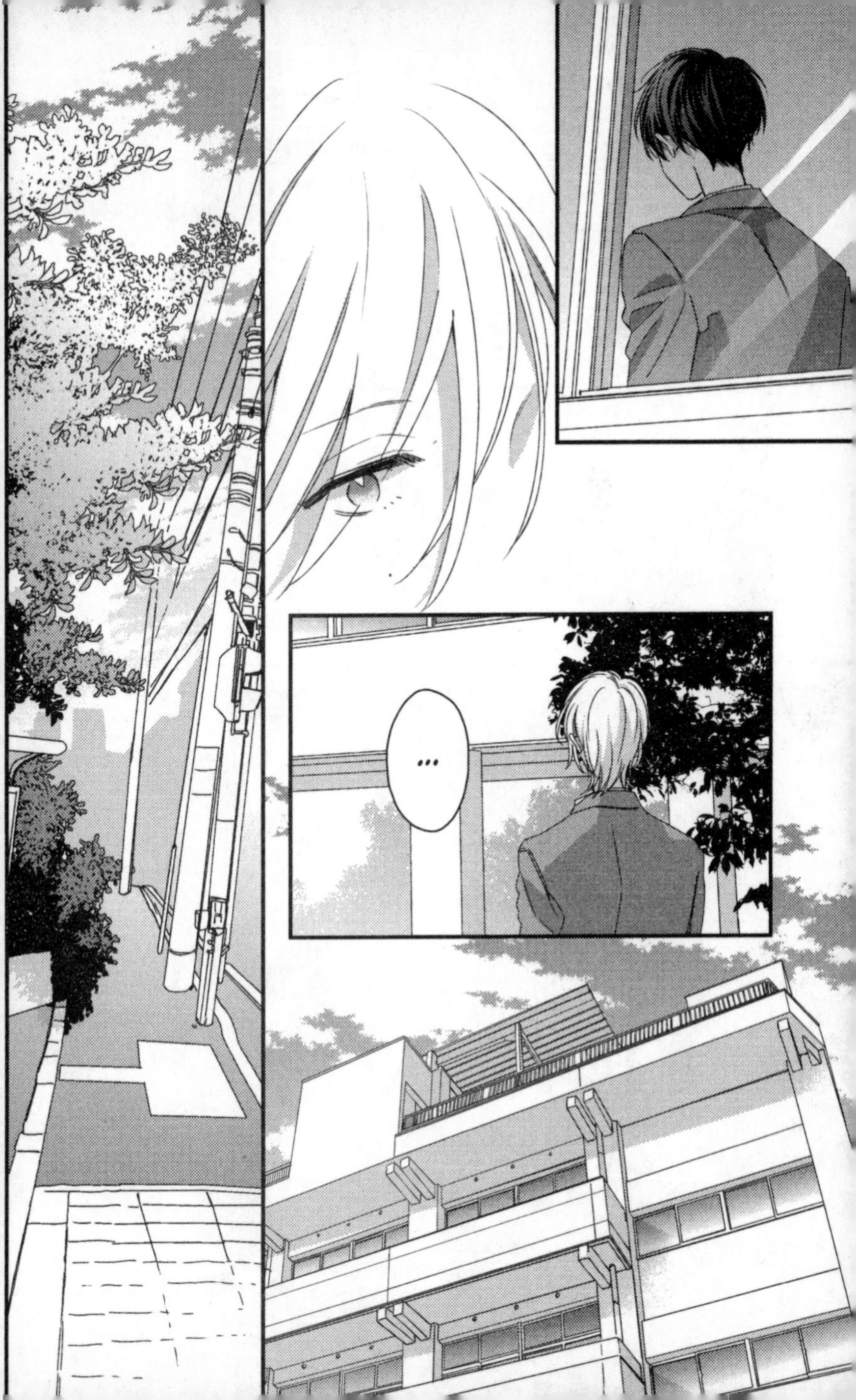
...

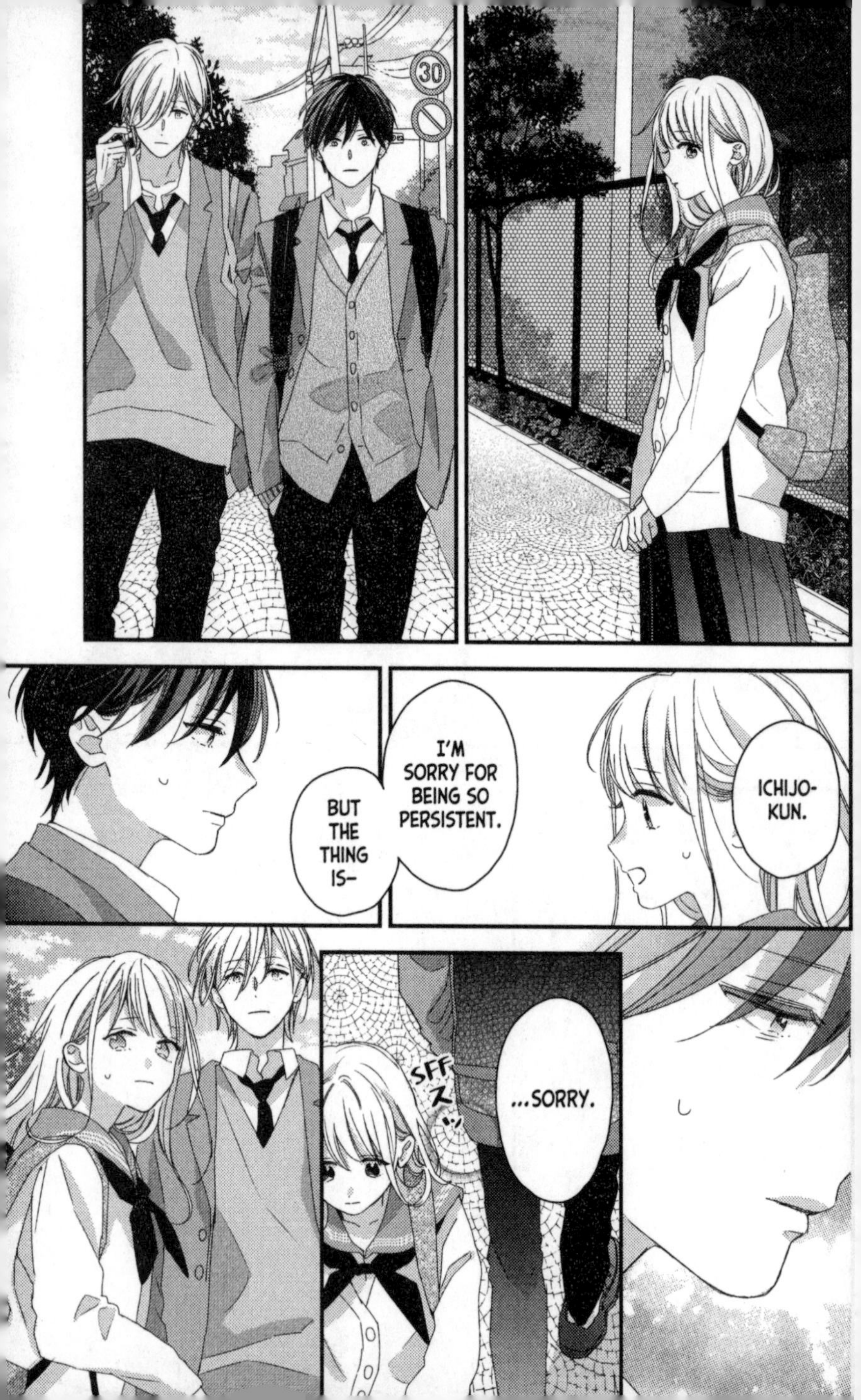
ICHIJO-KUN.
I'M SORRY FOR BEING SO PERSISTENT.
BUT THE THING IS–
...SORRY.
SFF
スッ

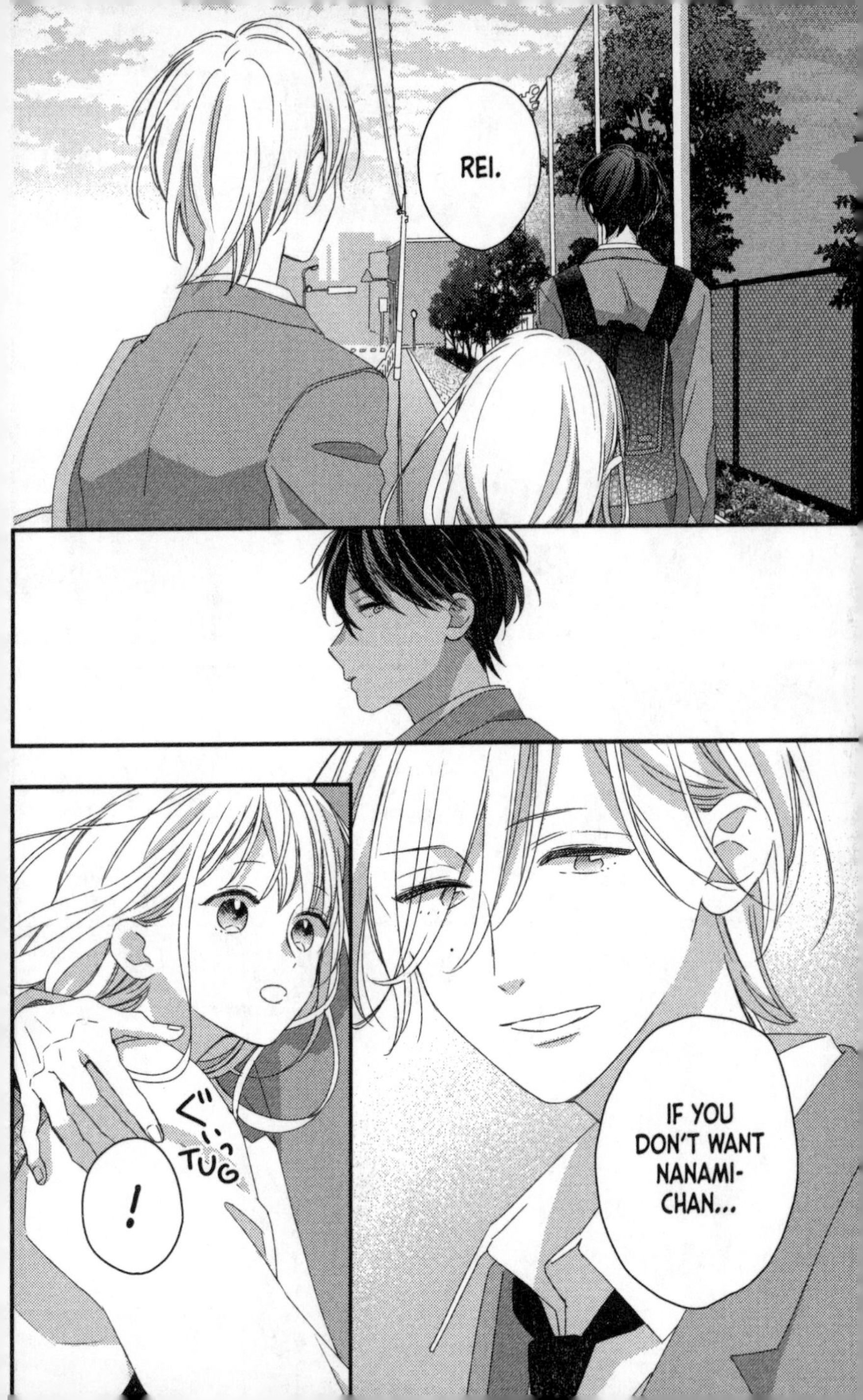
REI.
IF YOU DON'T WANT NANAMI-CHAN...
!
ぐいっ
TUG

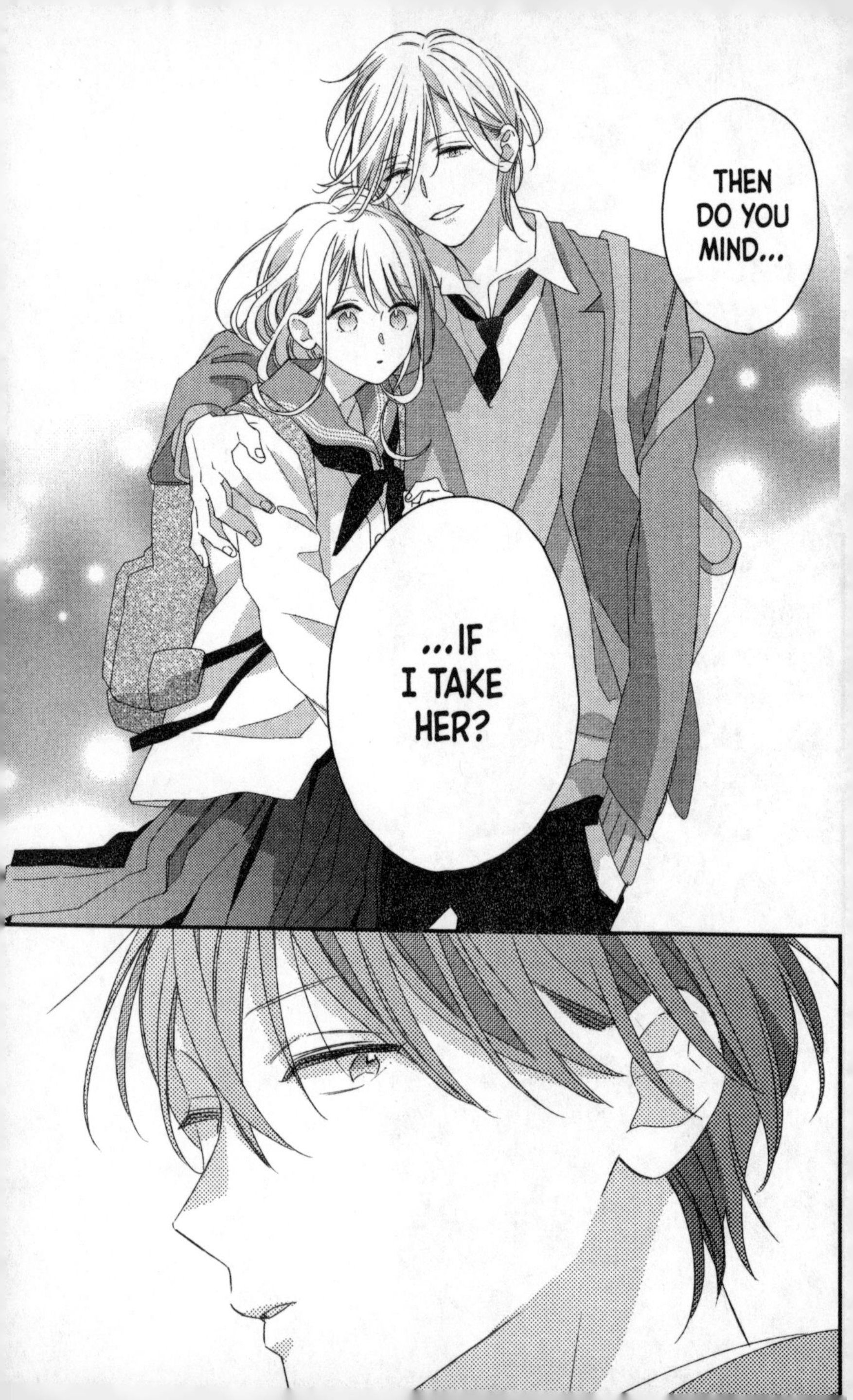
THEN DO YOU MIND...
...IF I TAKE HER?

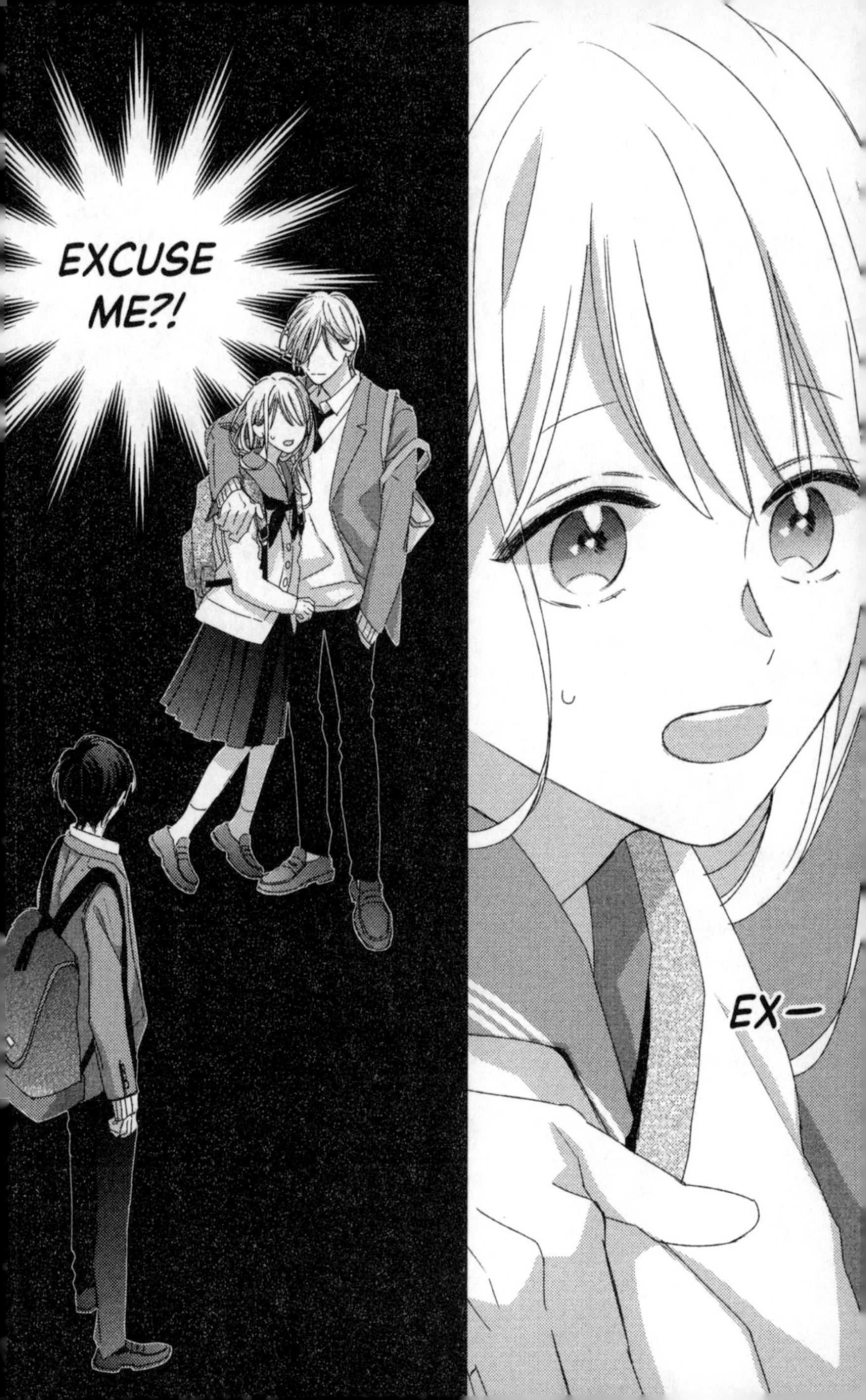
EX—
EXCUSE ME?!

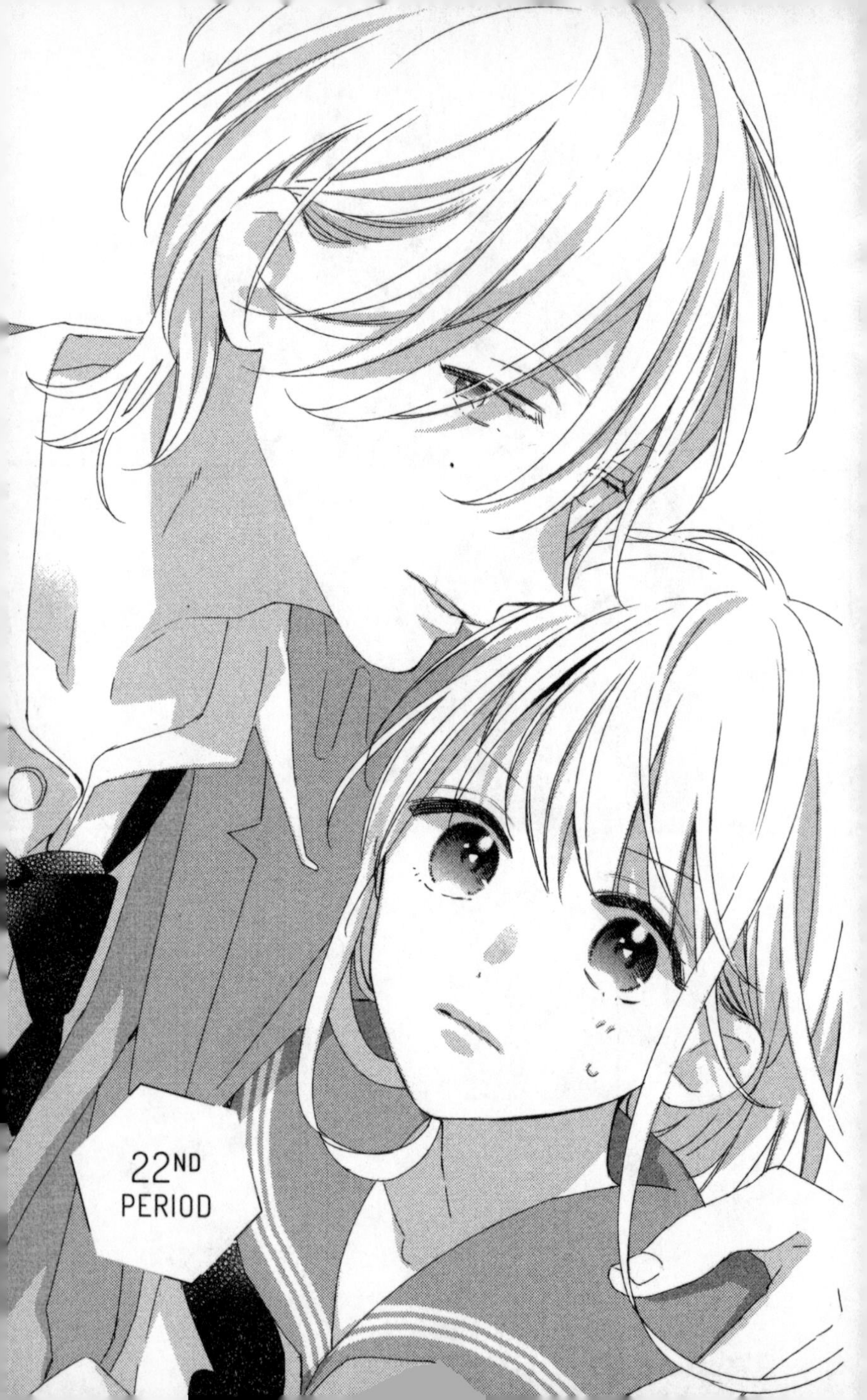
22ND
PERIOD

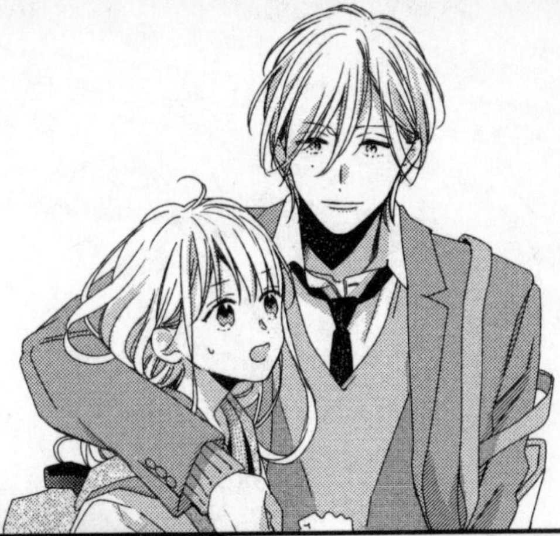

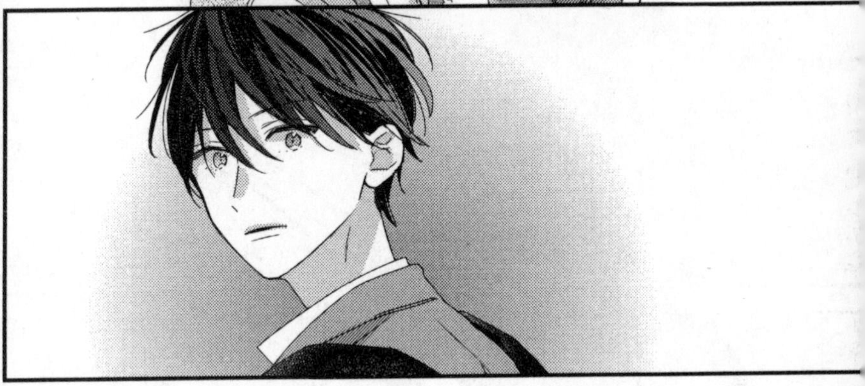

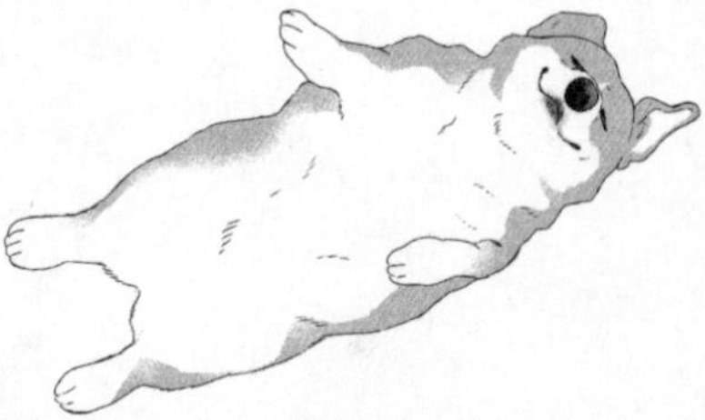

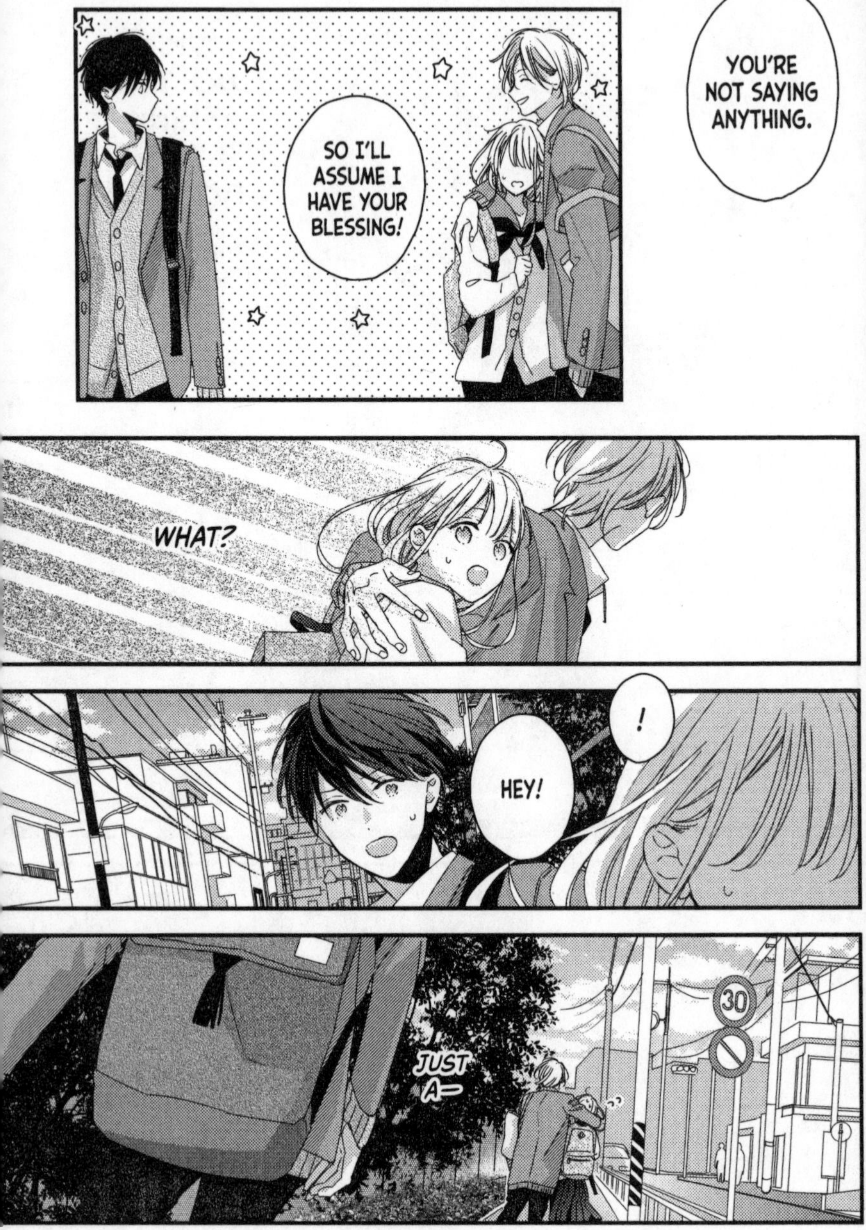
YOU'RE NOT SAYING ANYTHING.
SO I'LL ASSUME I HAVE YOUR BLESSING!
WHAT?
!
HEY!
JUST A—

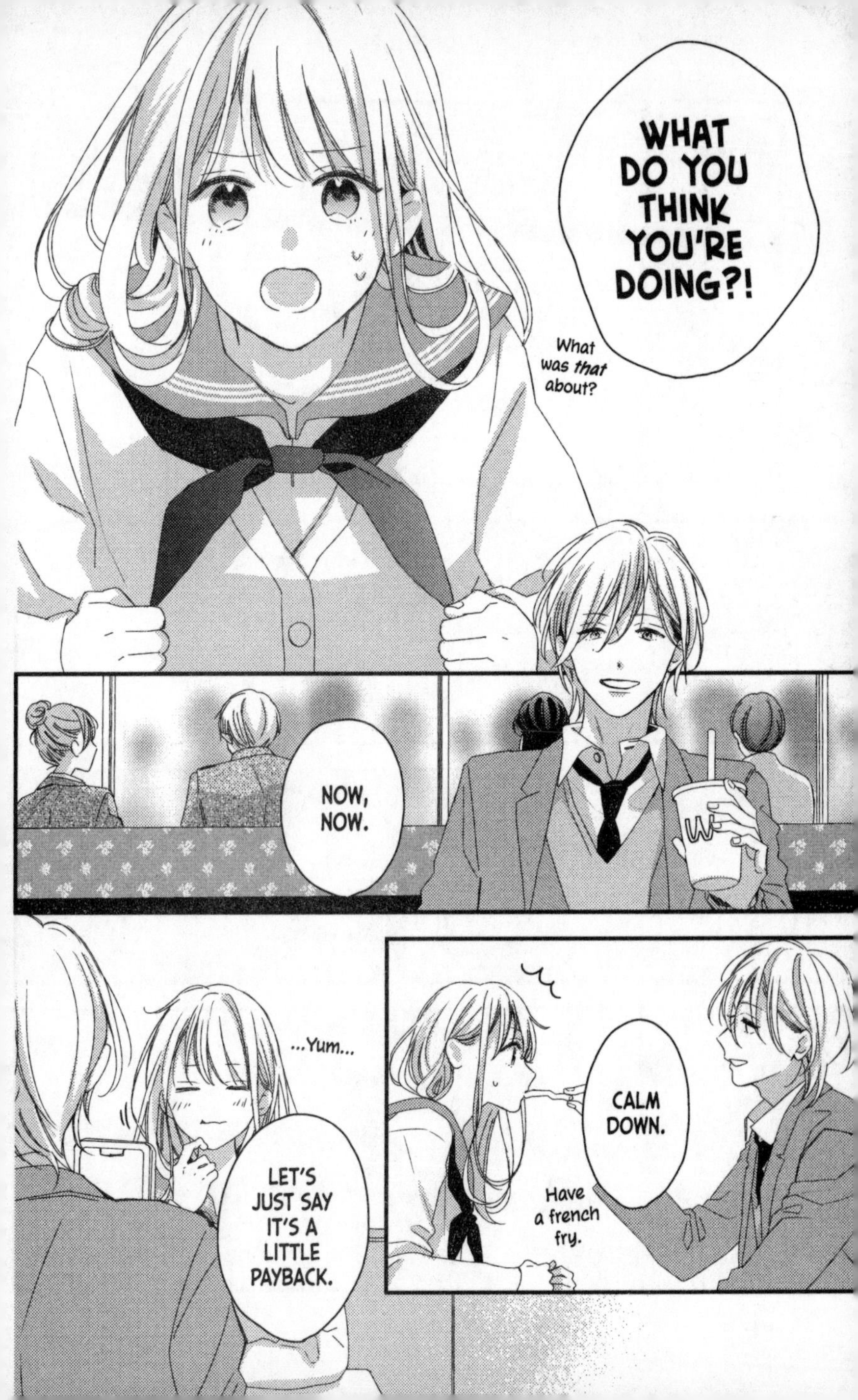
WHAT DO YOU THINK YOU'RE DOING?!
What was *that* about?
NOW, NOW.
CALM DOWN.
Have a french fry.
...Yum...
LET'S JUST SAY IT'S A LITTLE PAYBACK.

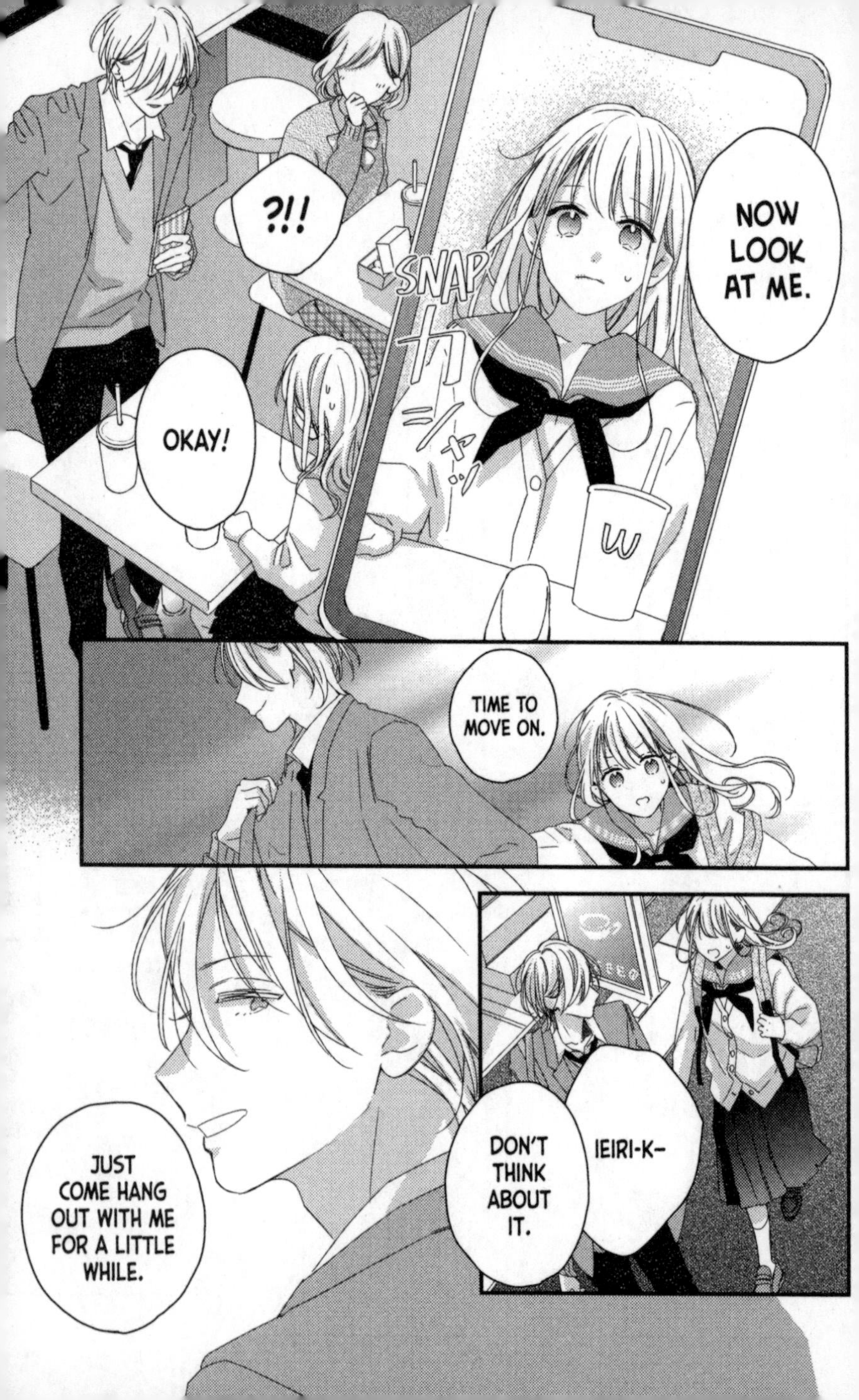
NOW LOOK AT ME.
SNAP
?!!
OKAY!
TIME TO MOVE ON.
IEIRI-K–
DON'T THINK ABOUT IT.
JUST COME HANG OUT WITH ME FOR A LITTLE WHILE.

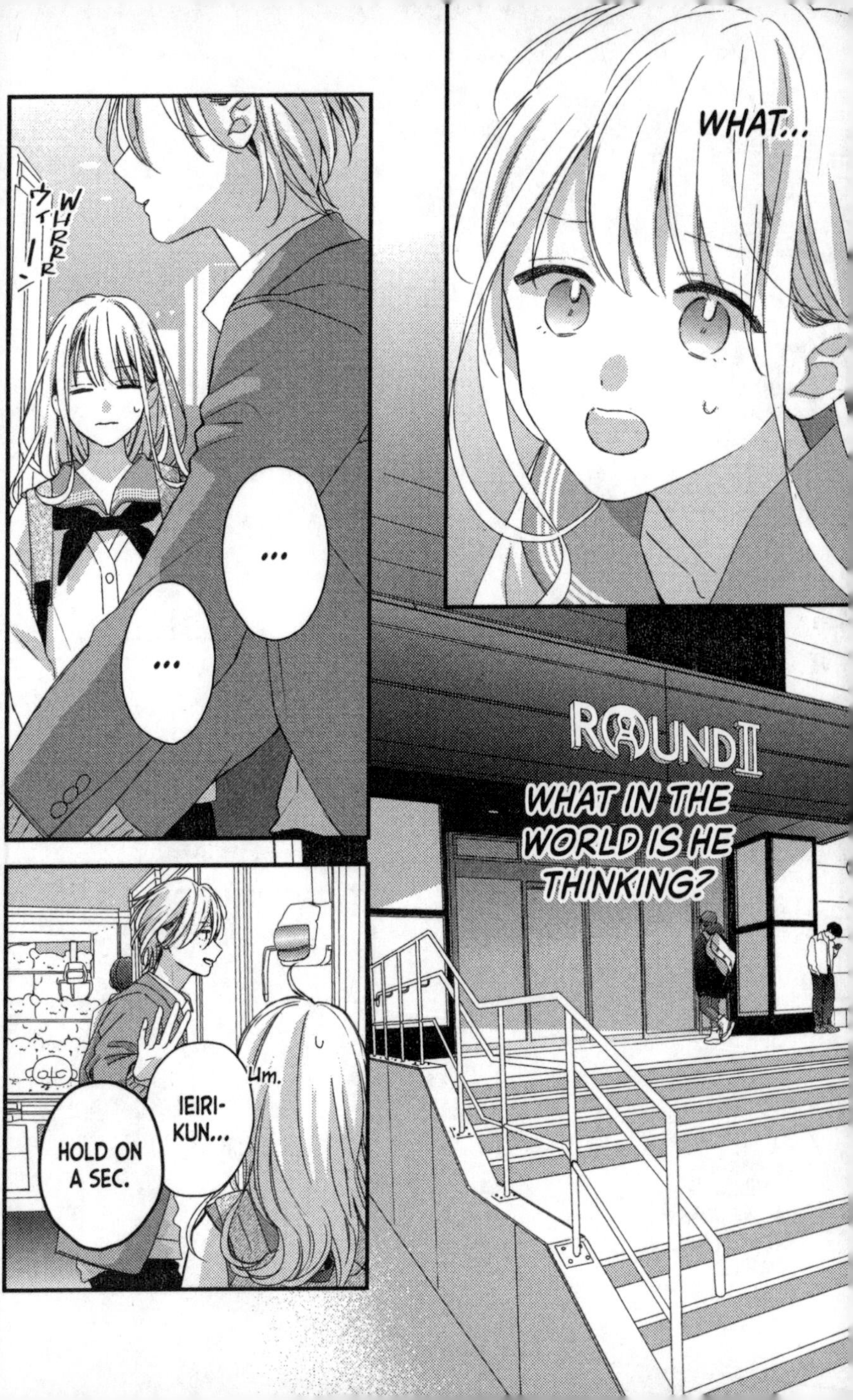
WHAT...
WHIRR
ウィーン
...
...
ROUND II
WHAT IN THE WORLD IS HE THINKING?
Um.
IEIRI-KUN...
HOLD ON A SEC.

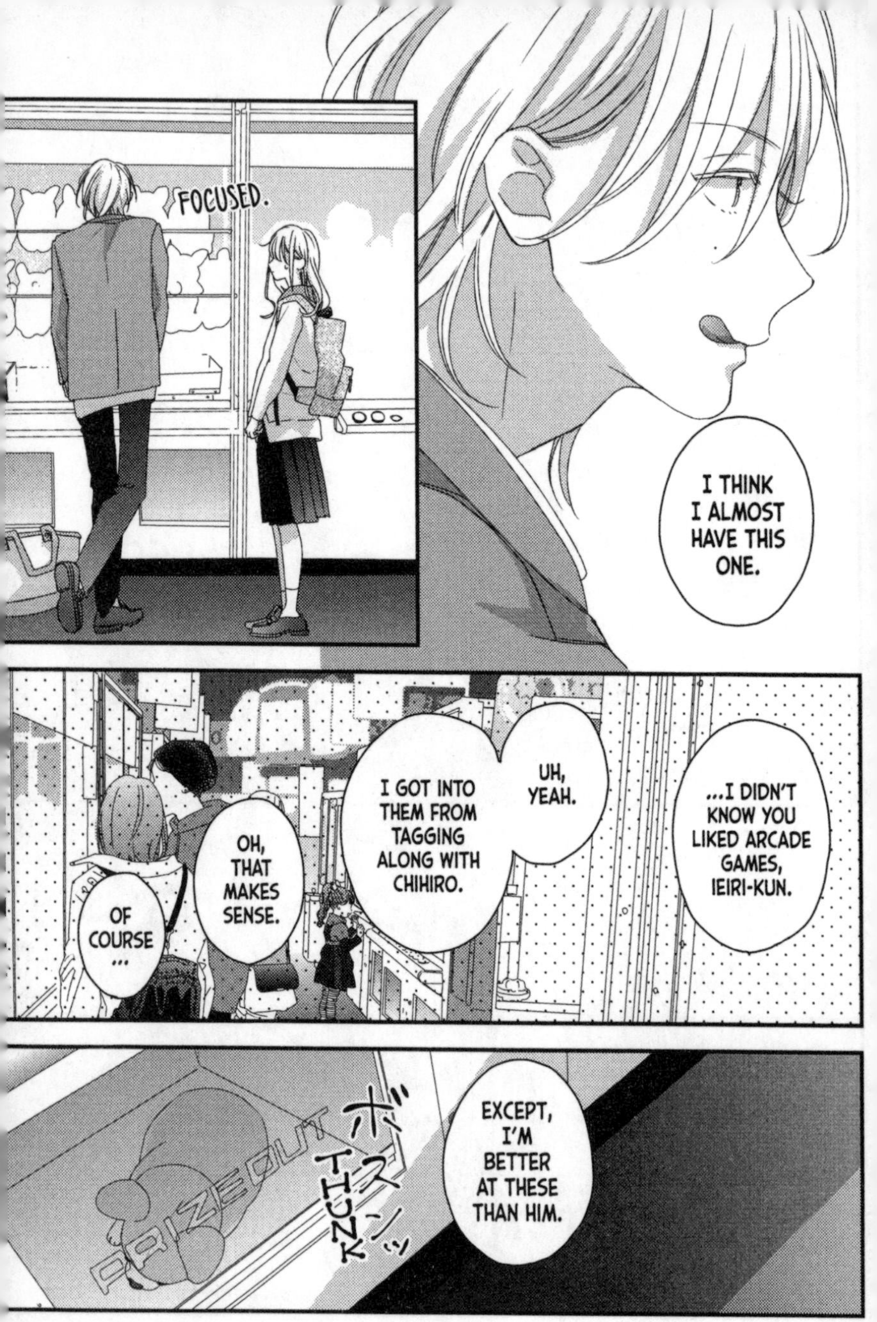
I THINK I ALMOST HAVE THIS ONE.
FOCUSED.
...I DIDN'T KNOW YOU LIKED ARCADE GAMES, IEIRI-KUN.
UH, YEAH.
I GOT INTO THEM FROM TAGGING ALONG WITH CHIHIRO.
OH, THAT MAKES SENSE.
OF COURSE...
EXCEPT, I'M BETTER AT THESE THAN HIM.
ボスーッ
THUNK
PRIZE OUT

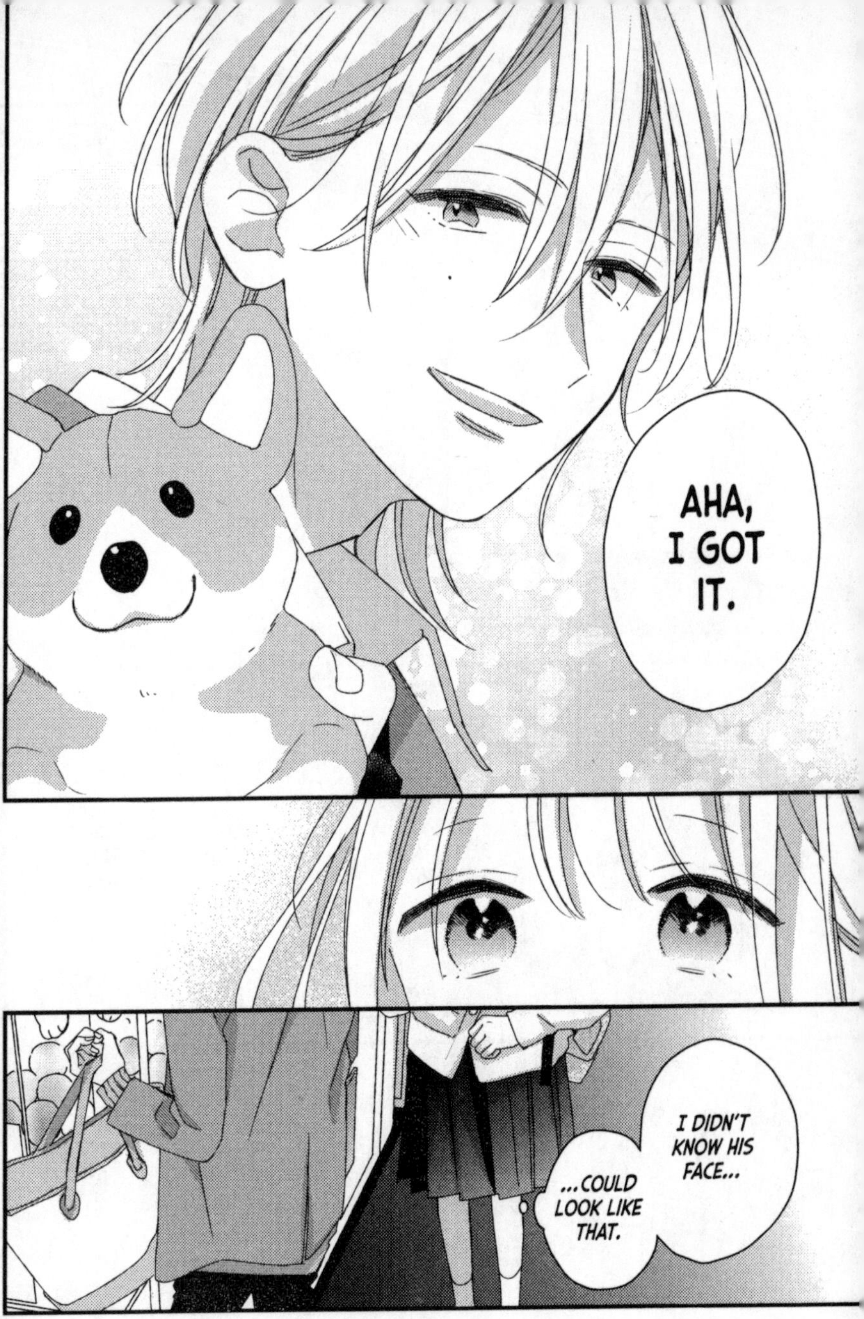
AHA, I GOT IT.
I DIDN'T KNOW HIS FACE...
...COULD LOOK LIKE THAT.

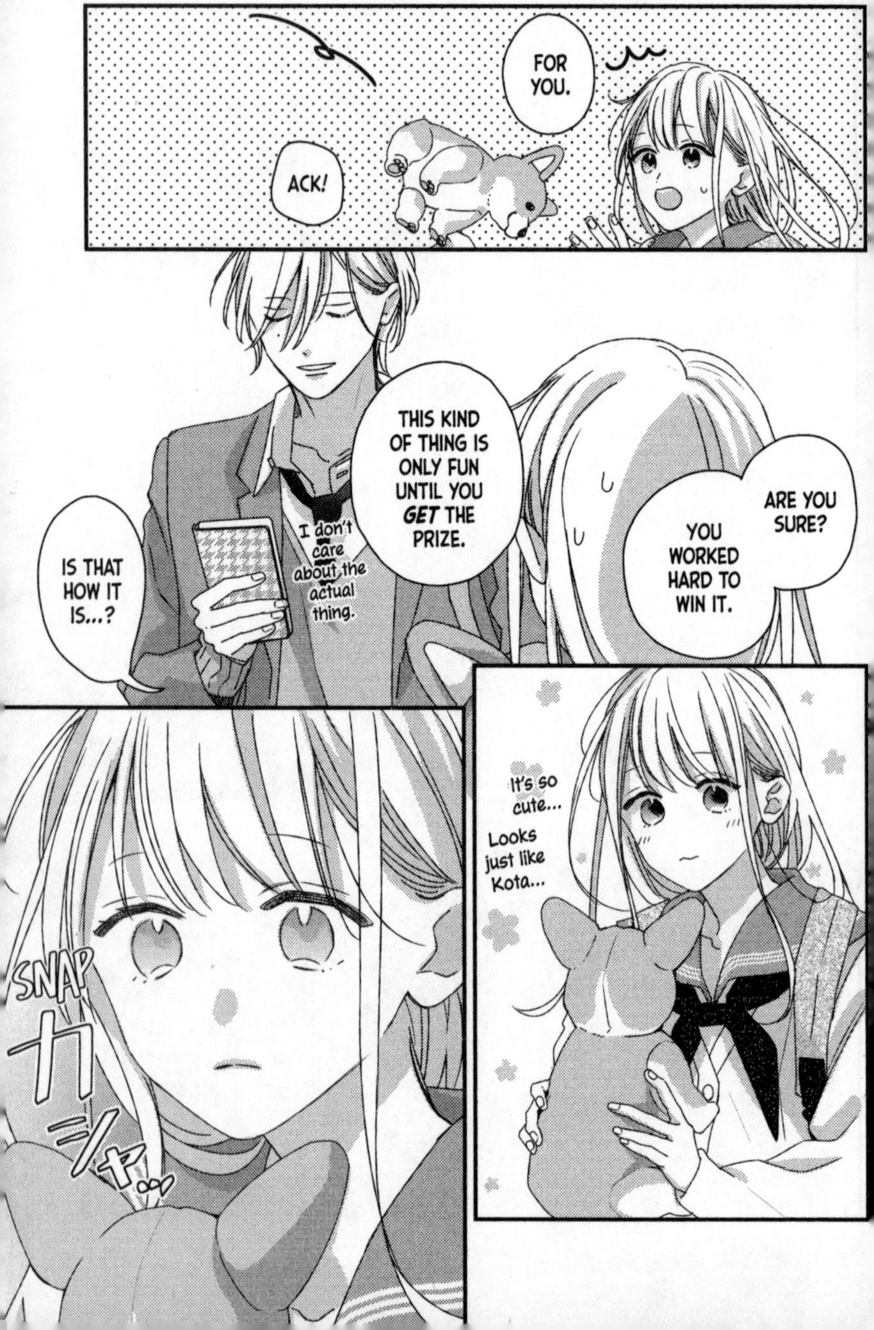
FOR YOU.
ACK!
ARE YOU SURE?
YOU WORKED HARD TO WIN IT.
THIS KIND OF THING IS ONLY FUN UNTIL YOU *GET* THE PRIZE.
I don't care about the actual thing.
IS THAT HOW IT IS...?
It's so cute...
Looks just like Kota...
SNAP

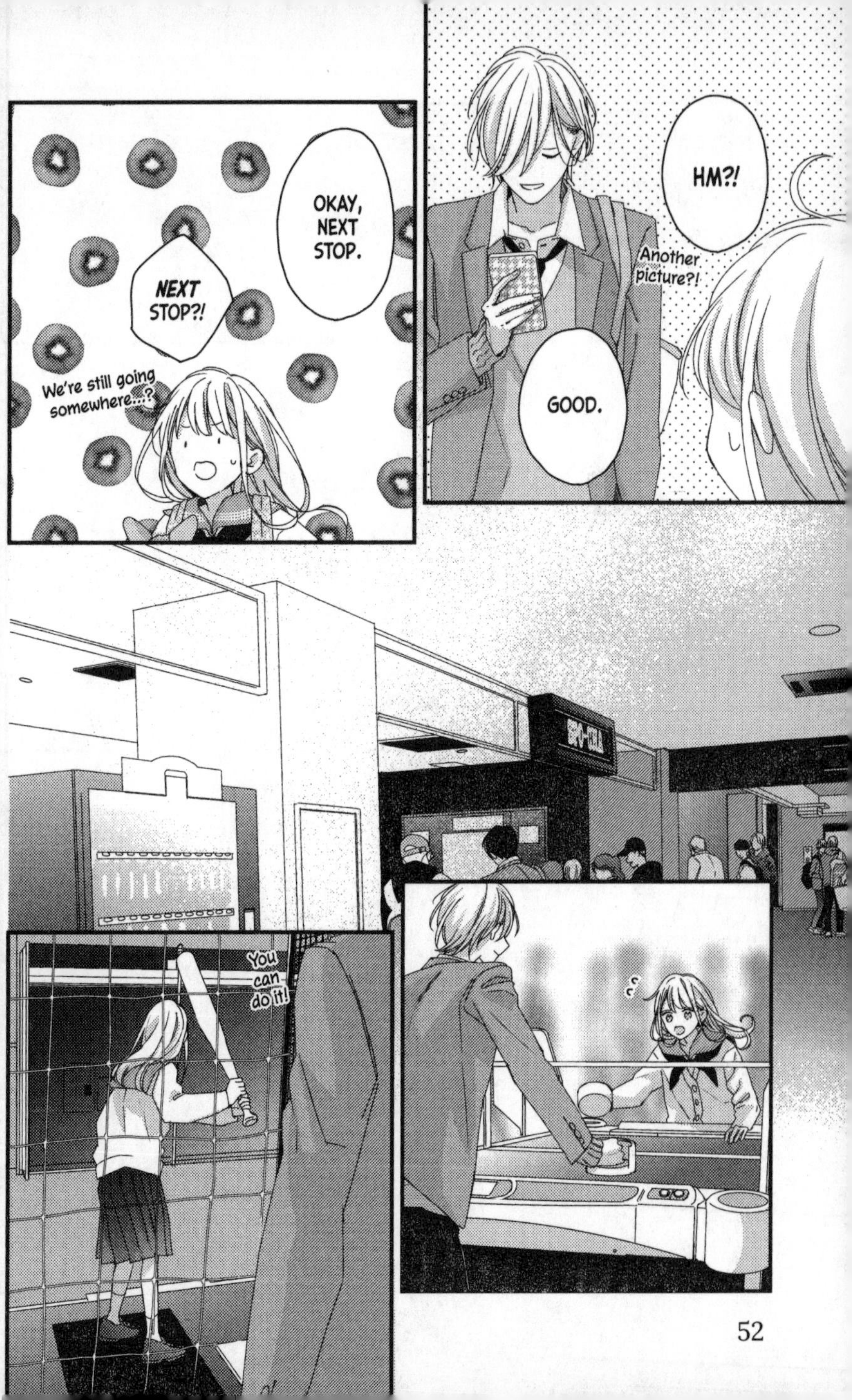
HM?!
Another picture?!
GOOD.
OKAY, NEXT STOP.
NEXT STOP?!
We're still going somewhere...?
You can do it!

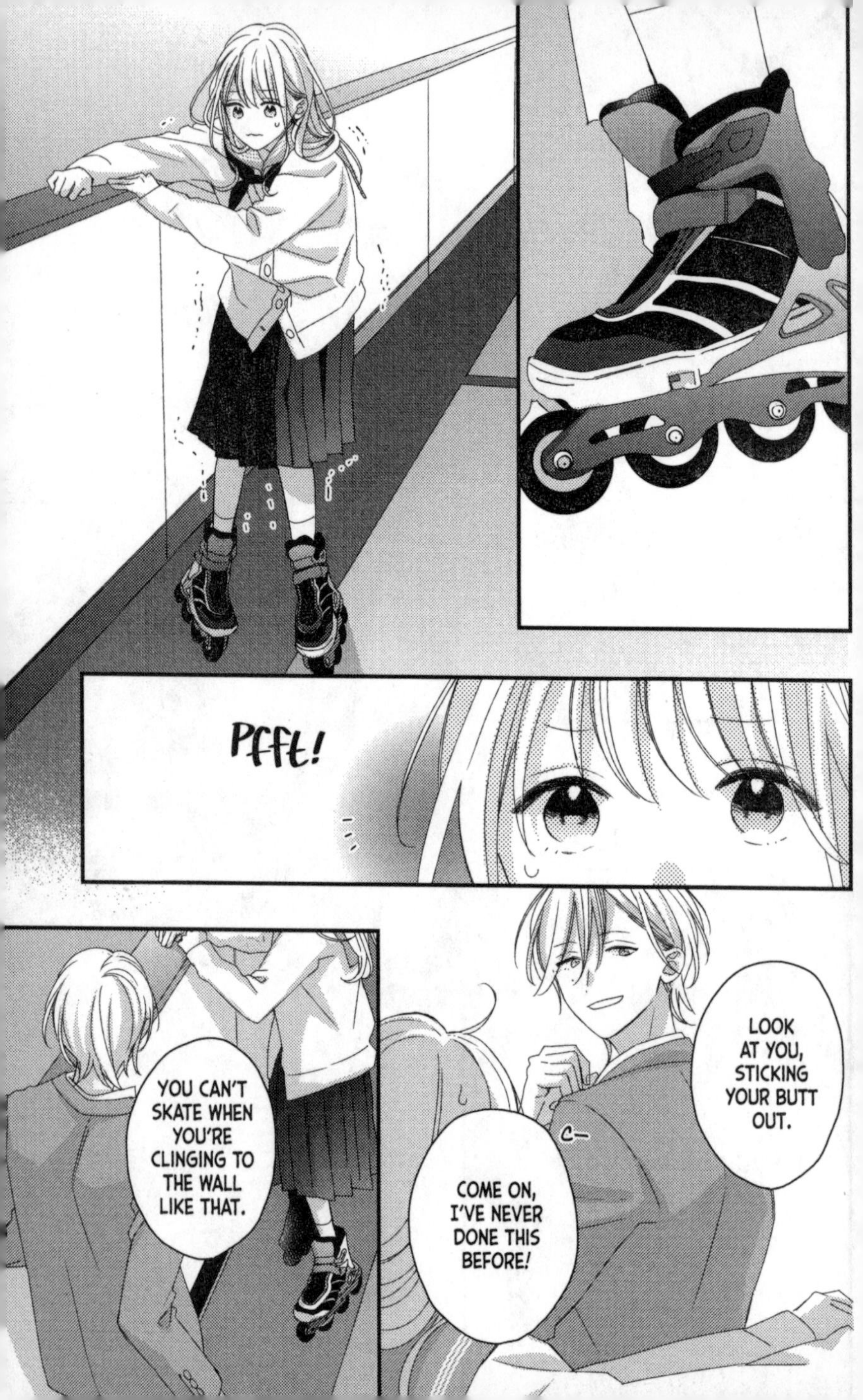
PFFT!
LOOK AT YOU, STICKING YOUR BUTT OUT.
C—
COME ON, I'VE NEVER DONE THIS BEFORE!
YOU CAN'T SKATE WHEN YOU'RE CLINGING TO THE WALL LIKE THAT.

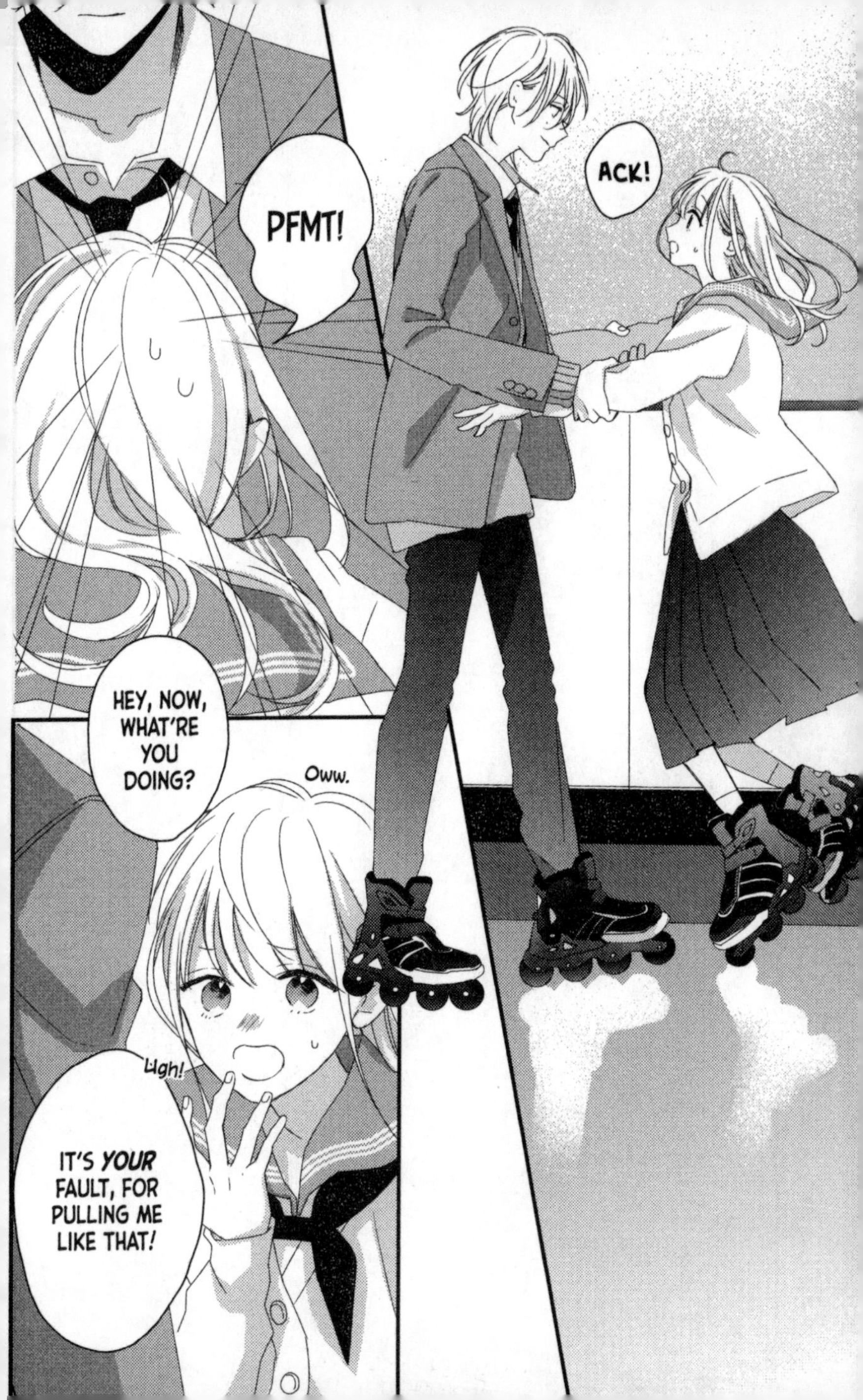
ACK!
PFMT!
HEY, NOW, WHAT'RE YOU DOING?
Oww.
Ugh!
IT'S *YOUR* FAULT, FOR PULLING ME LIKE THAT!

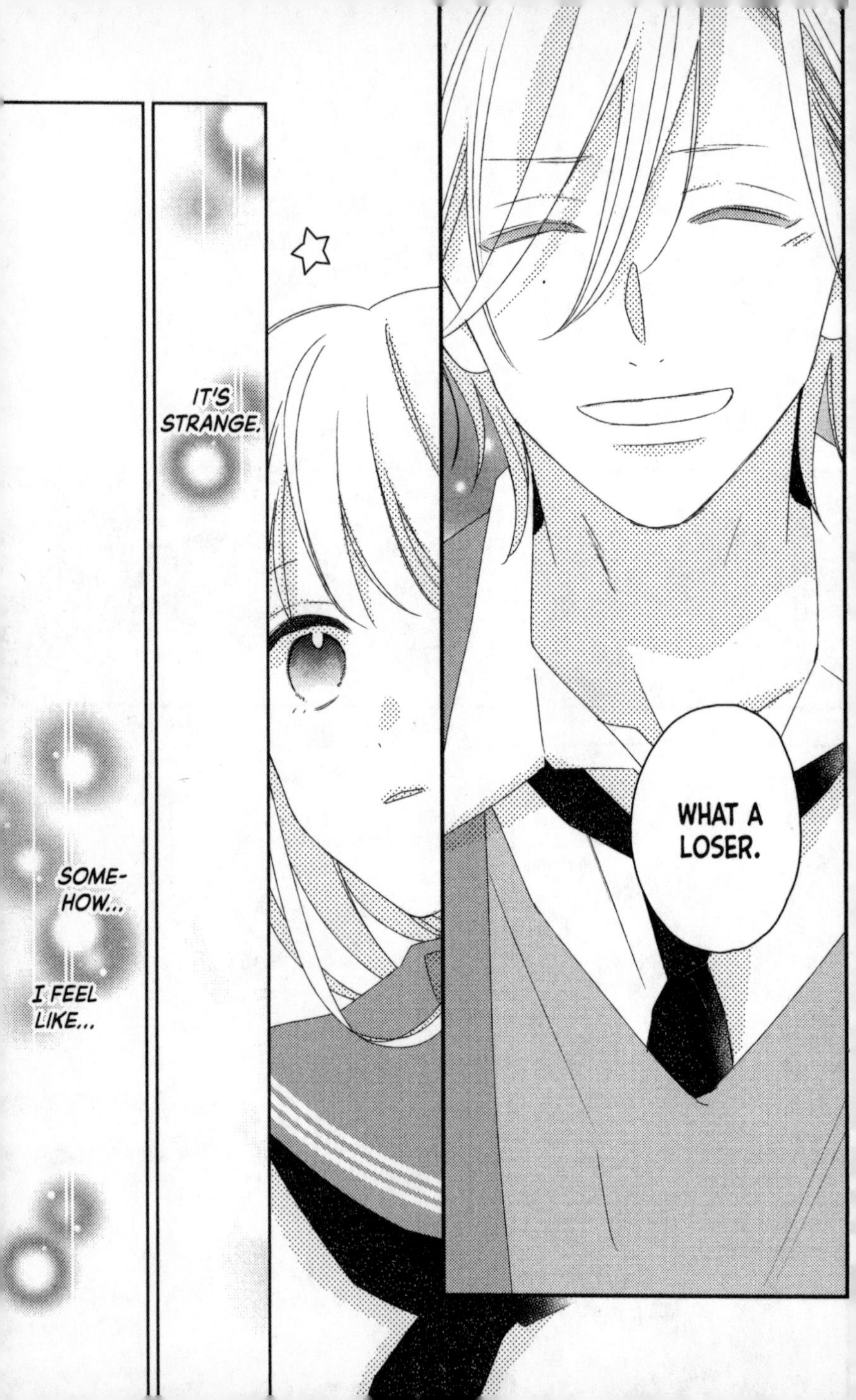
WHAT A LOSER.
IT'S STRANGE.
SOME-HOW...
I FEEL LIKE...

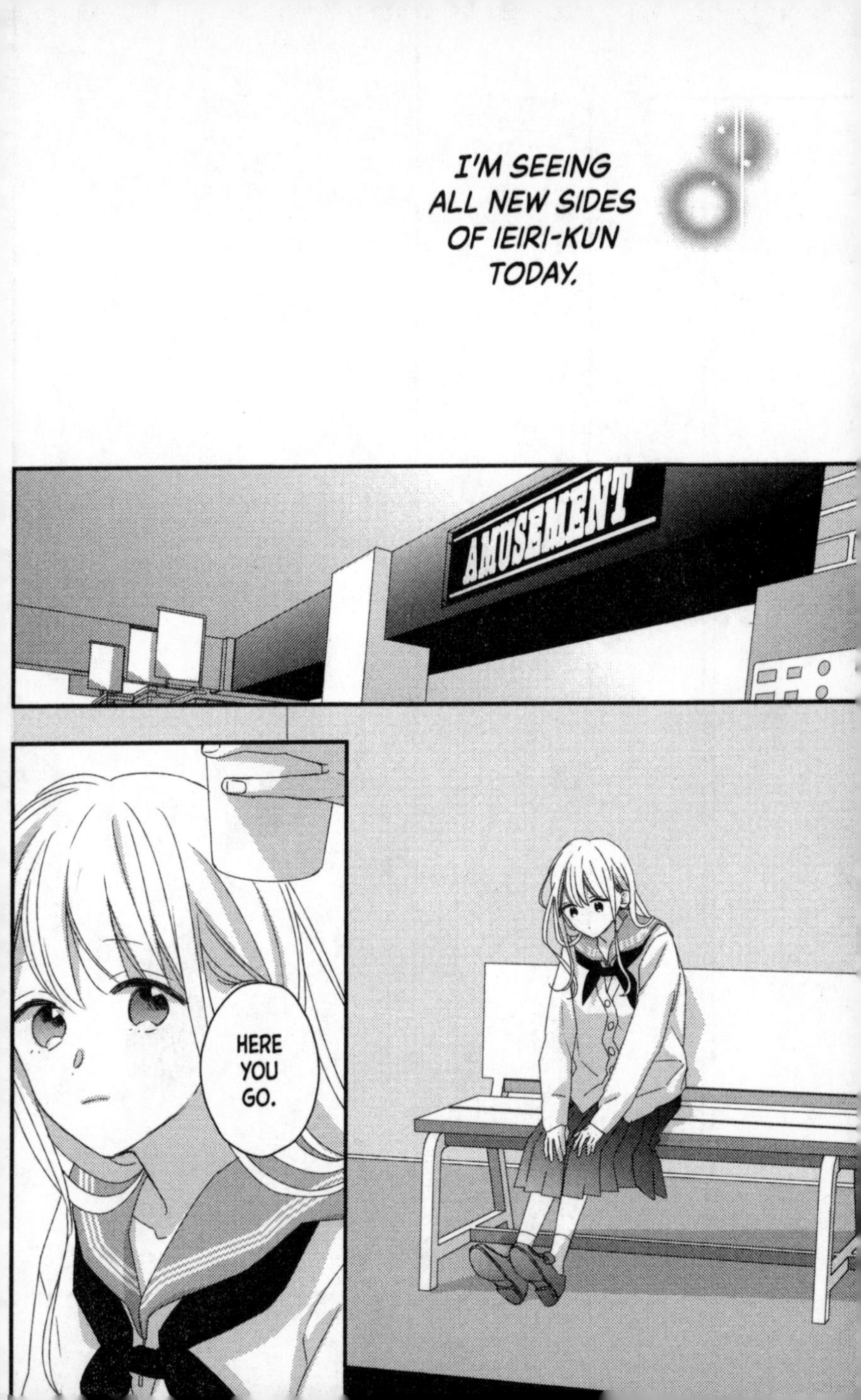
I'M SEEING ALL NEW SIDES OF IEIRI-KUN TODAY.
AMUSEMENT
HERE YOU GO.

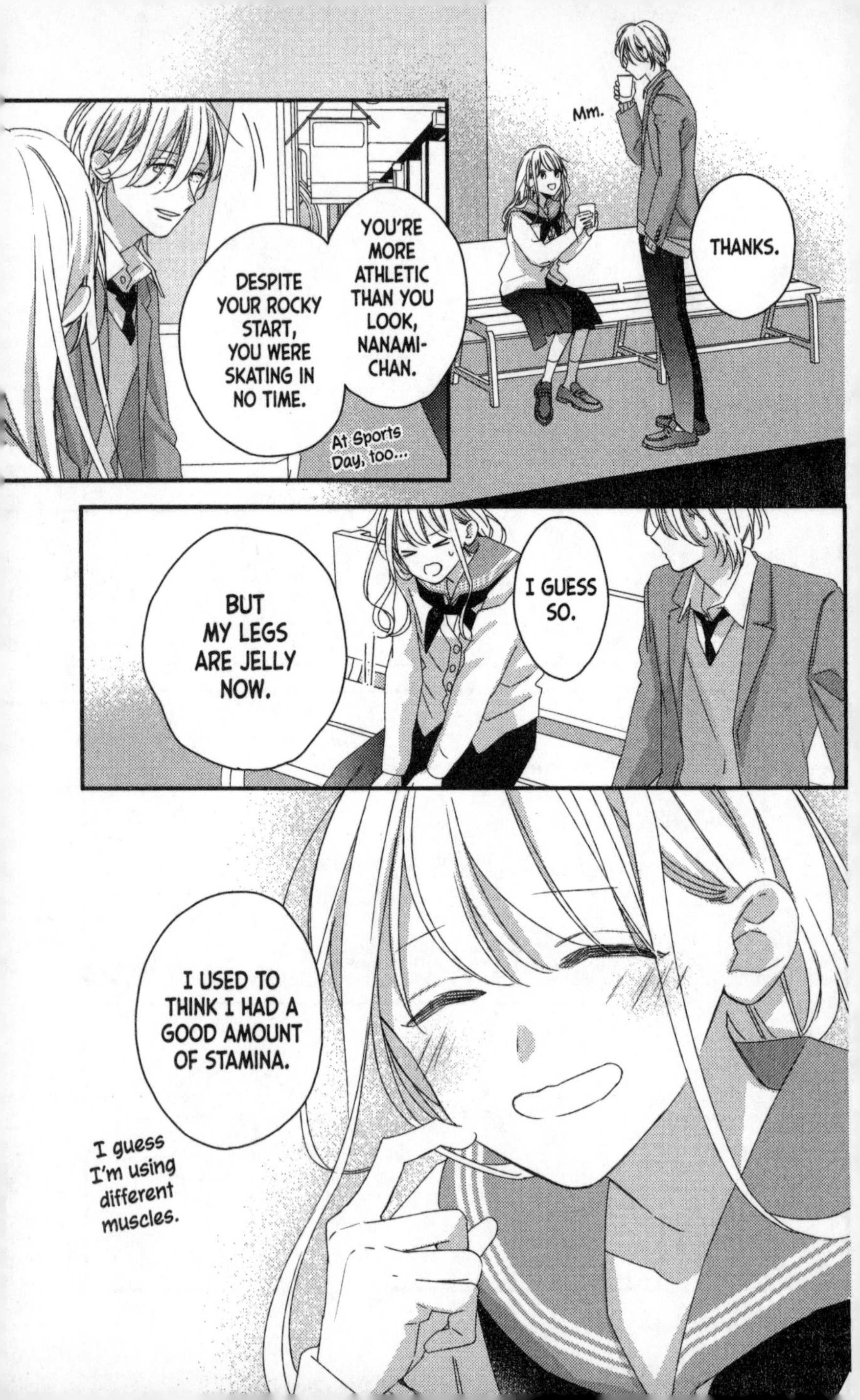
THANKS.
Mm.
YOU'RE MORE ATHLETIC THAN YOU LOOK, NANAMI-CHAN.
DESPITE YOUR ROCKY START, YOU WERE SKATING IN NO TIME.
At Sports Day, too...
I GUESS SO.
BUT MY LEGS ARE JELLY NOW.
I USED TO THINK I HAD A GOOD AMOUNT OF STAMINA.
I guess I'm using different muscles.

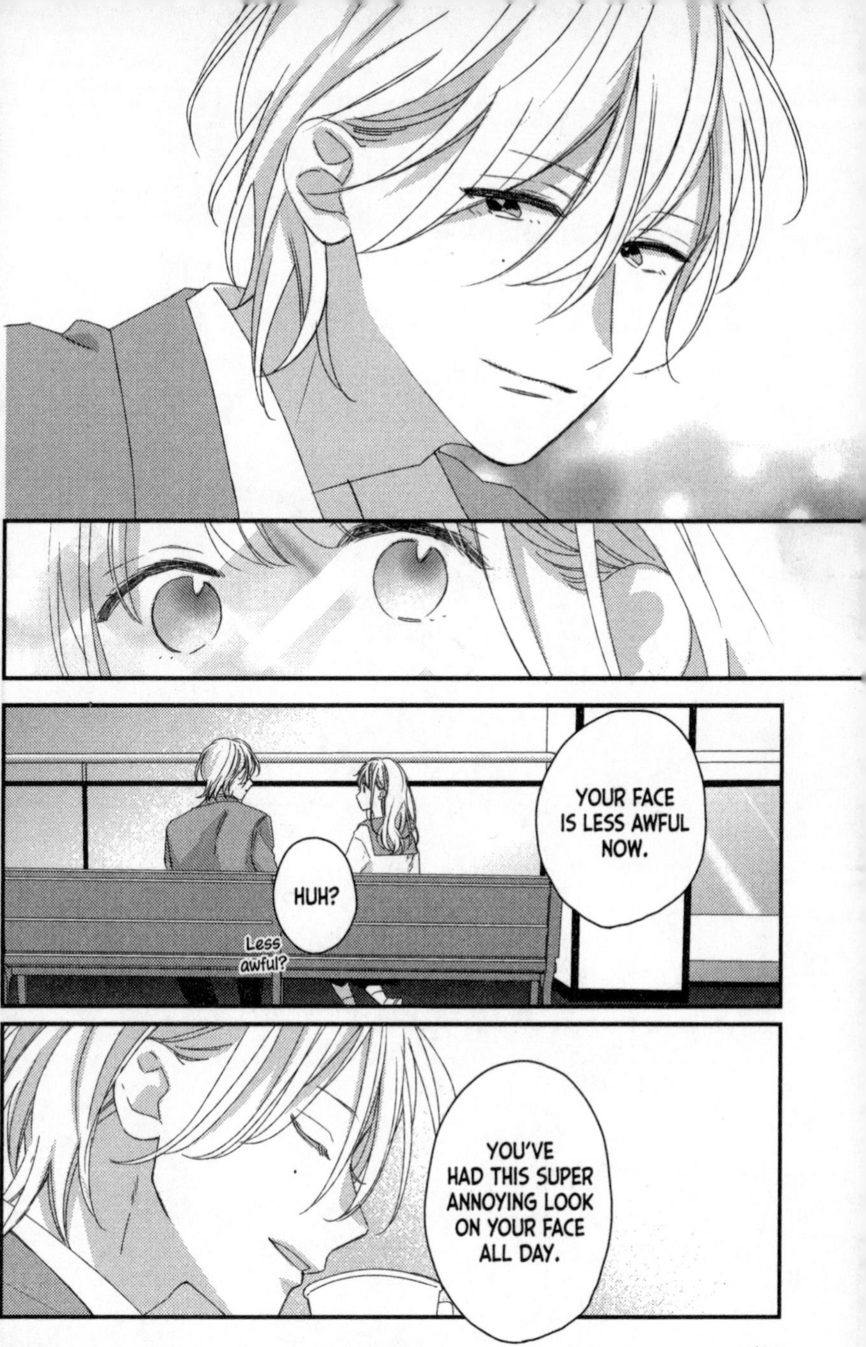
YOUR FACE IS LESS AWFUL NOW.
HUH?
Less awful?
YOU'VE HAD THIS SUPER ANNOYING LOOK ON YOUR FACE ALL DAY.

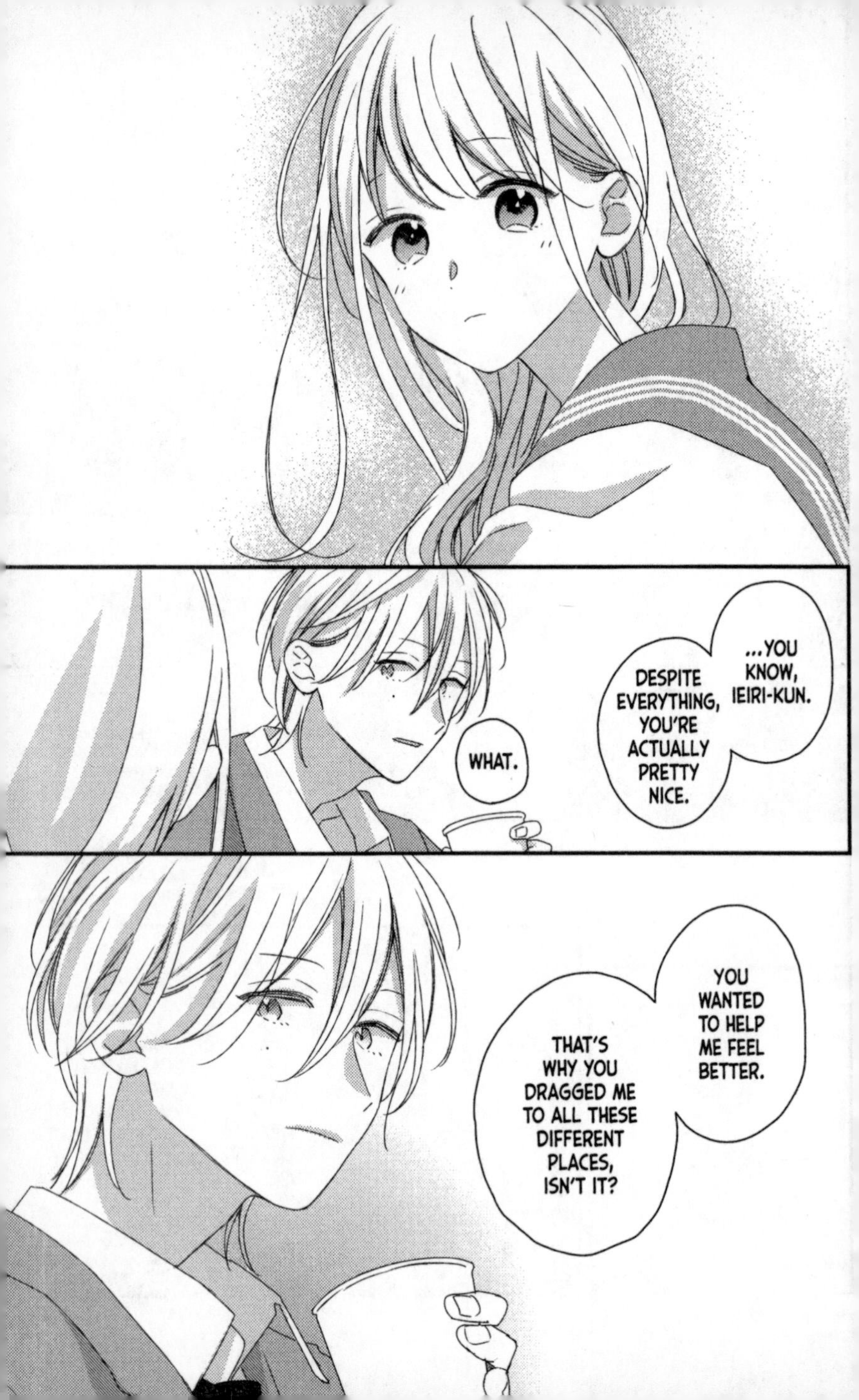
...YOU KNOW, IEIRI-KUN.
DESPITE EVERYTHING, YOU'RE ACTUALLY PRETTY NICE.
WHAT.
YOU WANTED TO HELP ME FEEL BETTER.
THAT'S WHY YOU DRAGGED ME TO ALL THESE DIFFERENT PLACES, ISN'T IT?

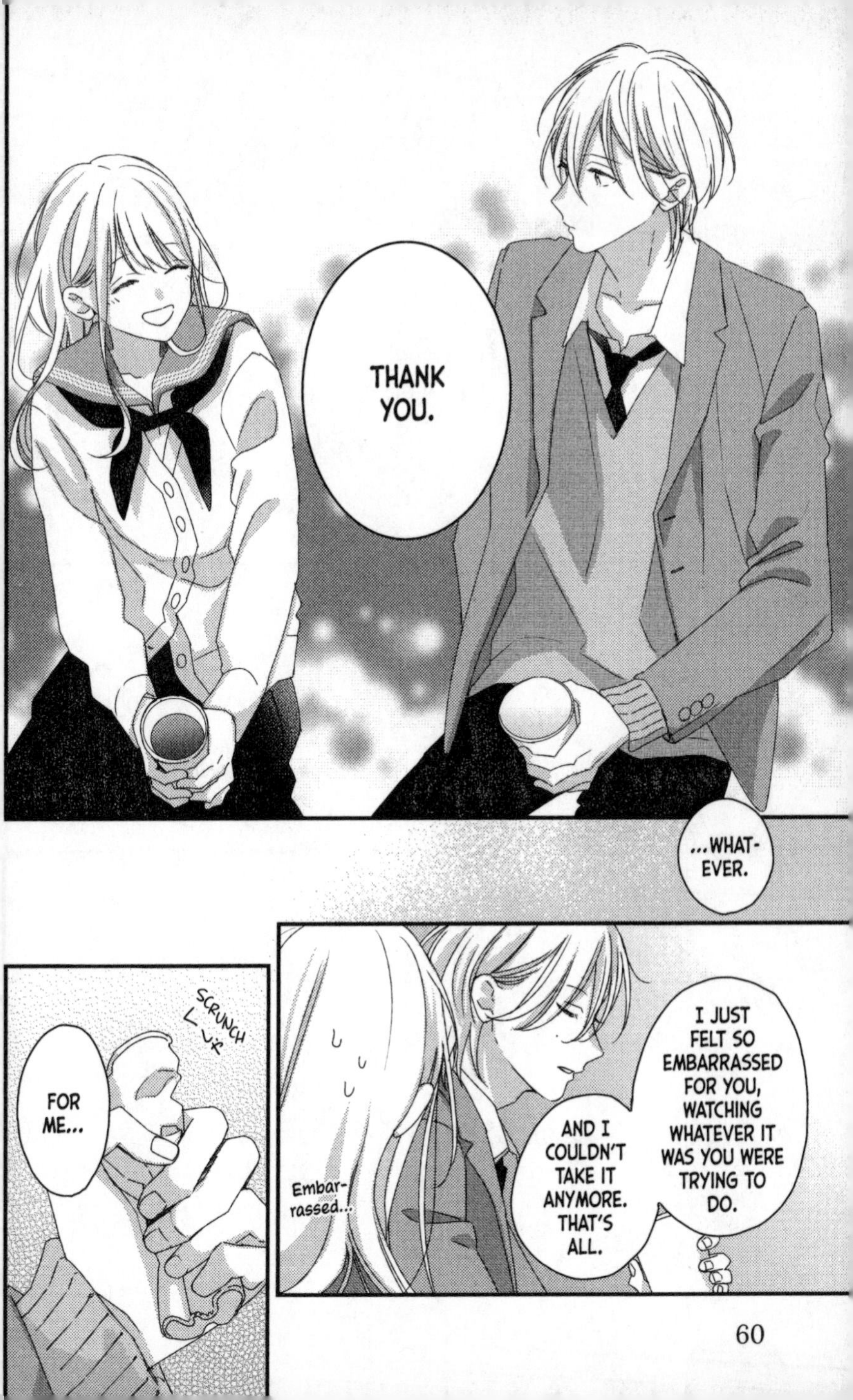
THANK YOU.
...WHAT-EVER.
I JUST FELT SO EMBARRASSED FOR YOU, WATCHING WHATEVER IT WAS YOU WERE TRYING TO DO.
AND I COULDN'T TAKE IT ANYMORE. THAT'S ALL.
Embar-rassed...
SCRUNCH
FOR ME...

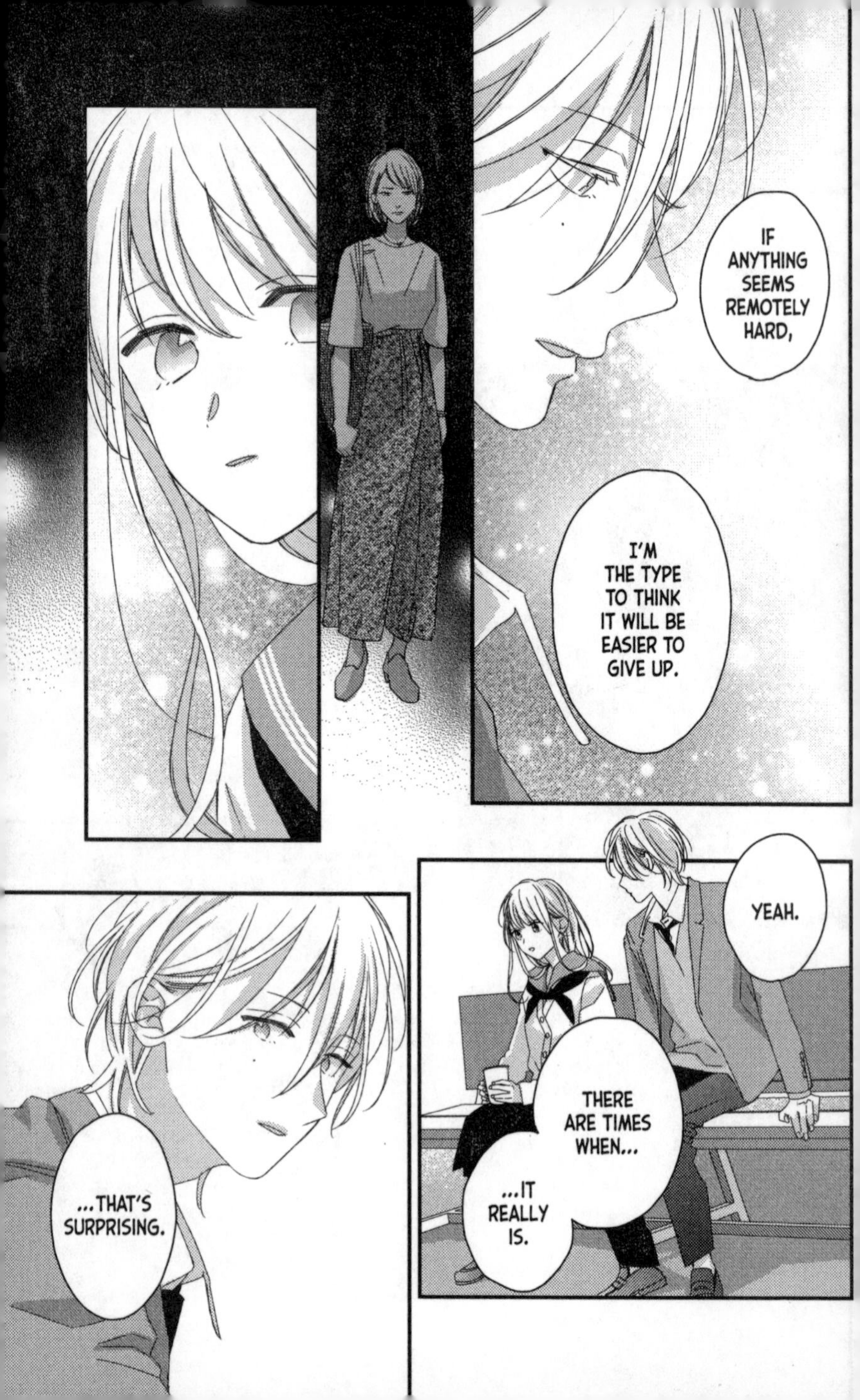
IF ANYTHING SEEMS REMOTELY HARD,
I'M THE TYPE TO THINK IT WILL BE EASIER TO GIVE UP.
YEAH.
THERE ARE TIMES WHEN...
...IT REALLY IS.
...THAT'S SURPRISING.

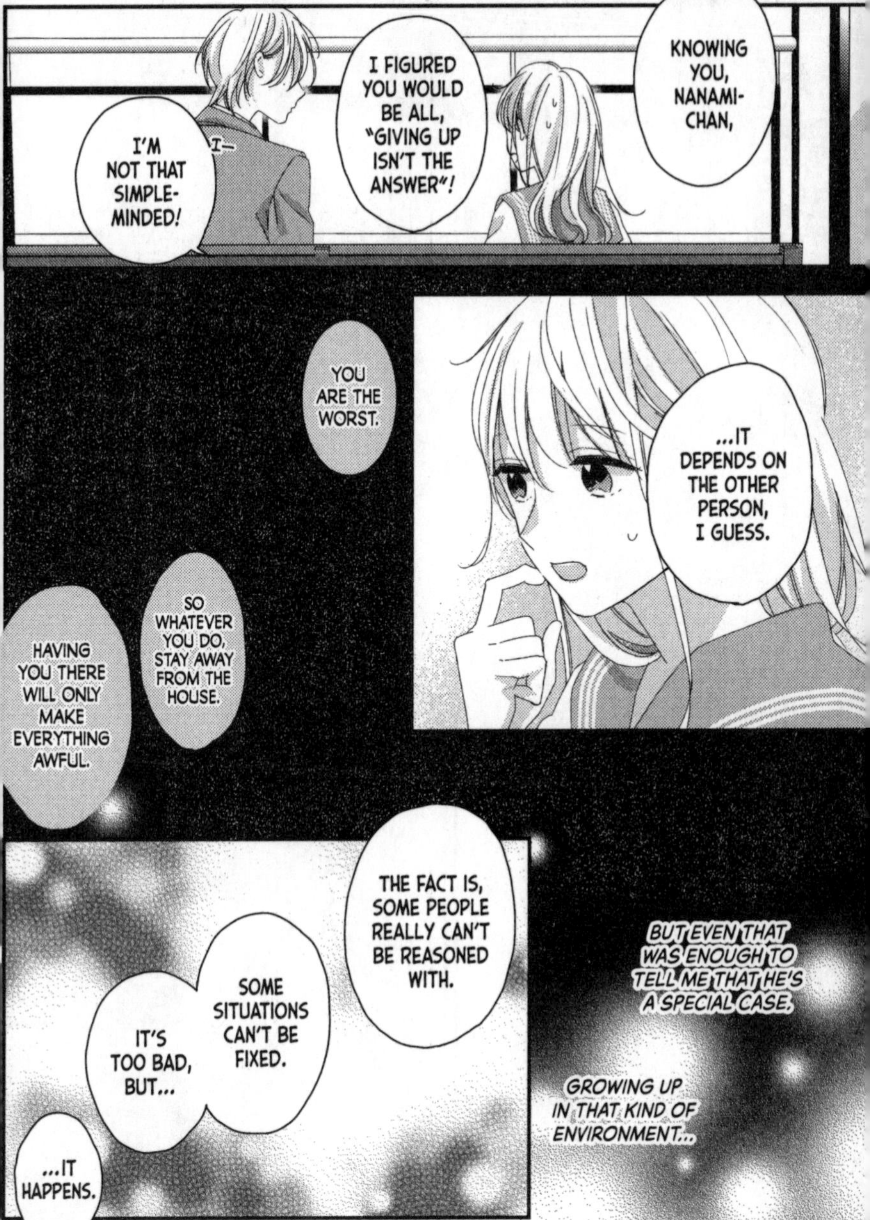
KNOWING YOU, NANAMI-CHAN,
I FIGURED YOU WOULD BE ALL, "GIVING UP ISN'T THE ANSWER"!
I—
I'M NOT THAT SIMPLE-MINDED!
...IT DEPENDS ON THE OTHER PERSON, I GUESS.
YOU ARE THE WORST.
SO WHATEVER YOU DO, STAY AWAY FROM THE HOUSE.
HAVING YOU THERE WILL ONLY MAKE EVERYTHING AWFUL.
BUT EVEN THAT WAS ENOUGH TO TELL ME THAT HE'S A SPECIAL CASE.
GROWING UP IN THAT KIND OF ENVIRONMENT...
THE FACT IS, SOME PEOPLE REALLY CAN'T BE REASONED WITH.
SOME SITUATIONS CAN'T BE FIXED.
IT'S TOO BAD, BUT...
...IT HAPPENS.

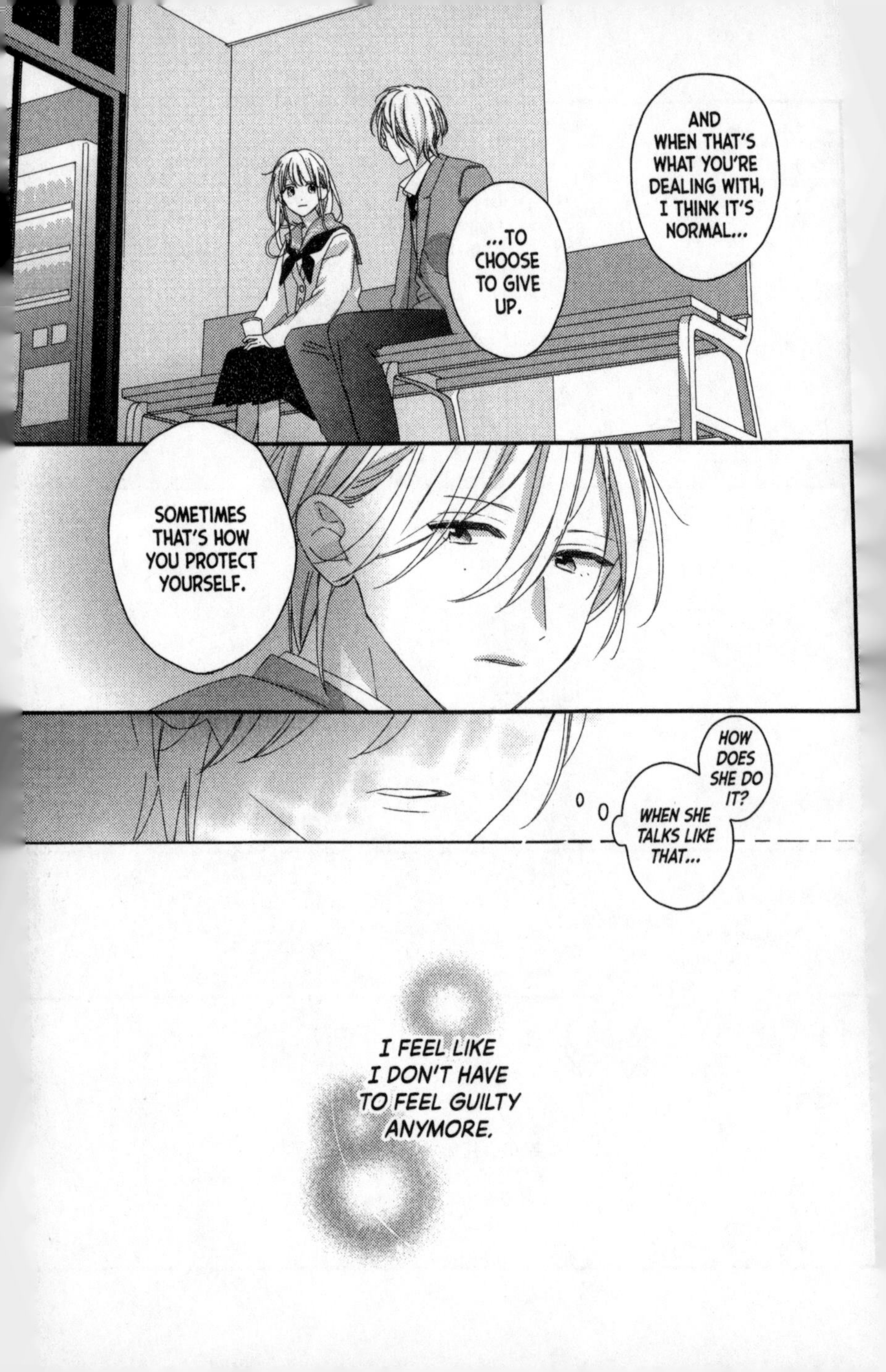
AND WHEN THAT'S WHAT YOU'RE DEALING WITH, I THINK IT'S NORMAL...
...TO CHOOSE TO GIVE UP.
SOMETIMES THAT'S HOW YOU PROTECT YOURSELF.
HOW DOES SHE DO IT?
WHEN SHE TALKS LIKE THAT...
I FEEL LIKE I DON'T HAVE TO FEEL GUILTY ANYMORE.

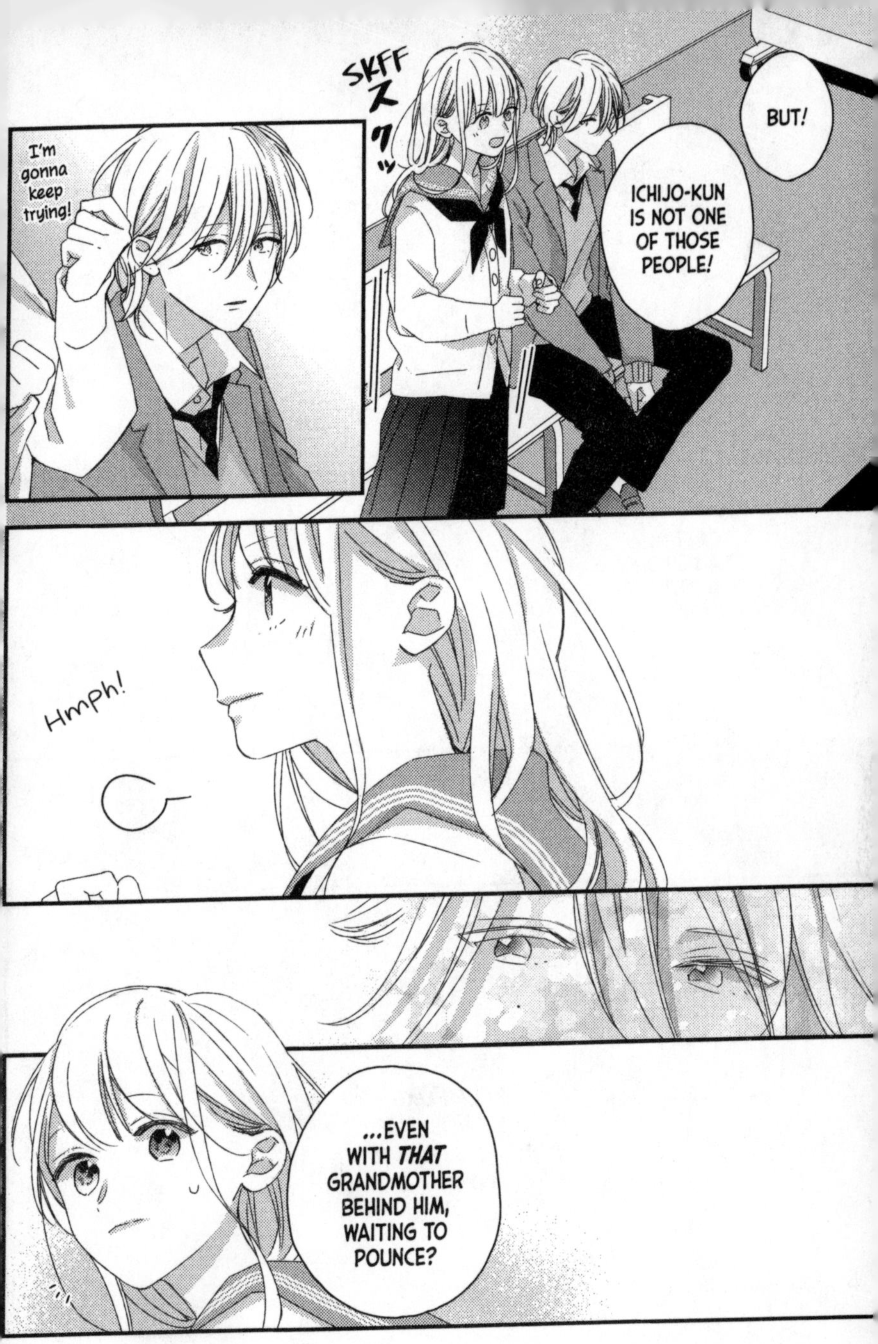
BUT!
ICHIJO-KUN IS NOT ONE OF THOSE PEOPLE!
SKFF
スクッ
I'm gonna keep trying!
Hmph!
...EVEN WITH *THAT* GRANDMOTHER BEHIND HIM, WAITING TO POUNCE?

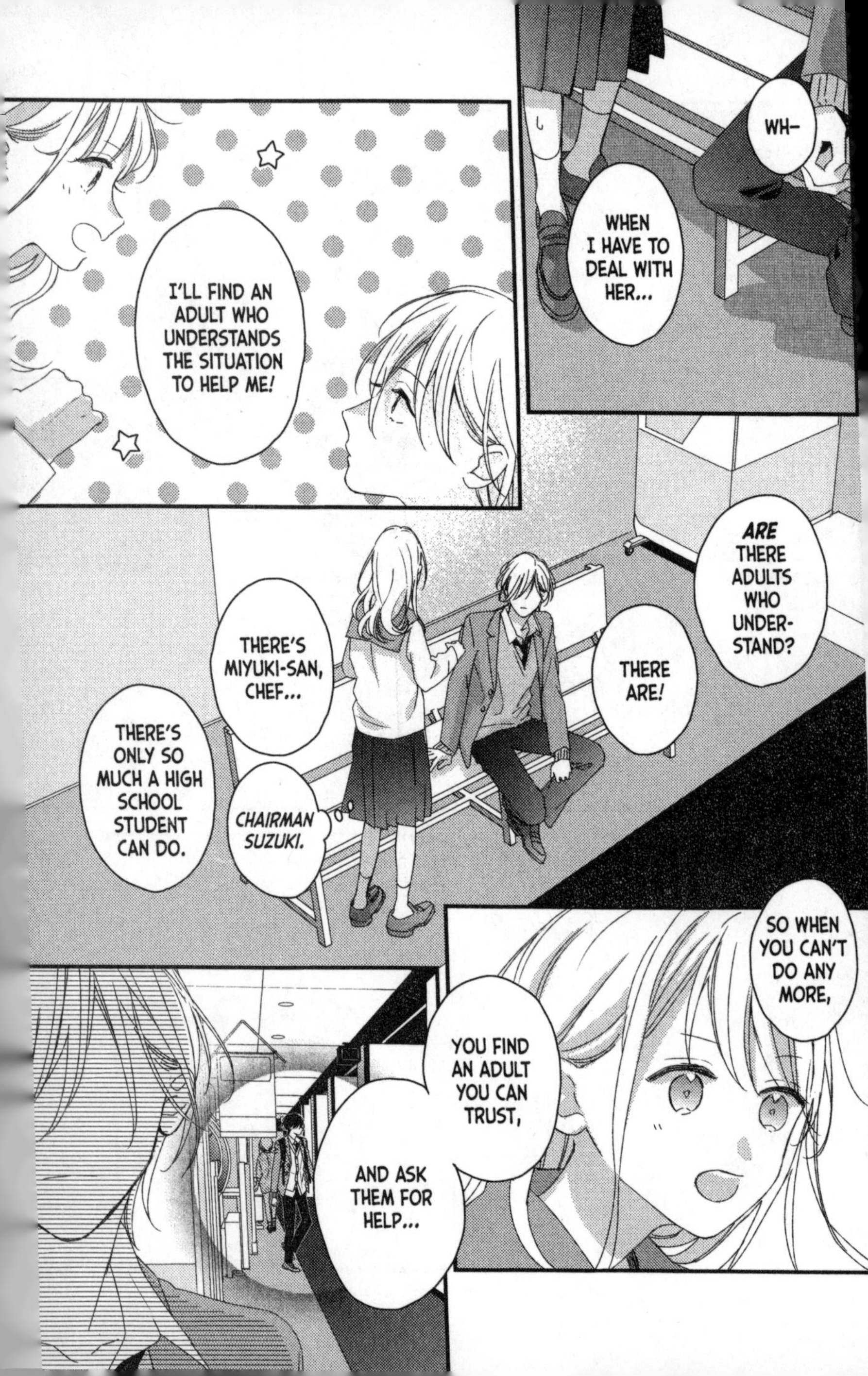
WH–
WHEN I HAVE TO DEAL WITH HER...
I'LL FIND AN ADULT WHO UNDERSTANDS THE SITUATION TO HELP ME!
*ARE* THERE ADULTS WHO UNDER-STAND?
THERE ARE!
THERE'S MIYUKI-SAN, CHEF...
*CHAIRMAN SUZUKI.*
THERE'S ONLY SO MUCH A HIGH SCHOOL STUDENT CAN DO.
SO WHEN YOU CAN'T DO ANY MORE,
YOU FIND AN ADULT YOU CAN TRUST,
AND ASK THEM FOR HELP...

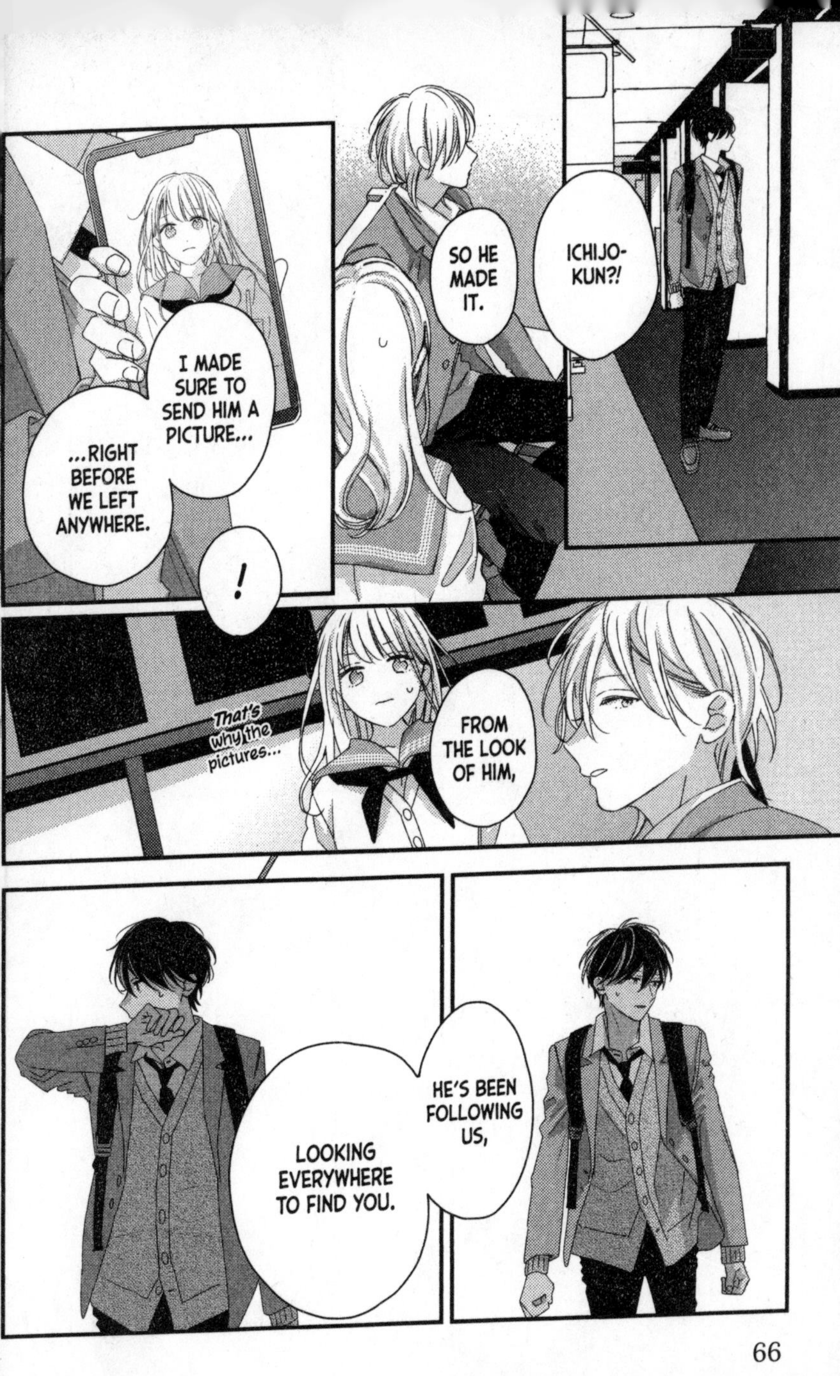
ICHIJO-KUN?!
SO HE MADE IT.
I MADE SURE TO SEND HIM A PICTURE...
...RIGHT BEFORE WE LEFT ANYWHERE.
!
FROM THE LOOK OF HIM,
That's why the pictures...
HE'S BEEN FOLLOWING US,
LOOKING EVERYWHERE TO FIND YOU.

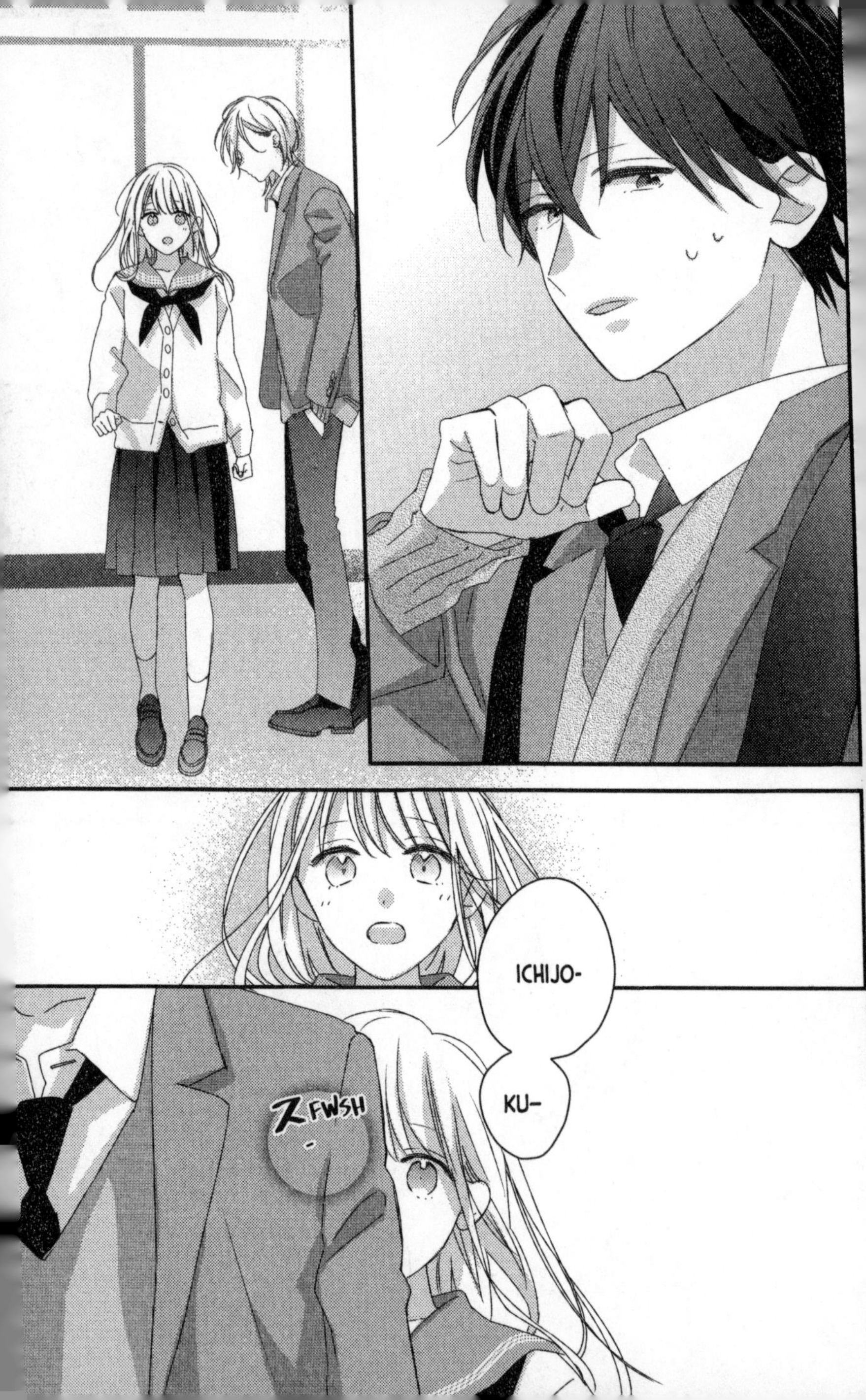
ICHIJO-
KU–
ス FWSH

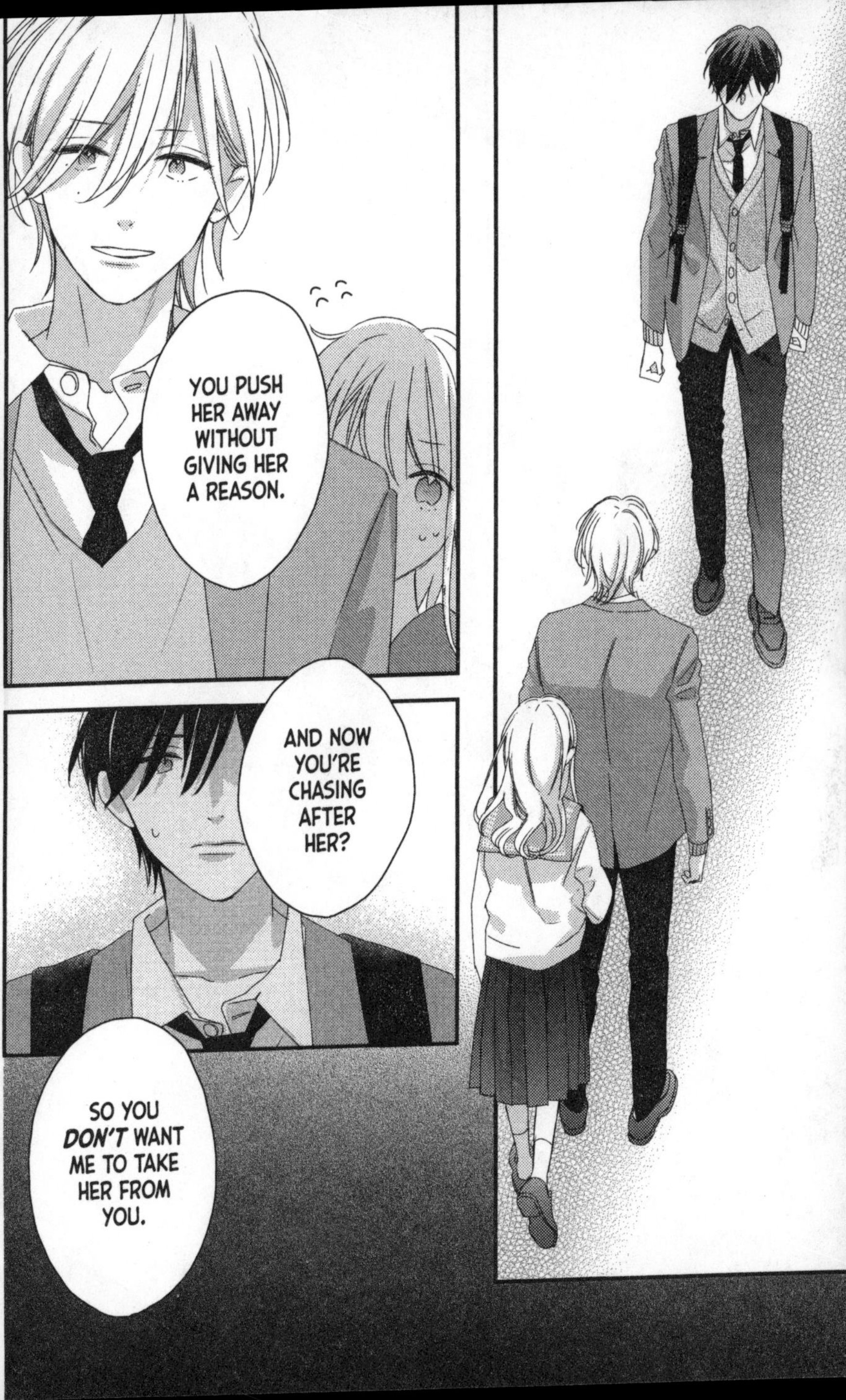
YOU PUSH HER AWAY WITHOUT GIVING HER A REASON.
AND NOW YOU'RE CHASING AFTER HER?
SO YOU *DON'T* WANT ME TO TAKE HER FROM YOU.

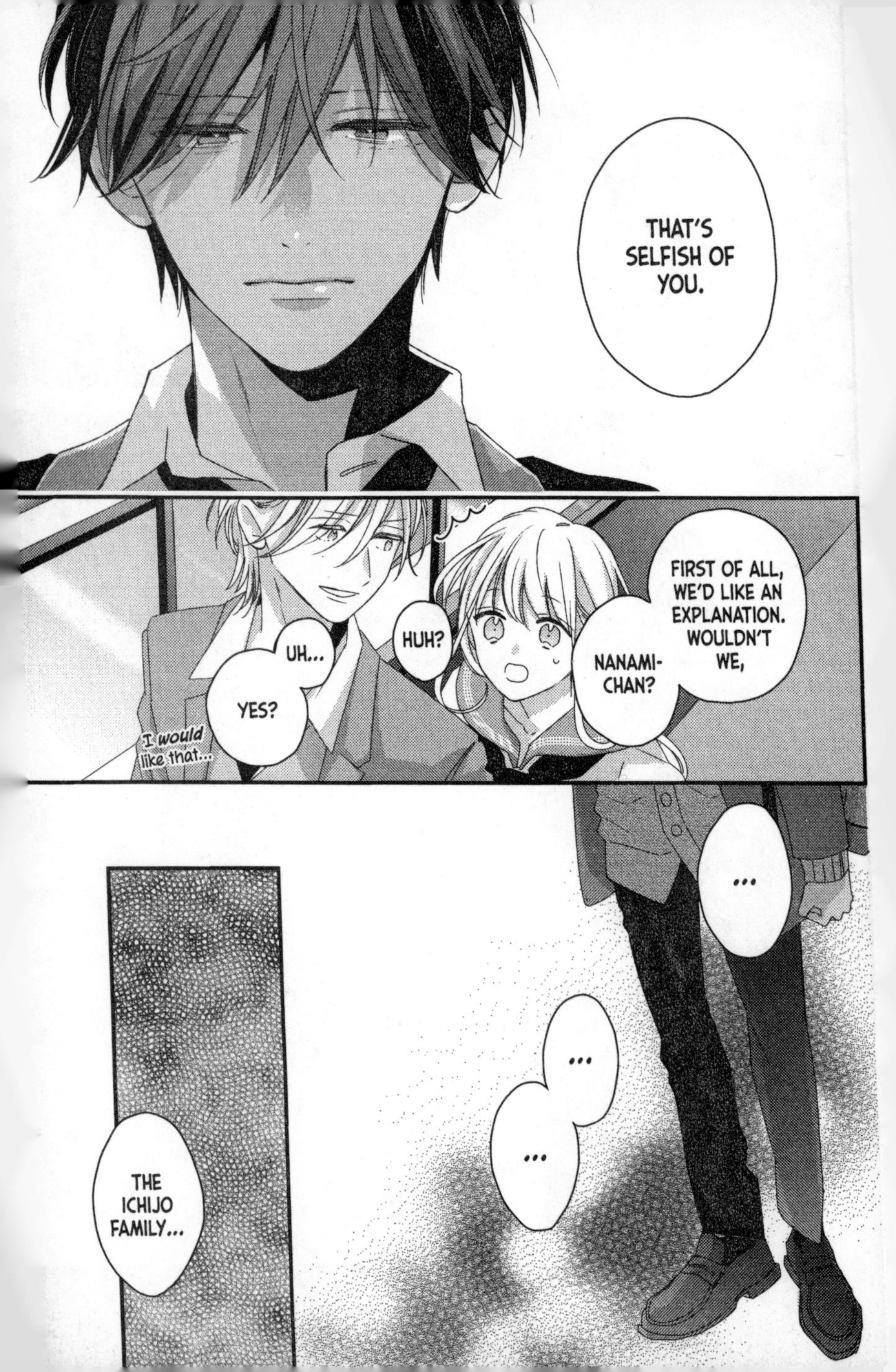
THAT'S SELFISH OF YOU.
FIRST OF ALL, WE'D LIKE AN EXPLANATION. WOULDN'T WE,
NANAMI-CHAN?
HUH?
UH...
YES?
I would like that...
...
...
...
THE ICHIJO FAMILY...

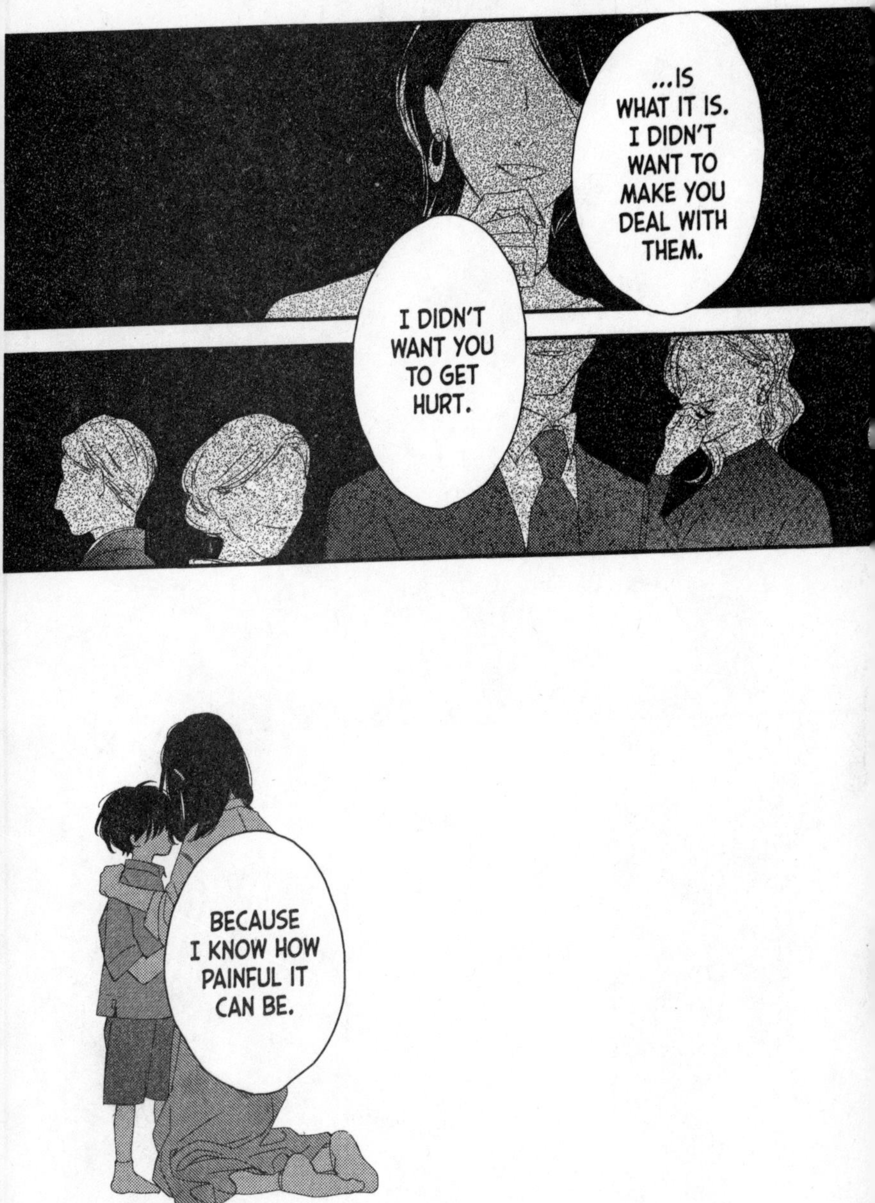
...IS WHAT IT IS. I DIDN'T WANT TO MAKE YOU DEAL WITH THEM.
I DIDN'T WANT YOU TO GET HURT.
BECAUSE I KNOW HOW PAINFUL IT CAN BE.

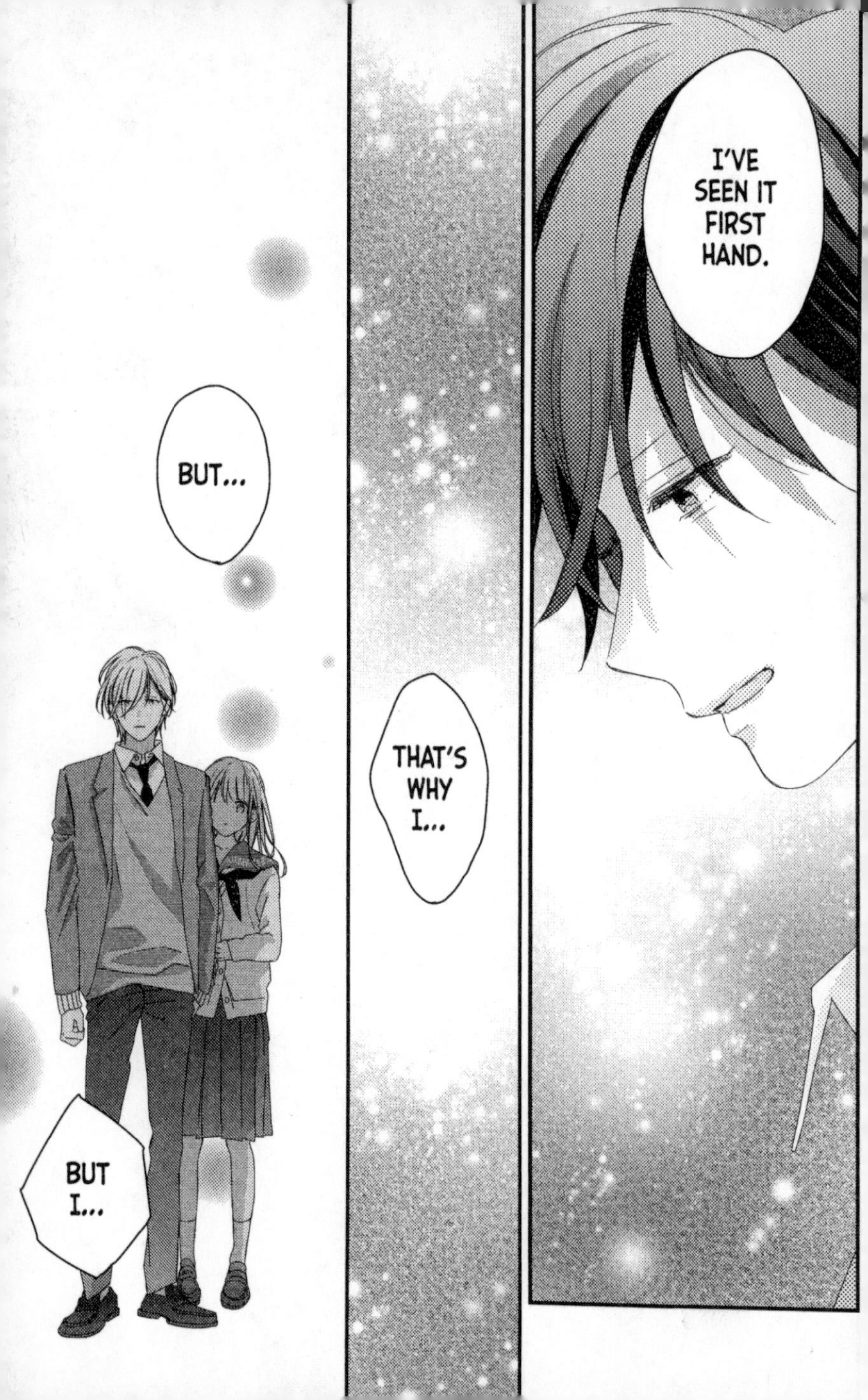
I'VE SEEN IT FIRST HAND.
THAT'S WHY I...
BUT...
BUT I...

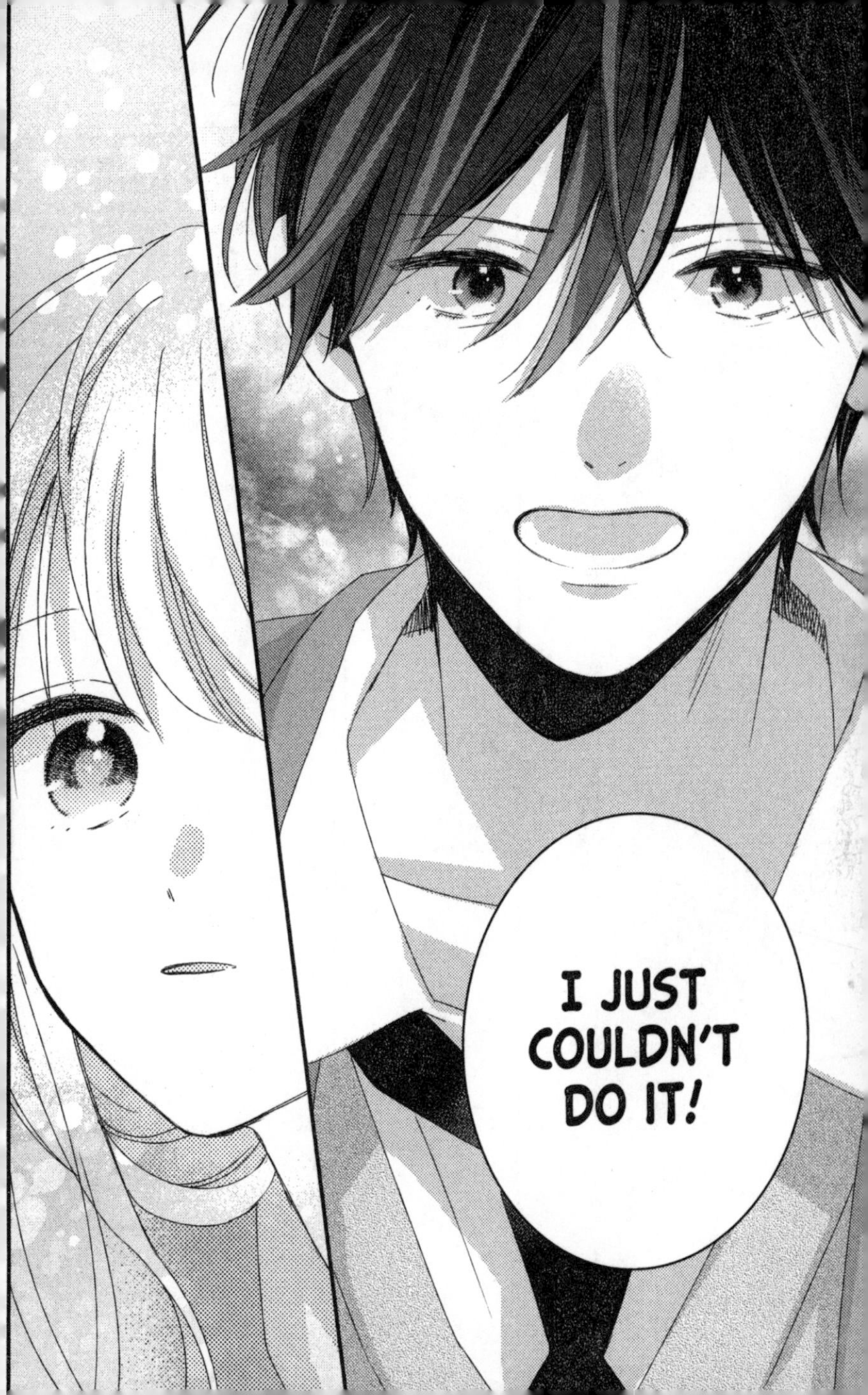
I JUST COULDN'T DO IT!

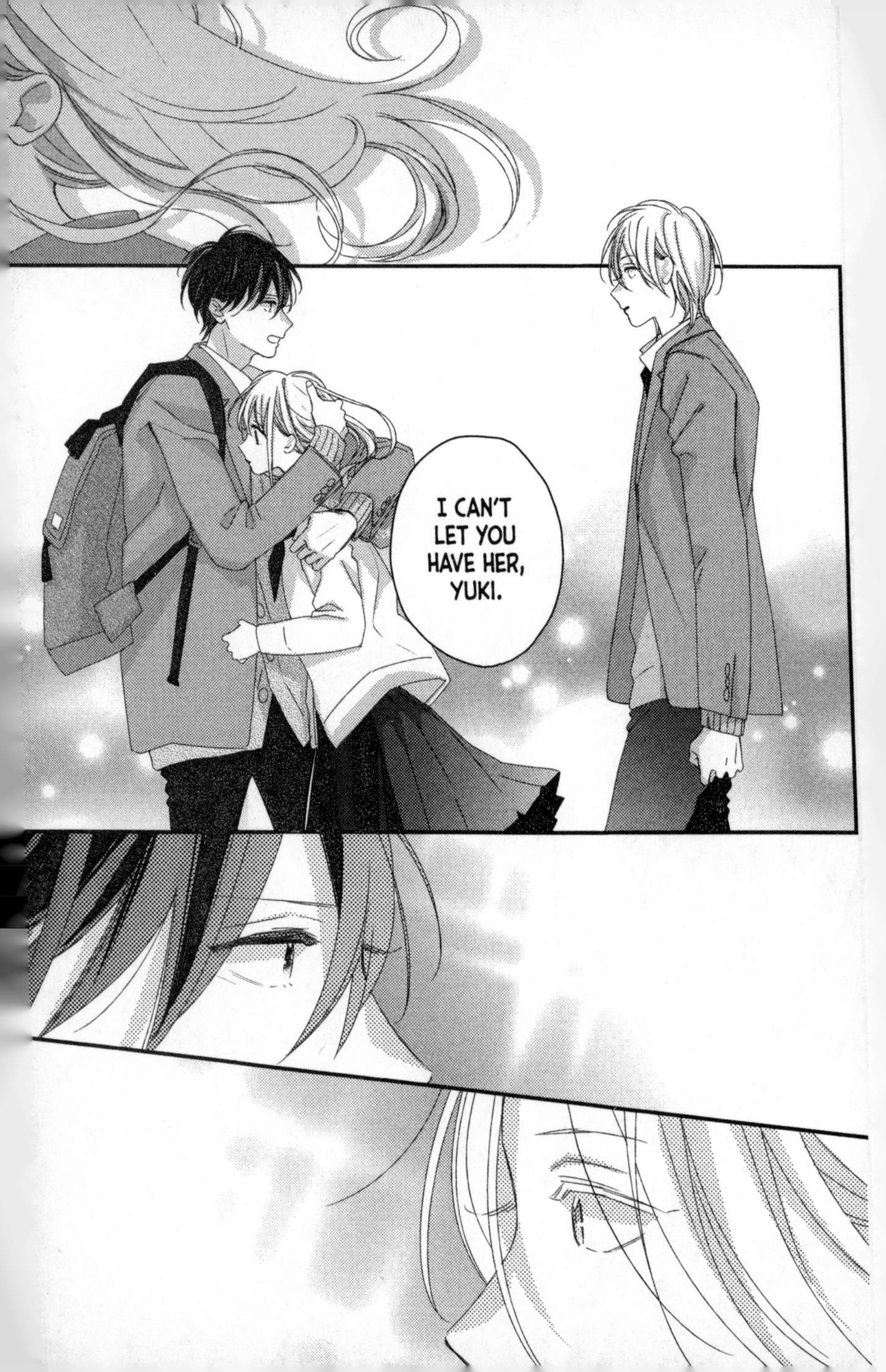
I CAN'T LET YOU HAVE HER, YUKI.

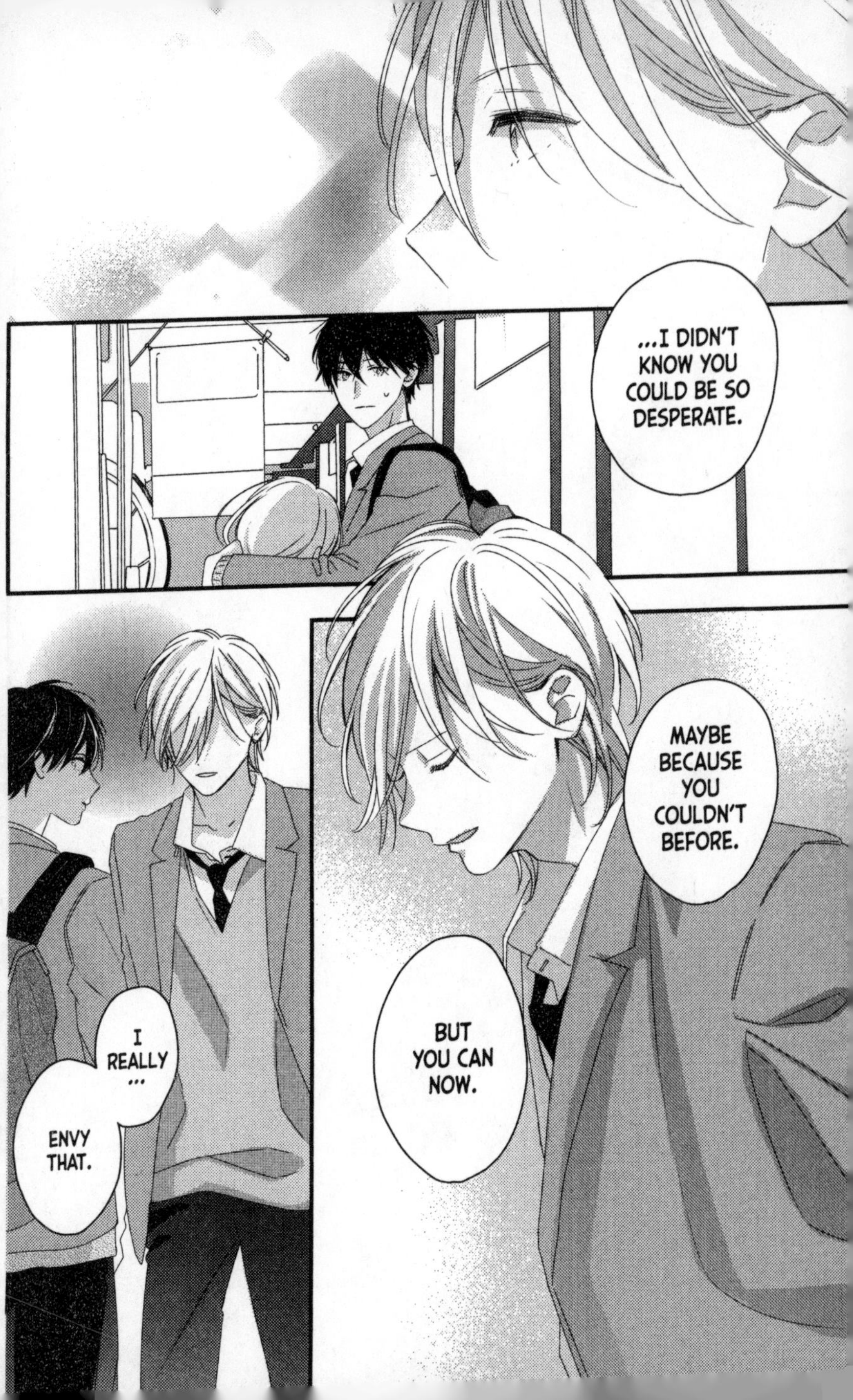
...I DIDN'T KNOW YOU COULD BE SO DESPERATE.
MAYBE BECAUSE YOU COULDN'T BEFORE.
BUT YOU CAN NOW.
I REALLY...
ENVY THAT.

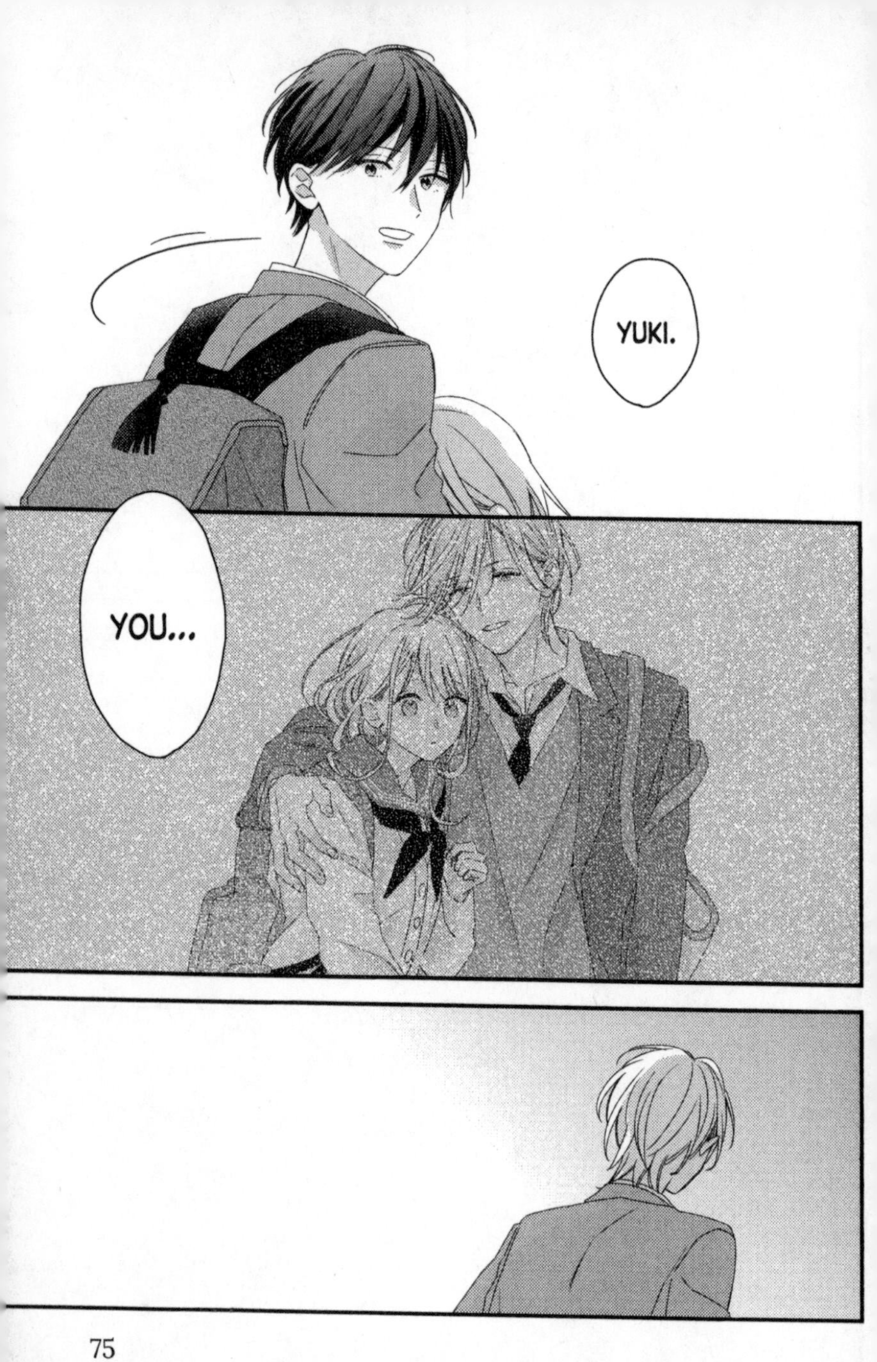
YUKI.
YOU...

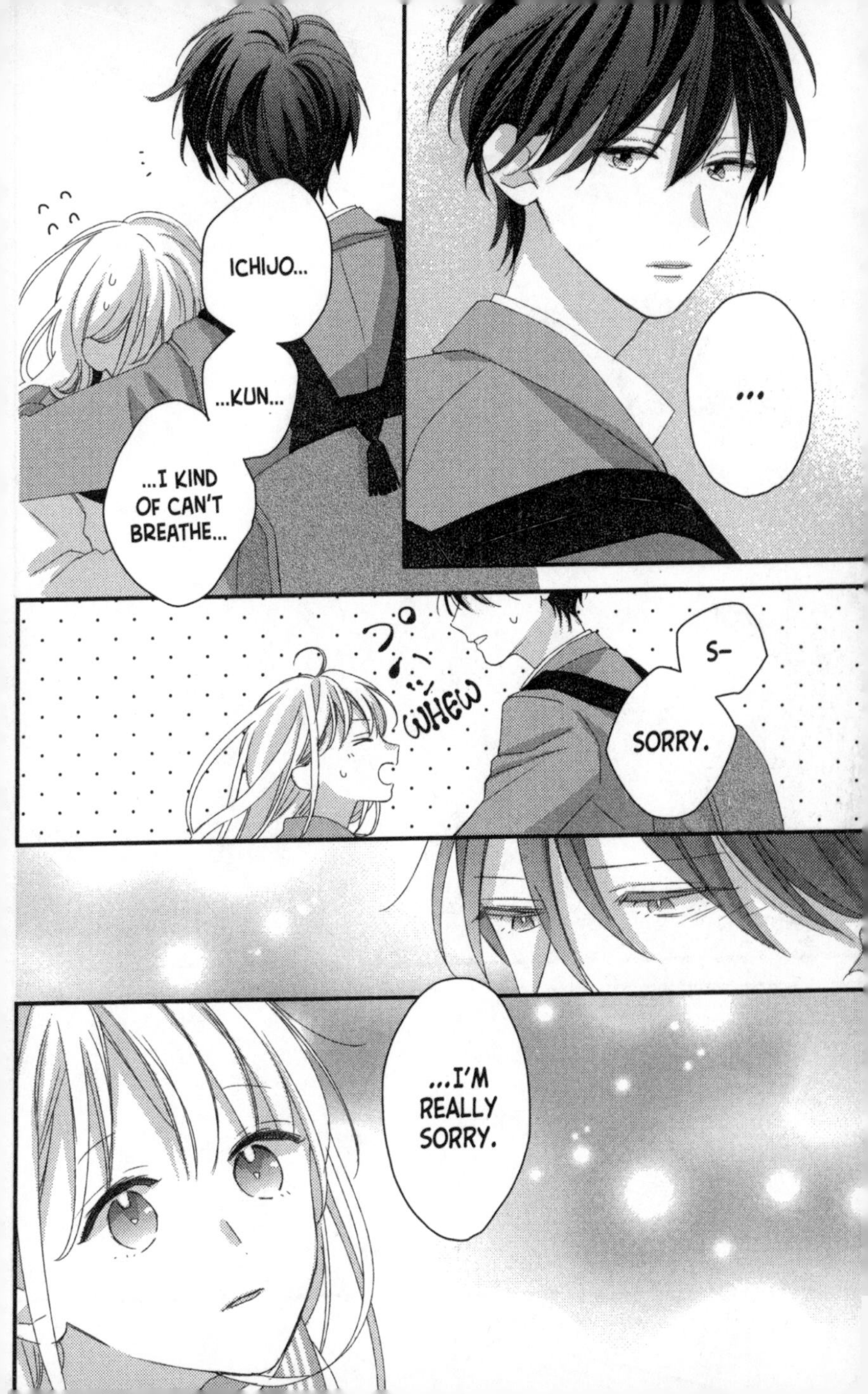
...
ICHIJO...
...KUN...
...I KIND OF CAN'T BREATHE...
S- SORRY.
WHEW
...I'M REALLY SORRY.

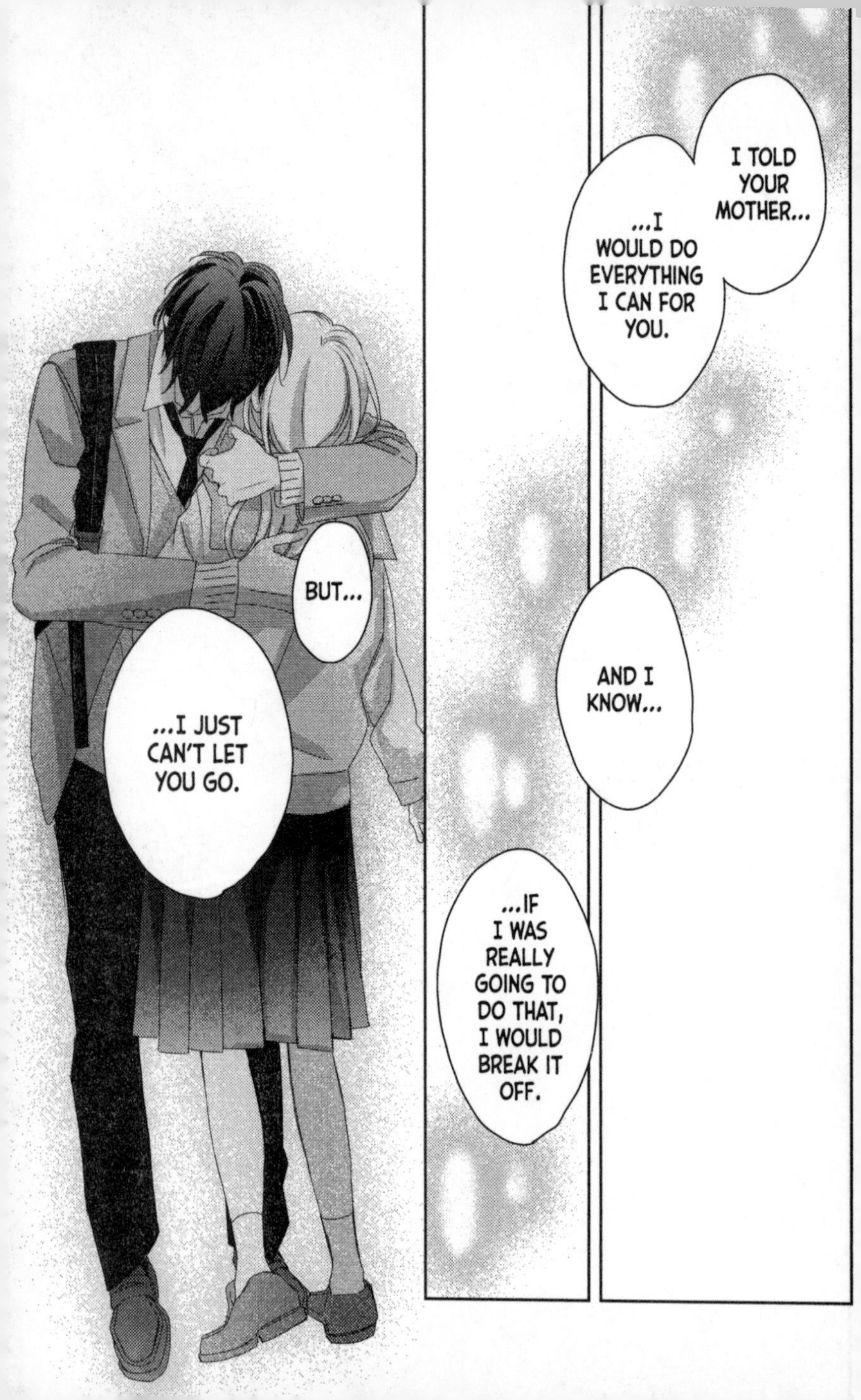
I TOLD YOUR MOTHER...
...I WOULD DO EVERYTHING I CAN FOR YOU.
AND I KNOW...
...IF I WAS REALLY GOING TO DO THAT, I WOULD BREAK IT OFF.
BUT...
...I JUST CAN'T LET YOU GO.

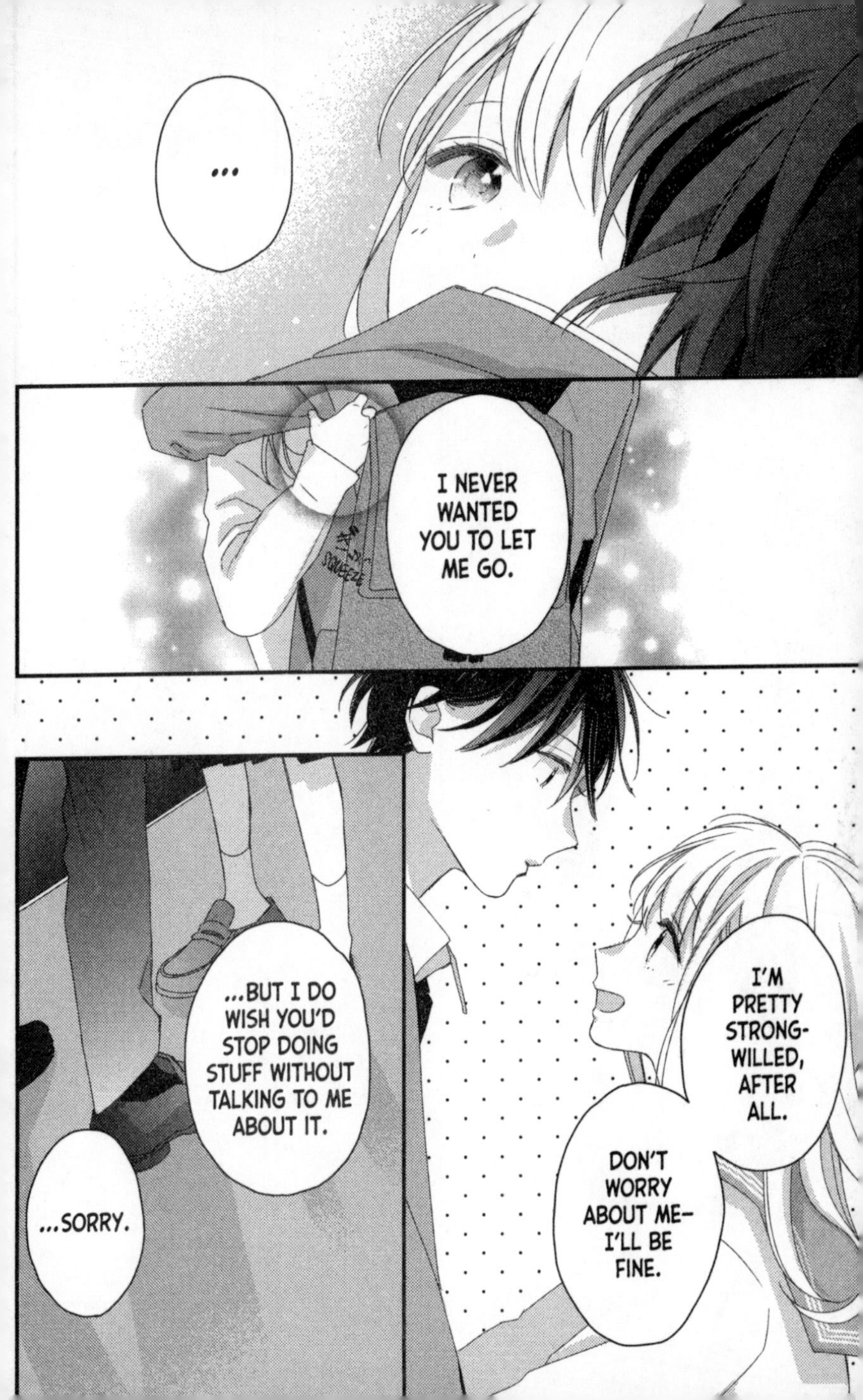
...
I NEVER WANTED YOU TO LET ME GO.
SQUEEZE
I'M PRETTY STRONG-WILLED, AFTER ALL.
DON'T WORRY ABOUT ME— I'LL BE FINE.
...BUT I DO WISH YOU'D STOP DOING STUFF WITHOUT TALKING TO ME ABOUT IT.
...SORRY.

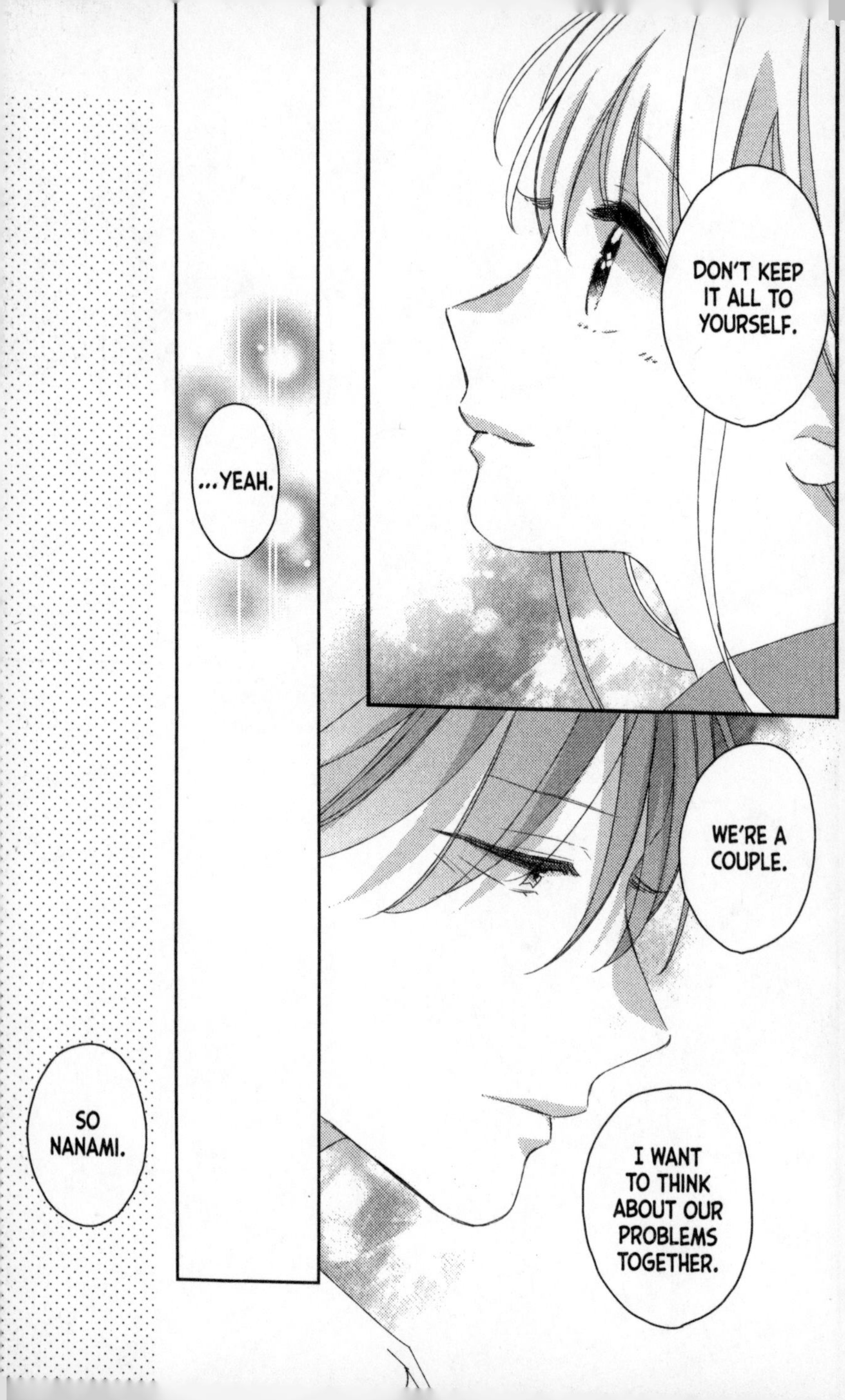
DON'T KEEP IT ALL TO YOURSELF.
WE'RE A COUPLE.
I WANT TO THINK ABOUT OUR PROBLEMS TOGETHER.
...YEAH.
SO NANAMI.

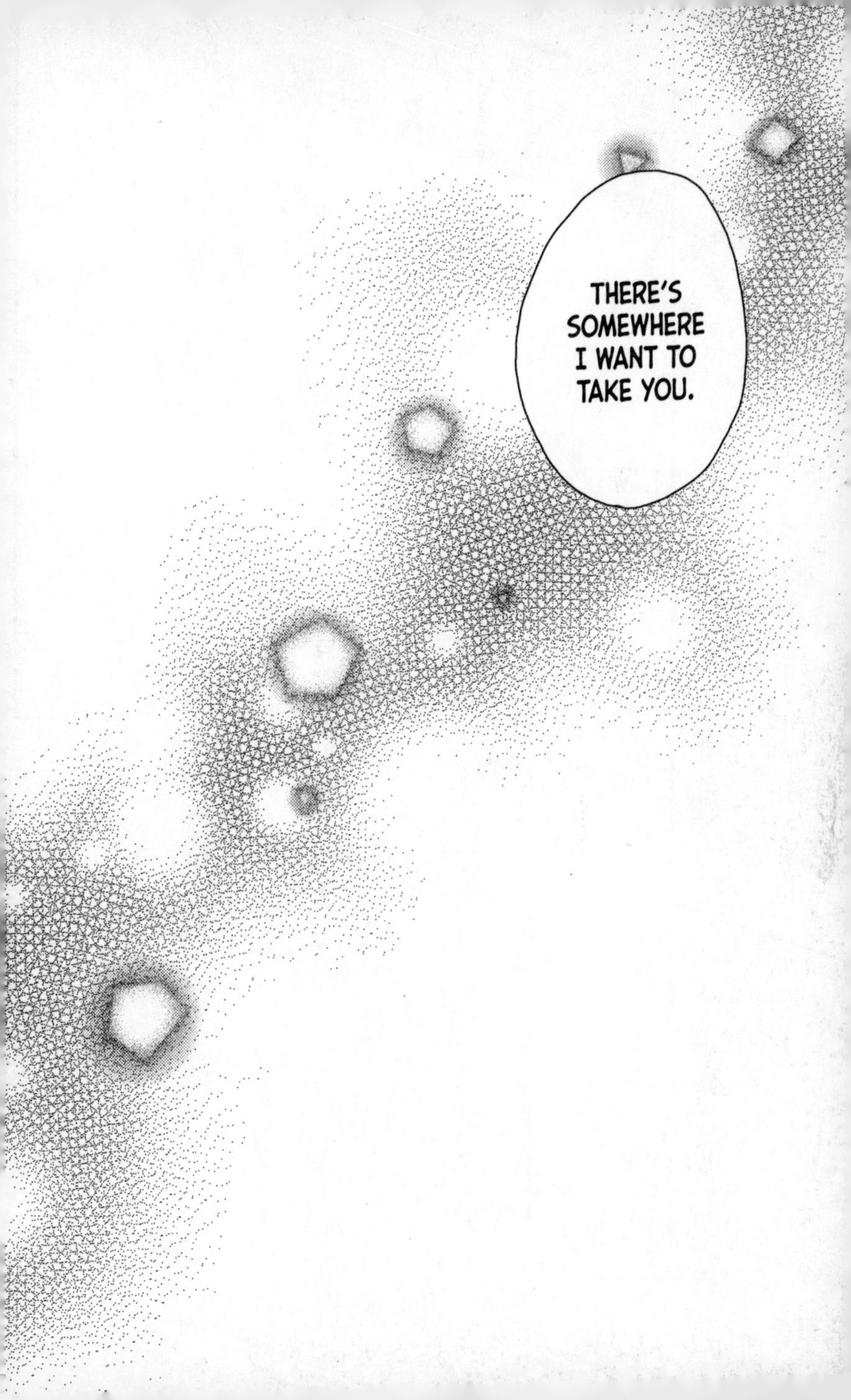
THERE'S SOMEWHERE I WANT TO TAKE YOU.

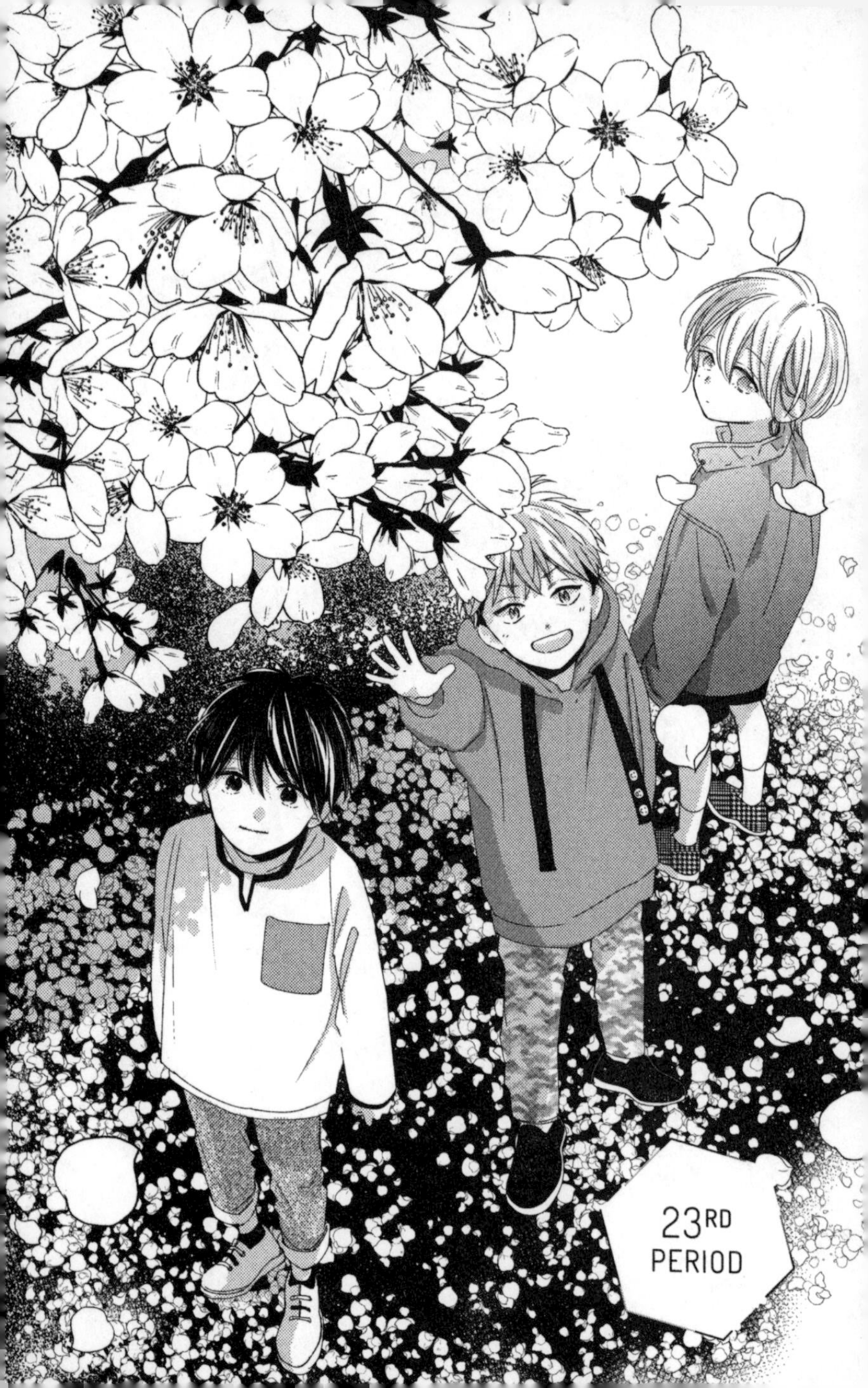
23RD PERIOD

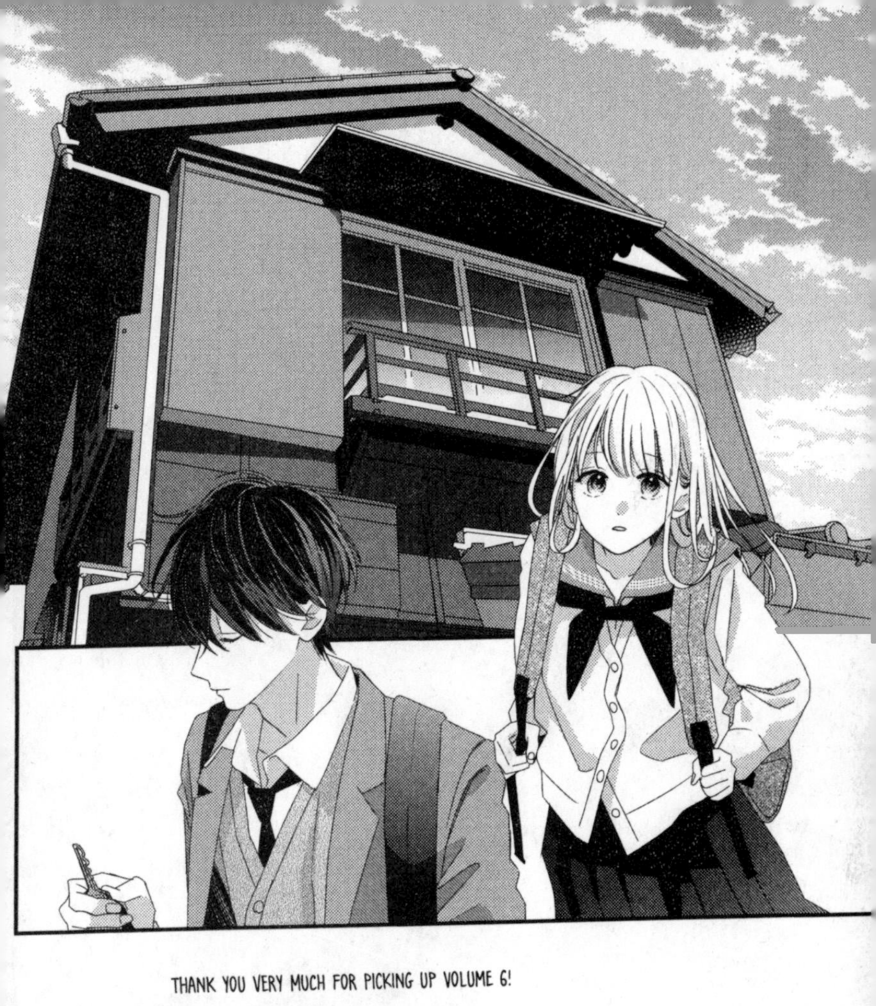

THANK YOU VERY MUCH FOR PICKING UP VOLUME 6!

THE SEASON IN THE CURRENT STORY OF THE MANGA, AND THE SEASON IN REAL LIFE, AND THE SEASON IN THE VOLUMES OF MANGA THAT ARE GOING ON SALE—THEY'RE ALL DIFFERENT, SO I'M ALWAYS GETTING CONFUSED, LIKE, "SHOULD THEY BE DRESSED LIKE THAT? IS THAT OKAY"...?

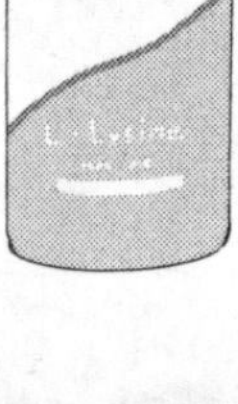

AN IMPORTED VITAMIN. THE PILLS ARE SO BIG I GET NERVOUS EVERY TIME I TAKE ONE.

I TAKE THEM BECAUSE THEY'RE SUPPOSED TO SUPPORT MY CONCENTRATION.

BUT THEY REALLY ARE SO BIG, I'M AFRAID I'M GOING TO CHOKE...

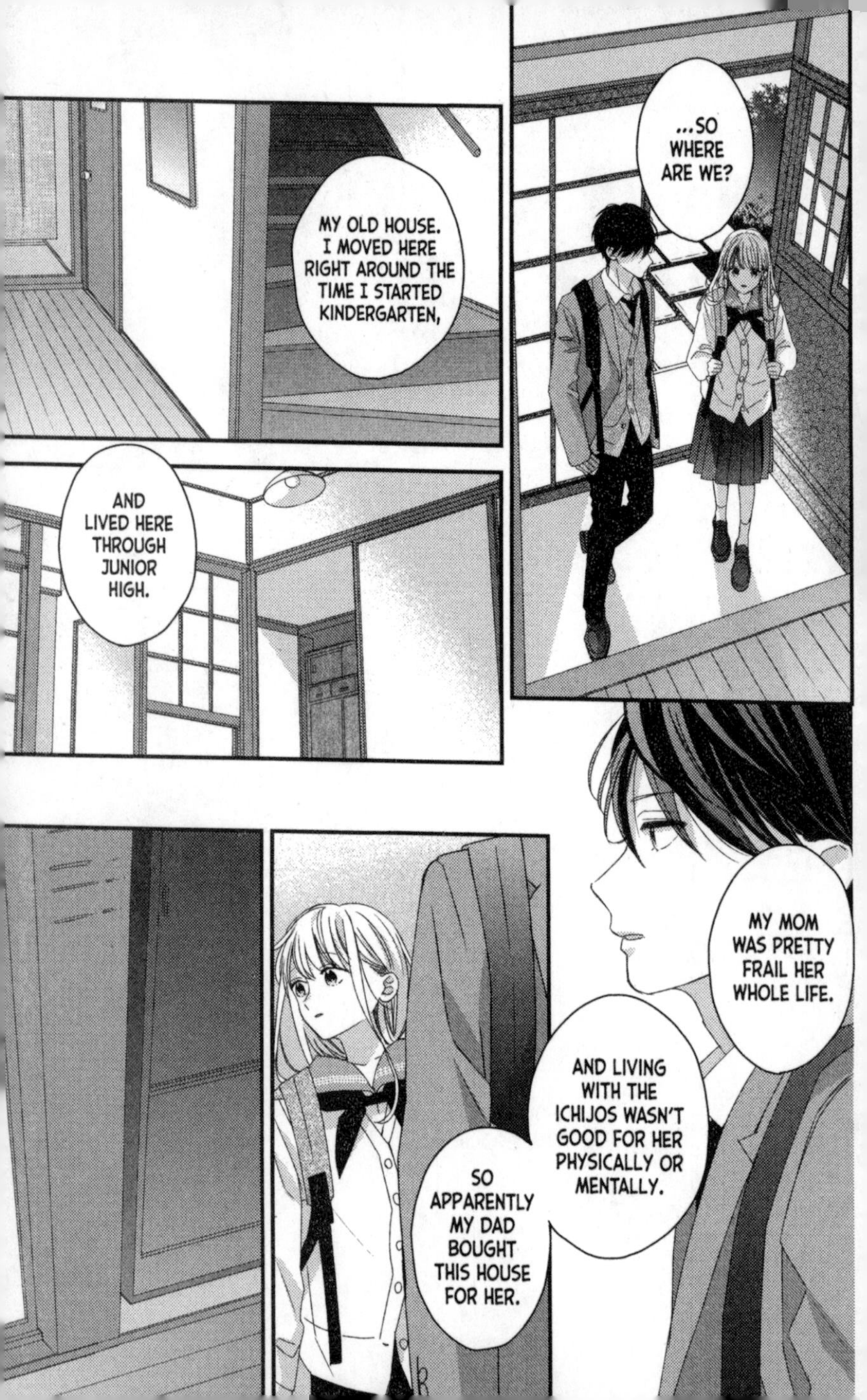
...SO WHERE ARE WE?
MY OLD HOUSE. I MOVED HERE RIGHT AROUND THE TIME I STARTED KINDERGARTEN,
AND LIVED HERE THROUGH JUNIOR HIGH.
MY MOM WAS PRETTY FRAIL HER WHOLE LIFE.
AND LIVING WITH THE ICHIJOS WASN'T GOOD FOR HER PHYSICALLY OR MENTALLY.
SO APPARENTLY MY DAD BOUGHT THIS HOUSE FOR HER.

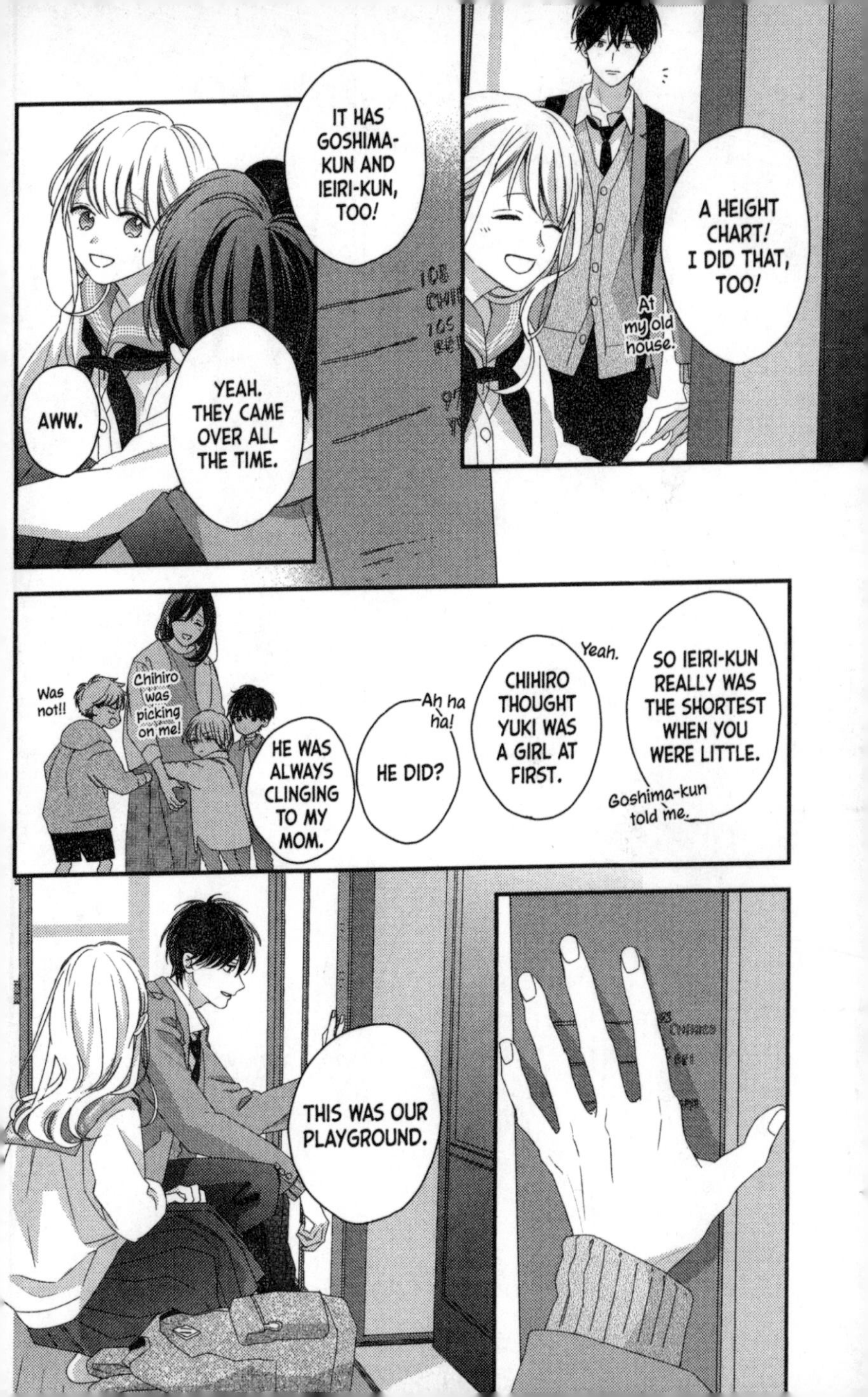
A HEIGHT CHART! I DID THAT, TOO!
At my old house.
IT HAS GOSHIMA-KUN AND IEIRI-KUN, TOO!
YEAH. THEY CAME OVER ALL THE TIME.
AWW.
SO IEIRI-KUN REALLY WAS THE SHORTEST WHEN YOU WERE LITTLE.
Goshima-kun told me.
Yeah.
CHIHIRO THOUGHT YUKI WAS A GIRL AT FIRST.
Ah ha ha!
HE DID?
HE WAS ALWAYS CLINGING TO MY MOM.
Chihiro was picking on me!
Was not!!
THIS WAS OUR PLAYGROUND.

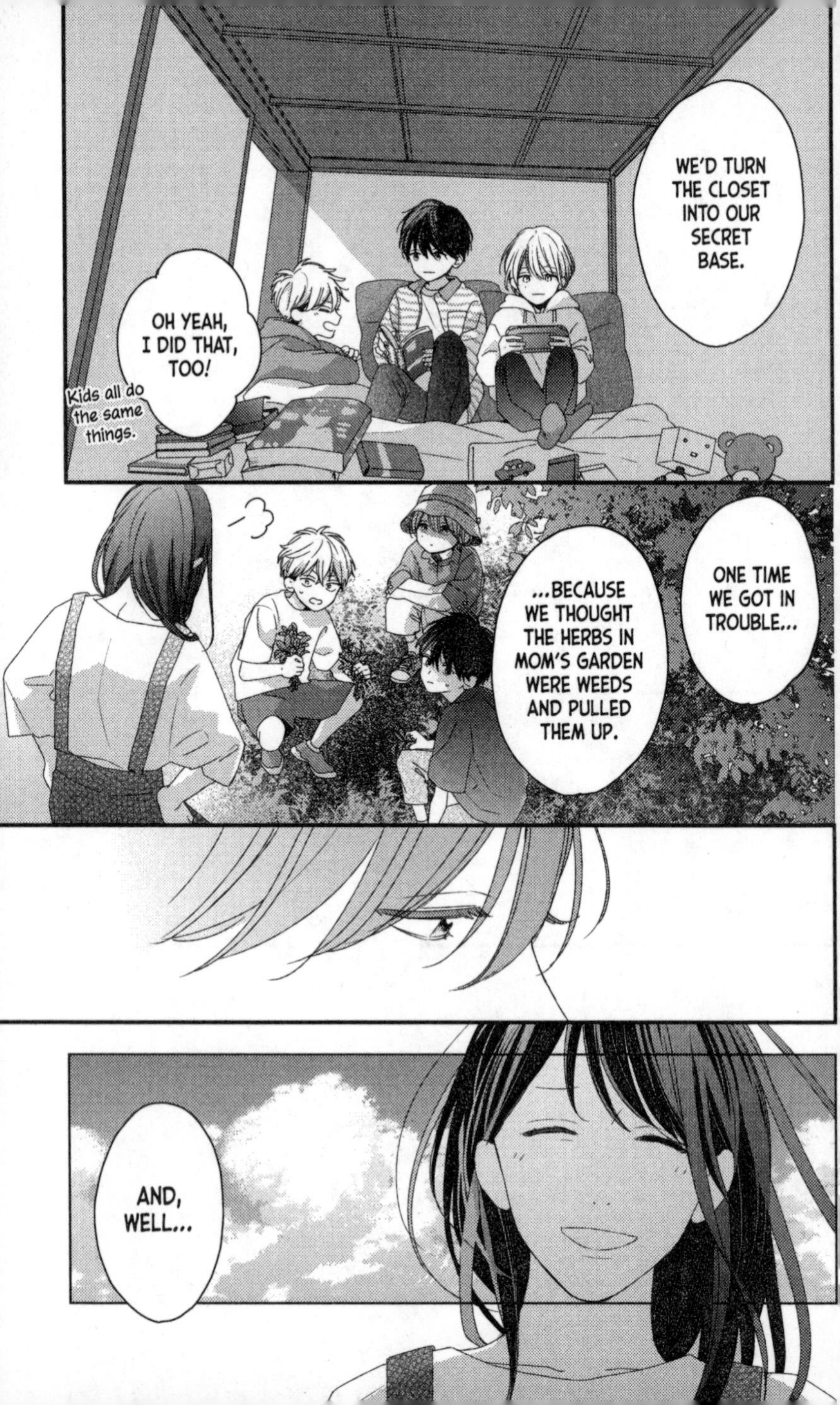

WE'D TURN THE CLOSET INTO OUR SECRET BASE.
OH YEAH, I DID THAT, TOO!
Kids all do the same things.
ONE TIME WE GOT IN TROUBLE...
...BECAUSE WE THOUGHT THE HERBS IN MOM'S GARDEN WERE WEEDS AND PULLED THEM UP.
AND, WELL...

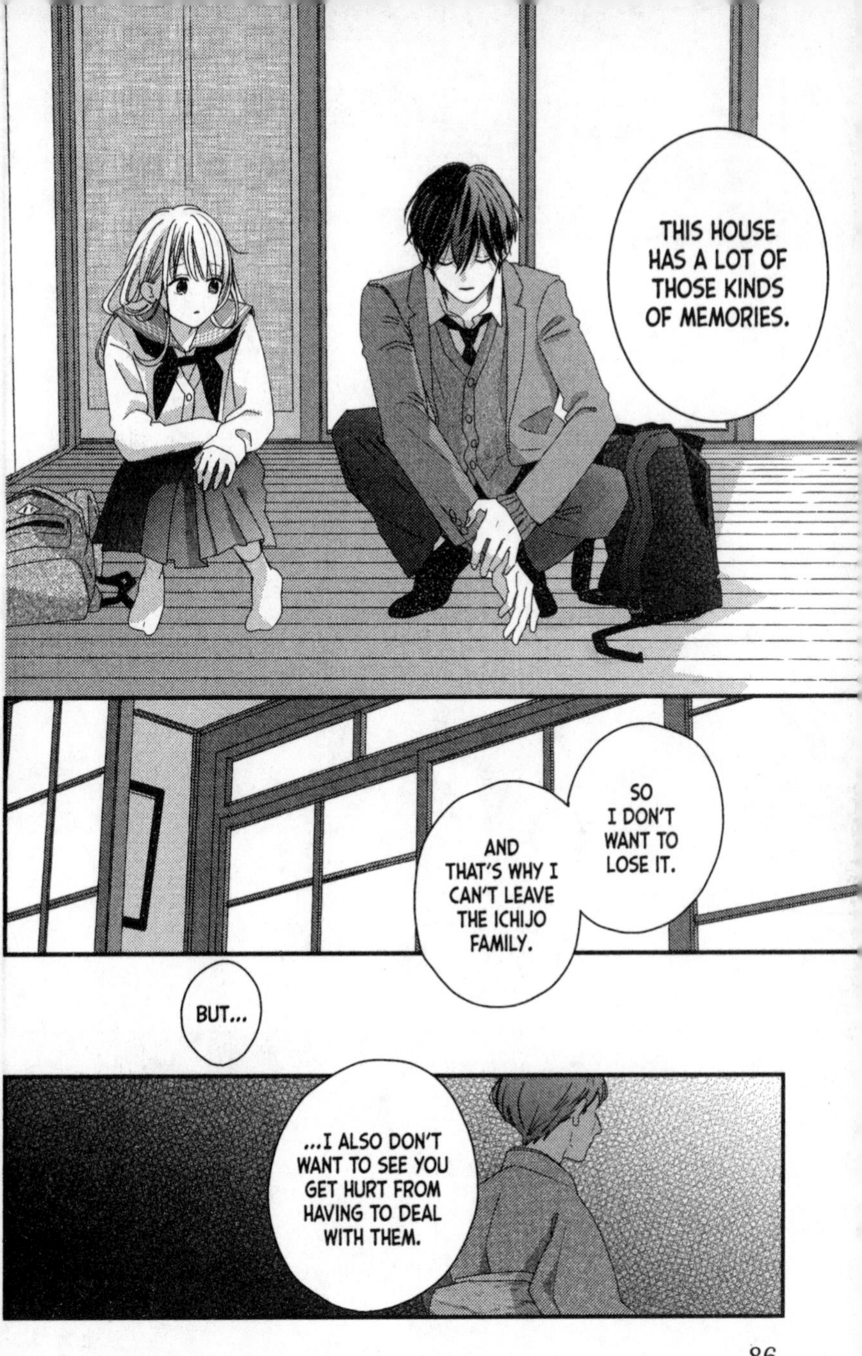
THIS HOUSE HAS A LOT OF THOSE KINDS OF MEMORIES.
SO I DON'T WANT TO LOSE IT.
AND THAT'S WHY I CAN'T LEAVE THE ICHIJO FAMILY.
BUT...
...I ALSO DON'T WANT TO SEE YOU GET HURT FROM HAVING TO DEAL WITH THEM.

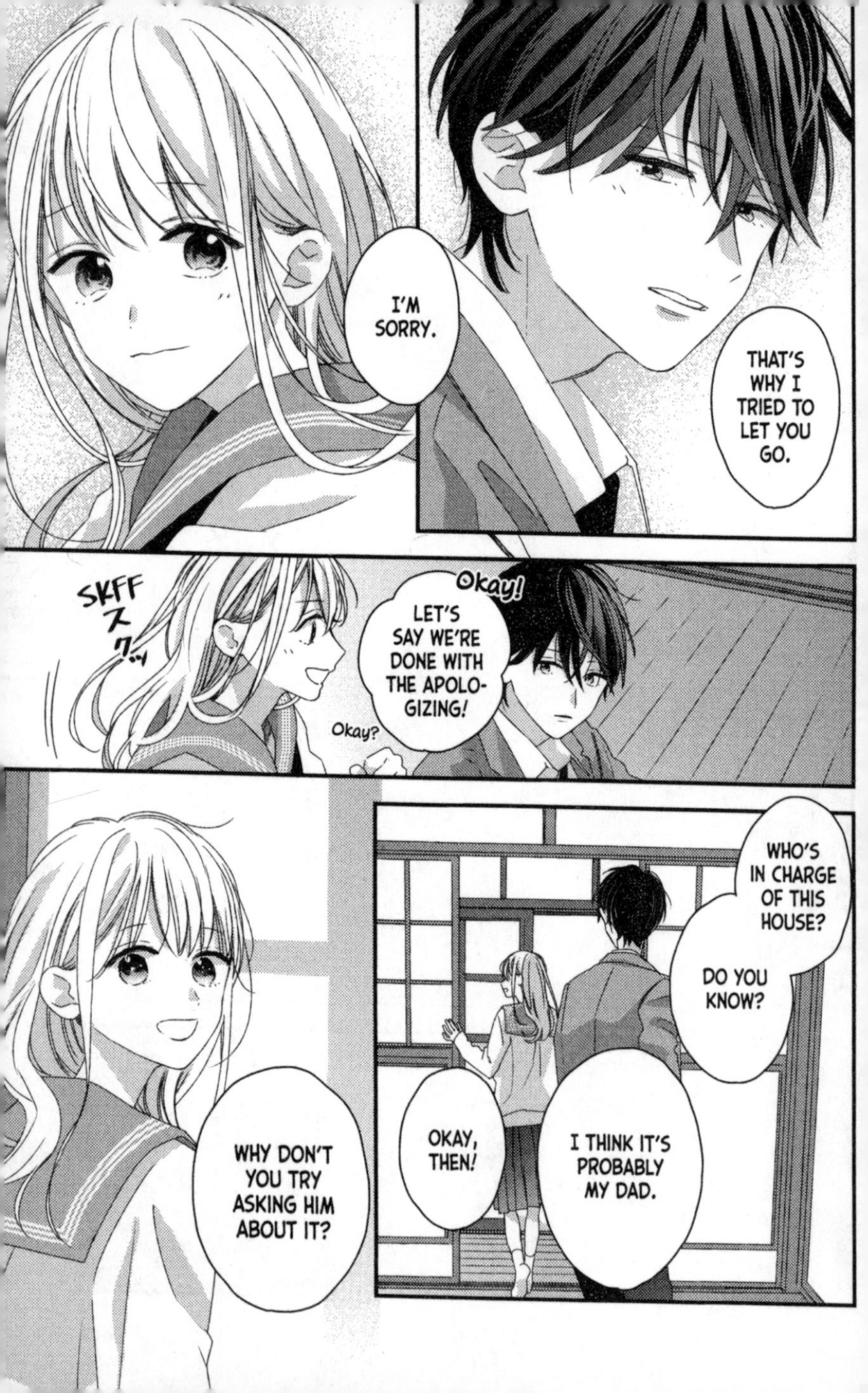
THAT'S WHY I TRIED TO LET YOU GO.
I'M SORRY.
Okay!
LET'S SAY WE'RE DONE WITH THE APOLO-GIZING!
Okay?
SKFF
スクッ
WHO'S IN CHARGE OF THIS HOUSE?
DO YOU KNOW?
I THINK IT'S PROBABLY MY DAD.
OKAY, THEN!
WHY DON'T YOU TRY ASKING HIM ABOUT IT?

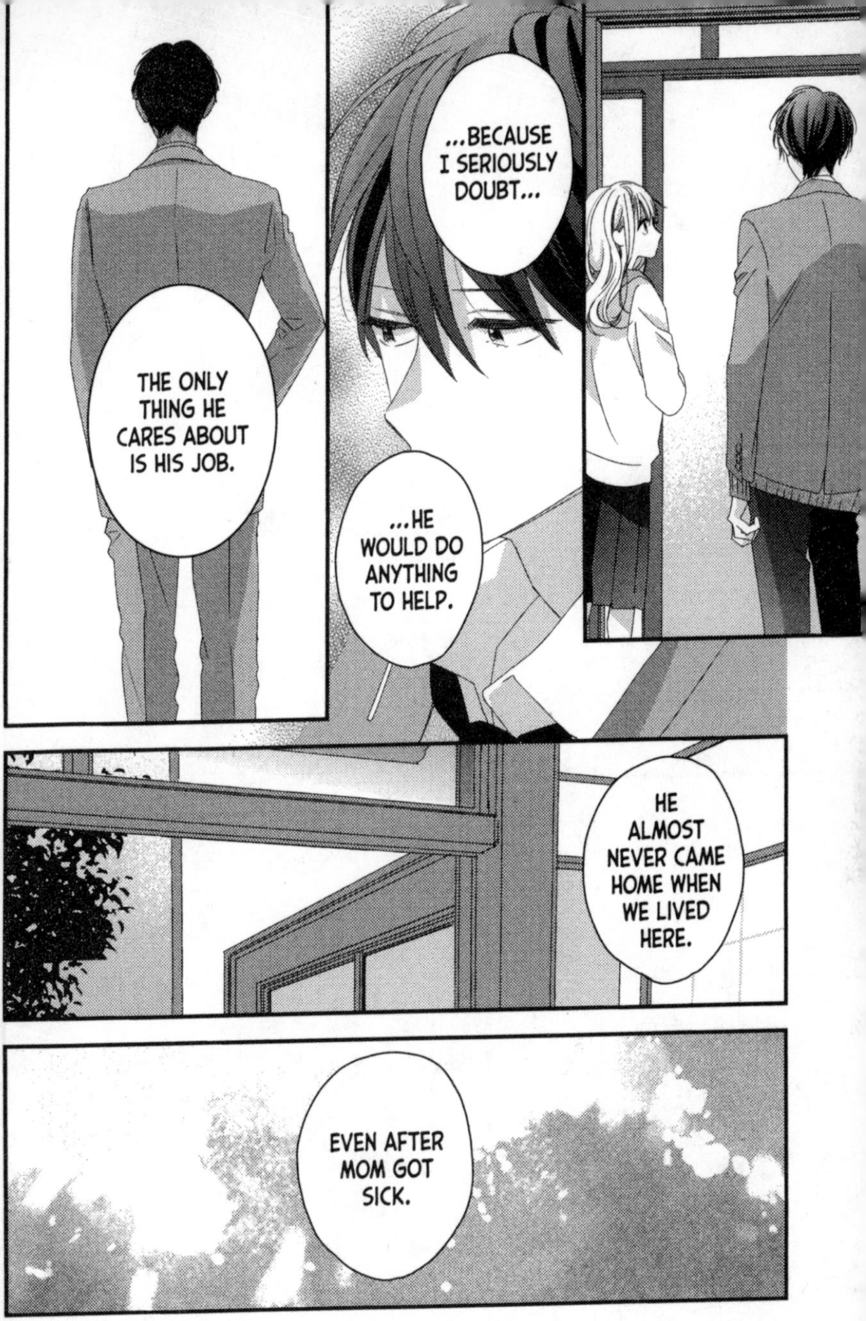
...BECAUSE I SERIOUSLY DOUBT...
...HE WOULD DO ANYTHING TO HELP.
THE ONLY THING HE CARES ABOUT IS HIS JOB.
HE ALMOST NEVER CAME HOME WHEN WE LIVED HERE.
EVEN AFTER MOM GOT SICK.

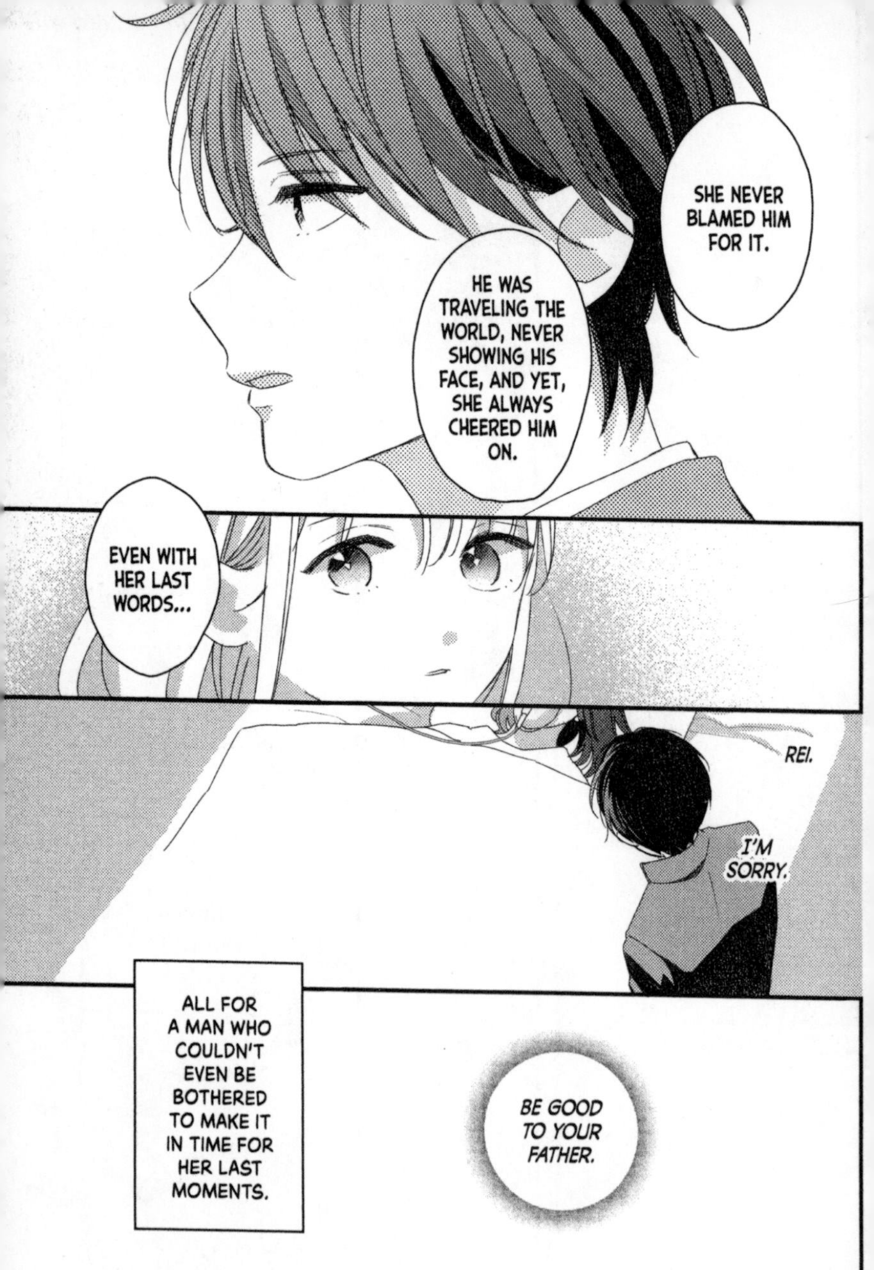
SHE NEVER BLAMED HIM FOR IT.
HE WAS TRAVELING THE WORLD, NEVER SHOWING HIS FACE, AND YET, SHE ALWAYS CHEERED HIM ON.
EVEN WITH HER LAST WORDS...
REI.
I'M SORRY.
BE GOOD TO YOUR FATHER.
ALL FOR A MAN WHO COULDN'T EVEN BE BOTHERED TO MAKE IT IN TIME FOR HER LAST MOMENTS.

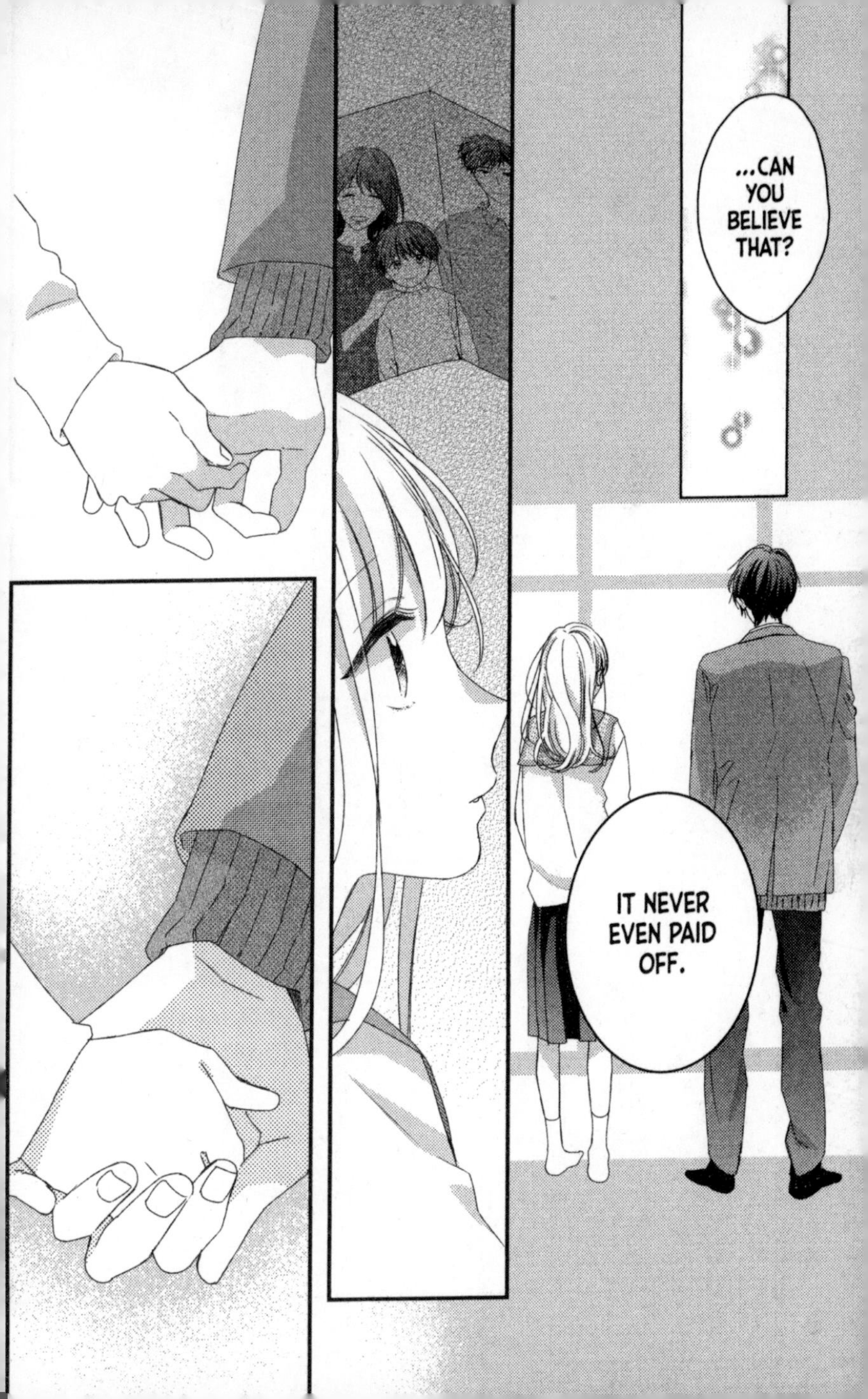
...CAN YOU BELIEVE THAT?
IT NEVER EVEN PAID OFF.

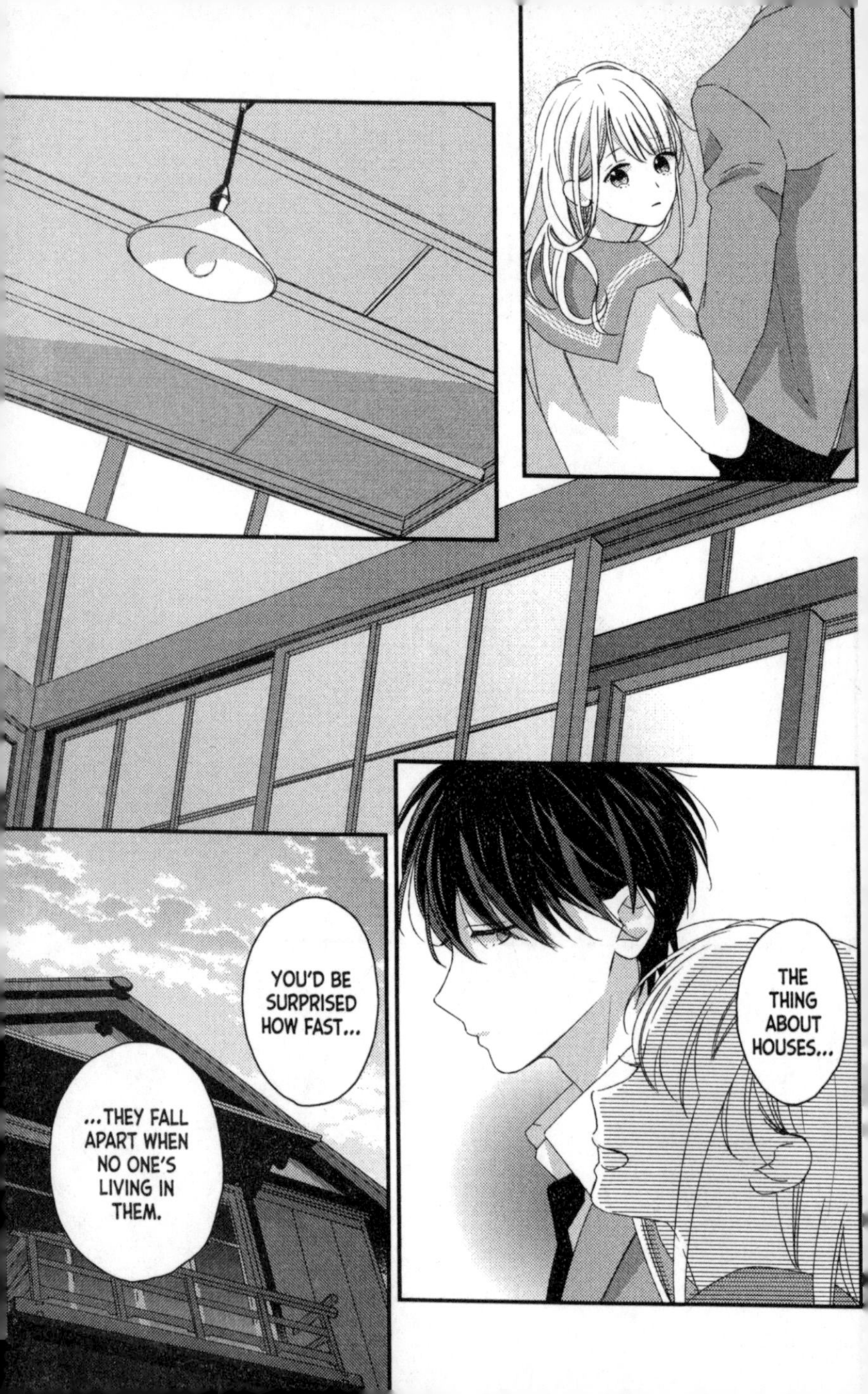
THE THING ABOUT HOUSES...
YOU'D BE SURPRISED HOW FAST...
...THEY FALL APART WHEN NO ONE'S LIVING IN THEM.

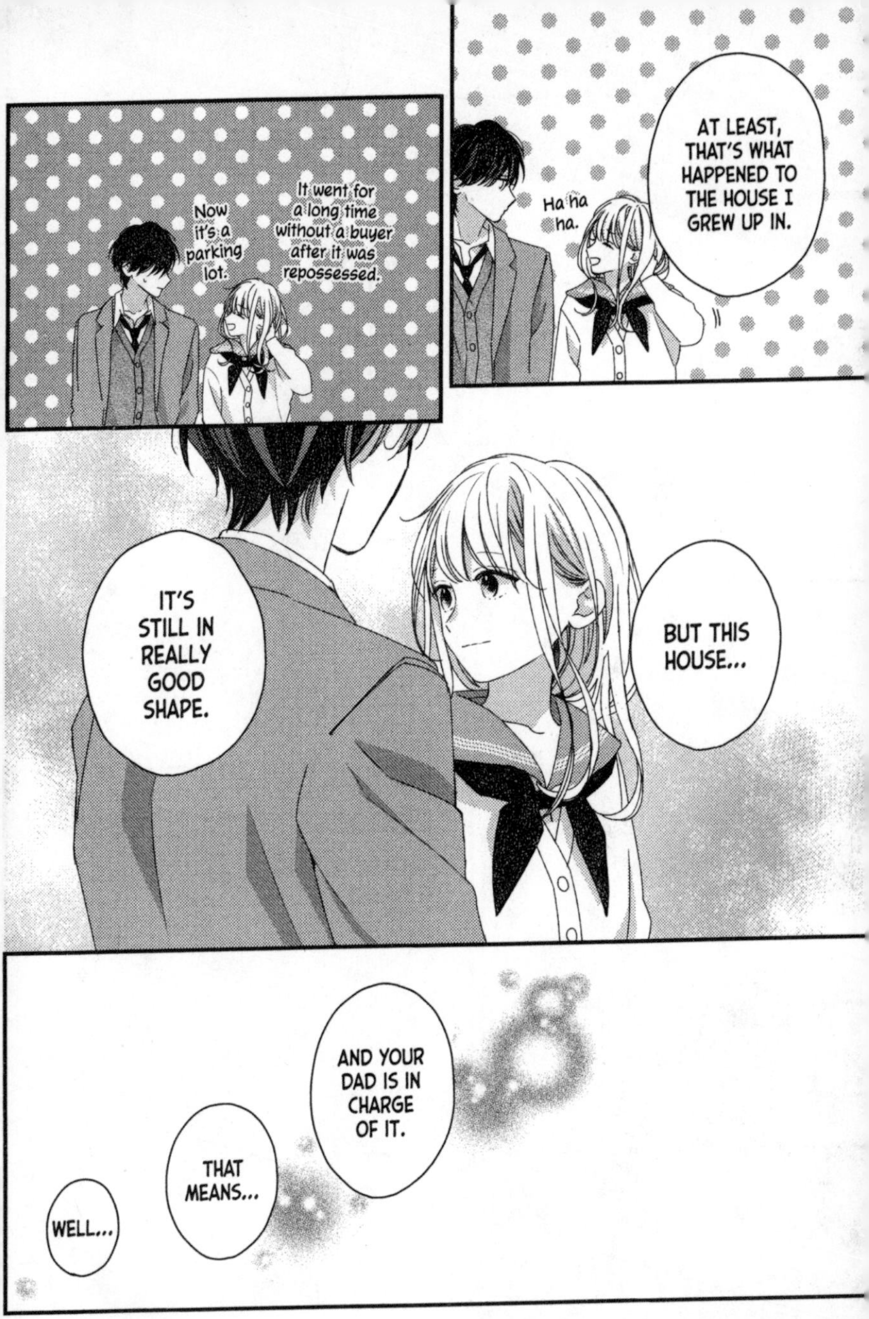
AT LEAST, THAT'S WHAT HAPPENED TO THE HOUSE I GREW UP IN.
Ha ha ha.
It went for a long time without a buyer after it was repossessed.
Now it's a parking lot.
BUT THIS HOUSE...
IT'S STILL IN REALLY GOOD SHAPE.
AND YOUR DAD IS IN CHARGE OF IT.
THAT MEANS...
WELL...

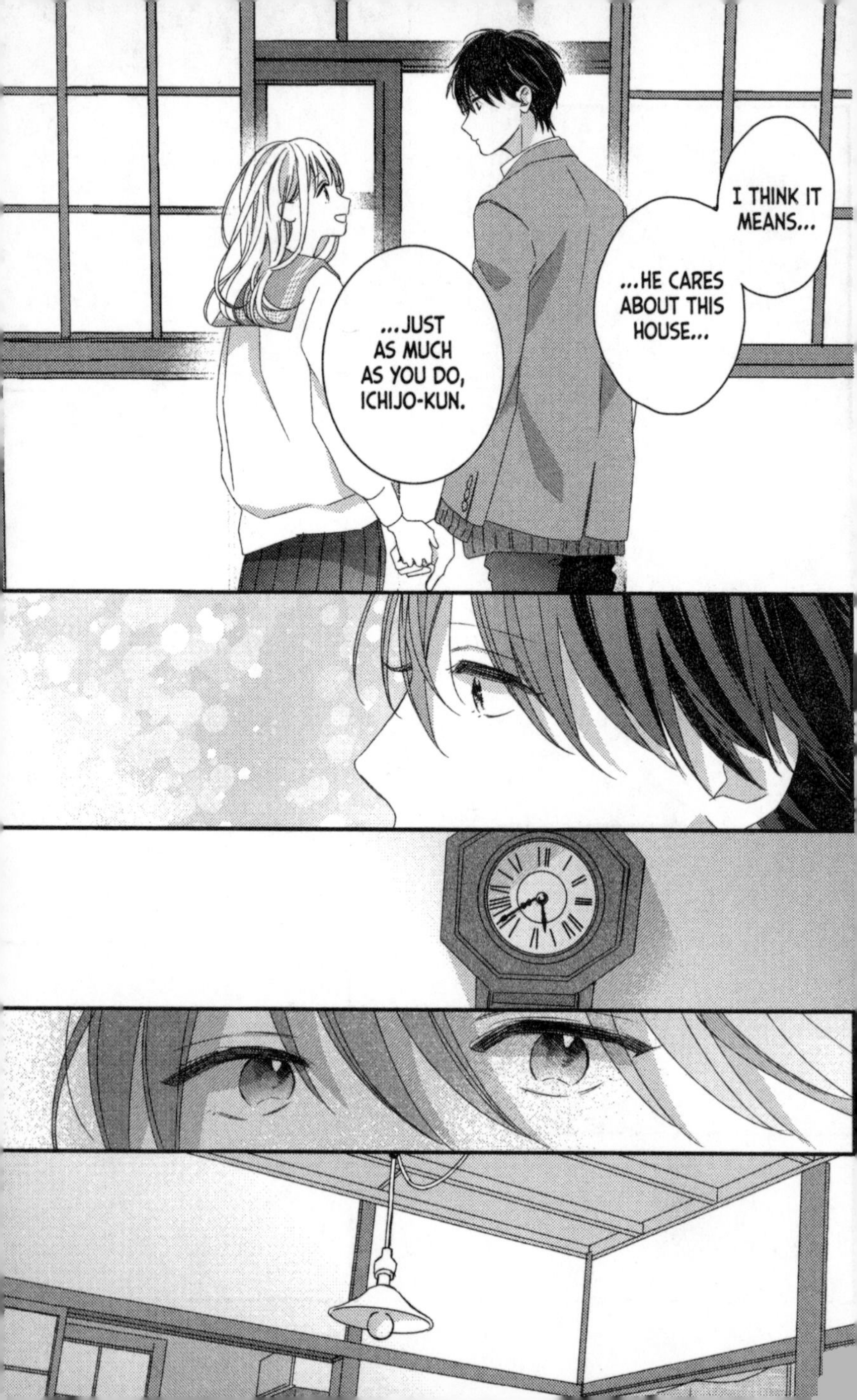
I THINK IT MEANS...
...HE CARES ABOUT THIS HOUSE...
...JUST AS MUCH AS YOU DO, ICHIJO-KUN.

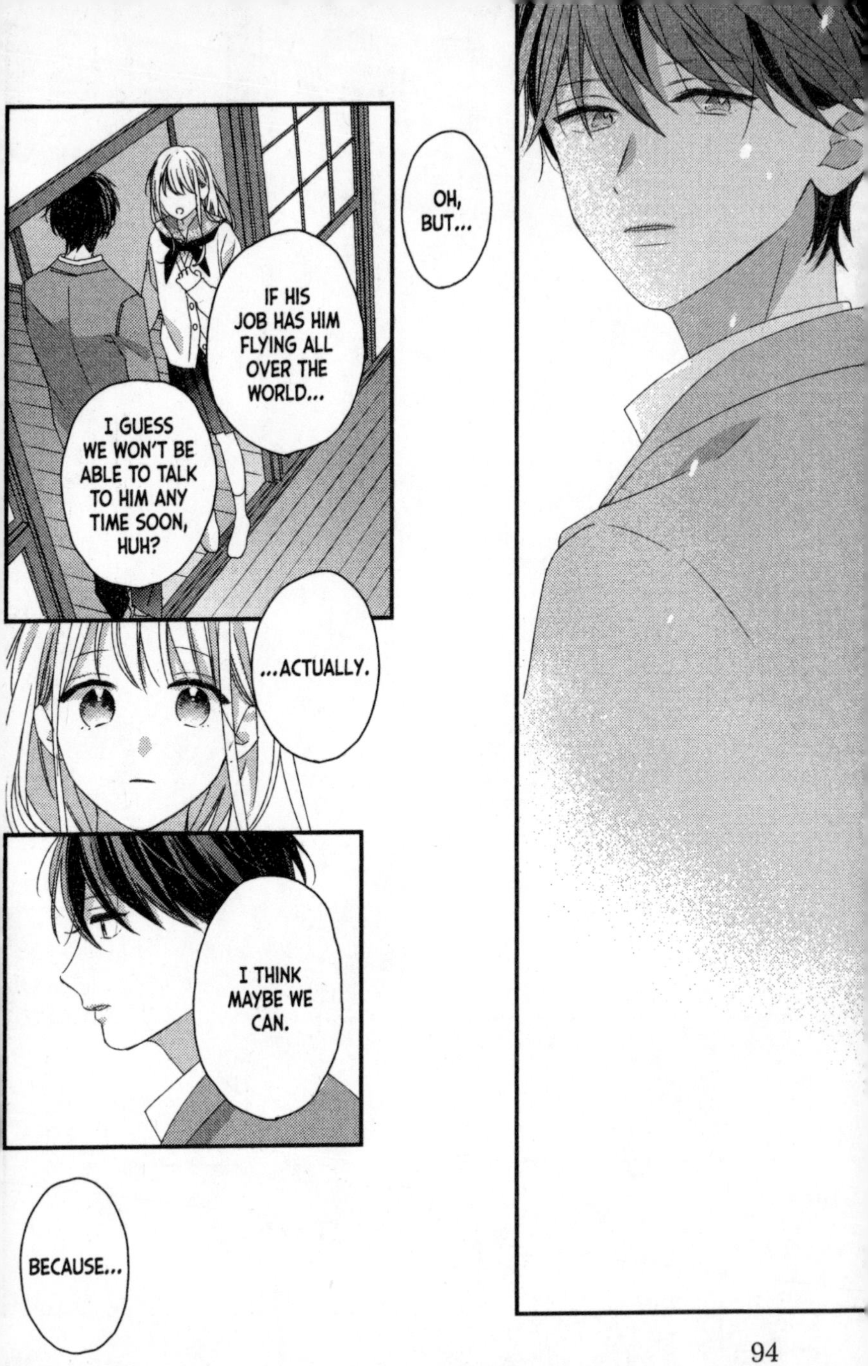
OH, BUT...
IF HIS JOB HAS HIM FLYING ALL OVER THE WORLD...
I GUESS WE WON'T BE ABLE TO TALK TO HIM ANY TIME SOON, HUH?
...ACTUALLY.
I THINK MAYBE WE CAN.
BECAUSE...

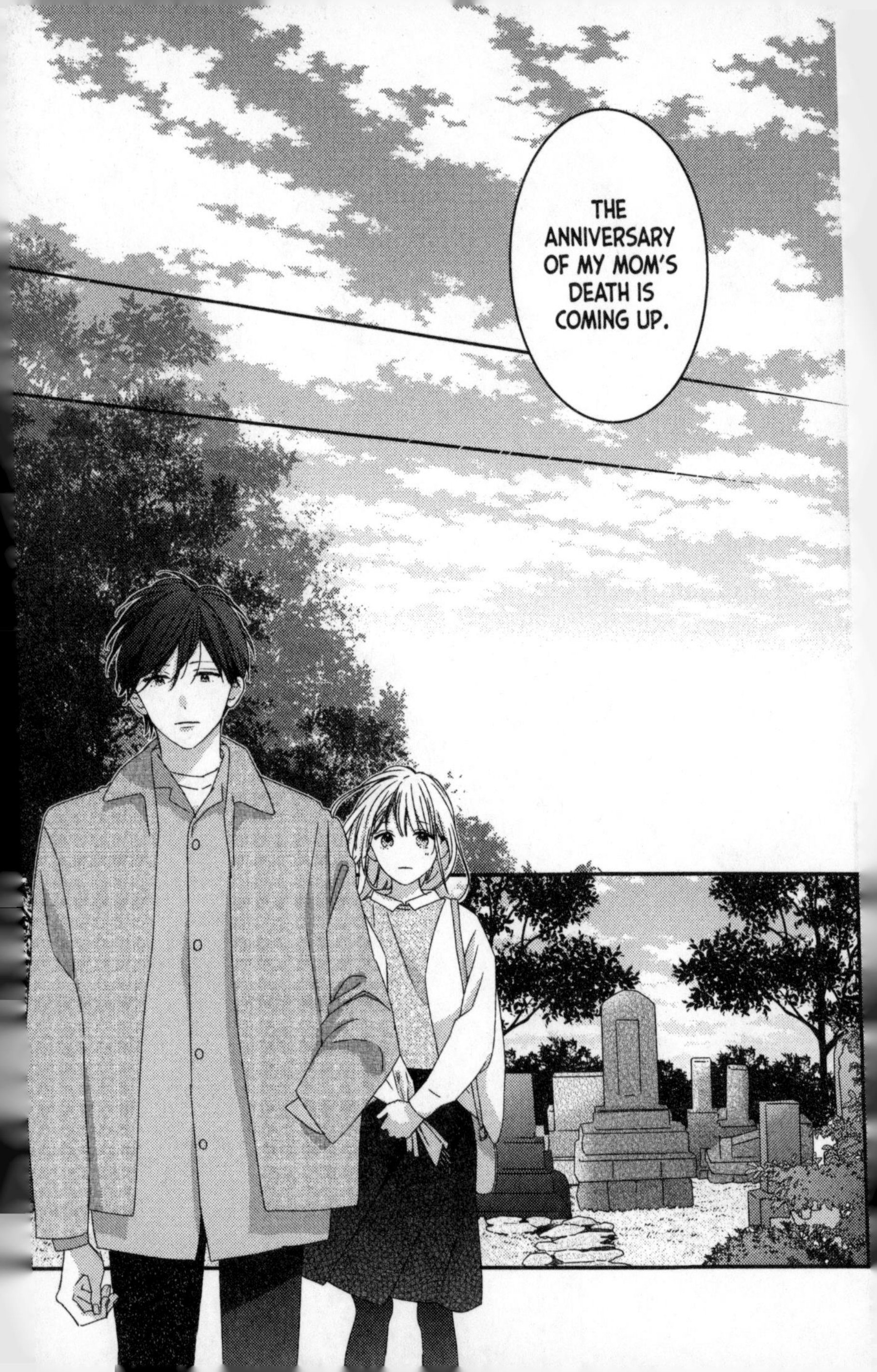
THE ANNIVERSARY OF MY MOM'S DEATH IS COMING UP.

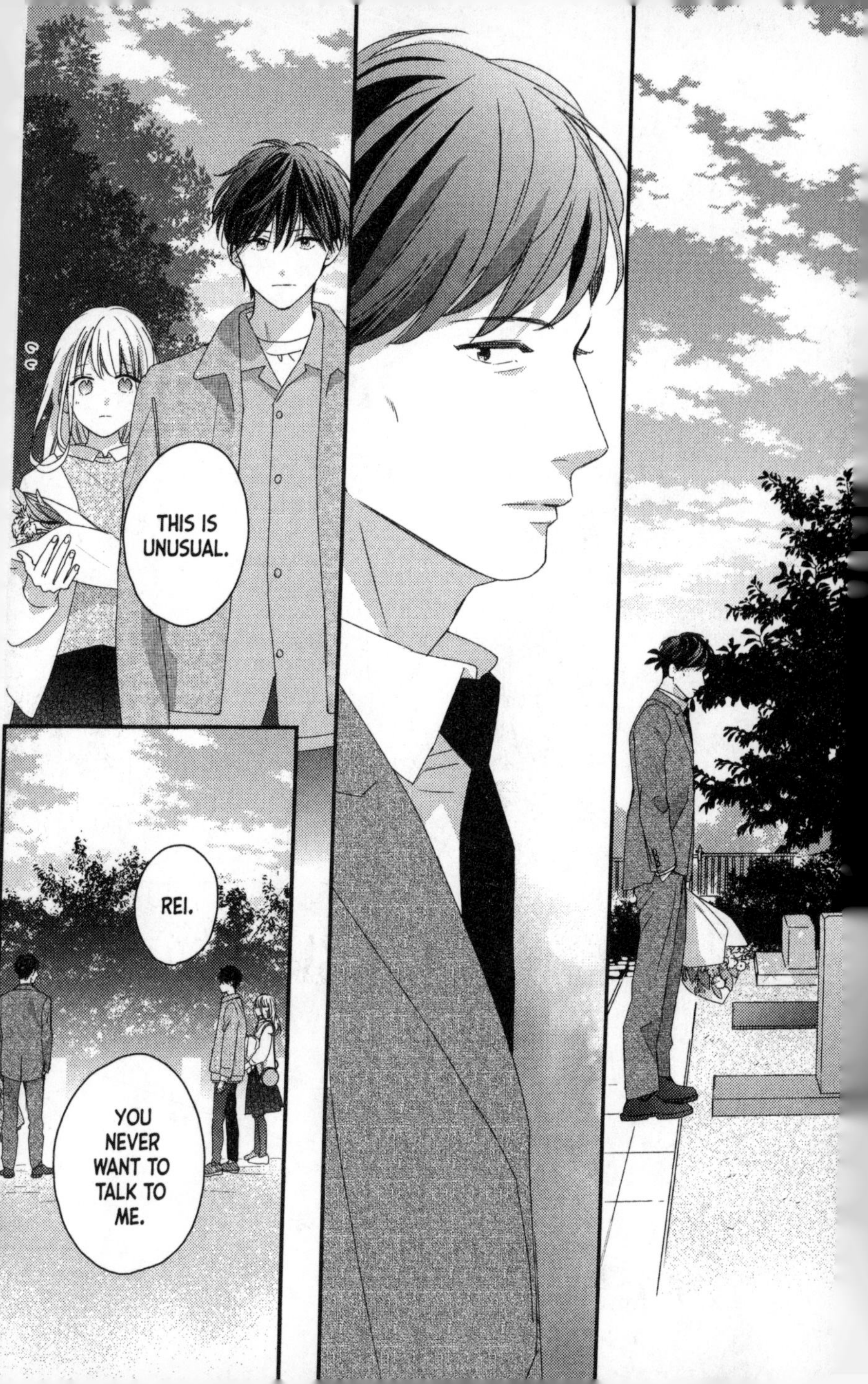
THIS IS UNUSUAL.
REI.
YOU NEVER WANT TO TALK TO ME.

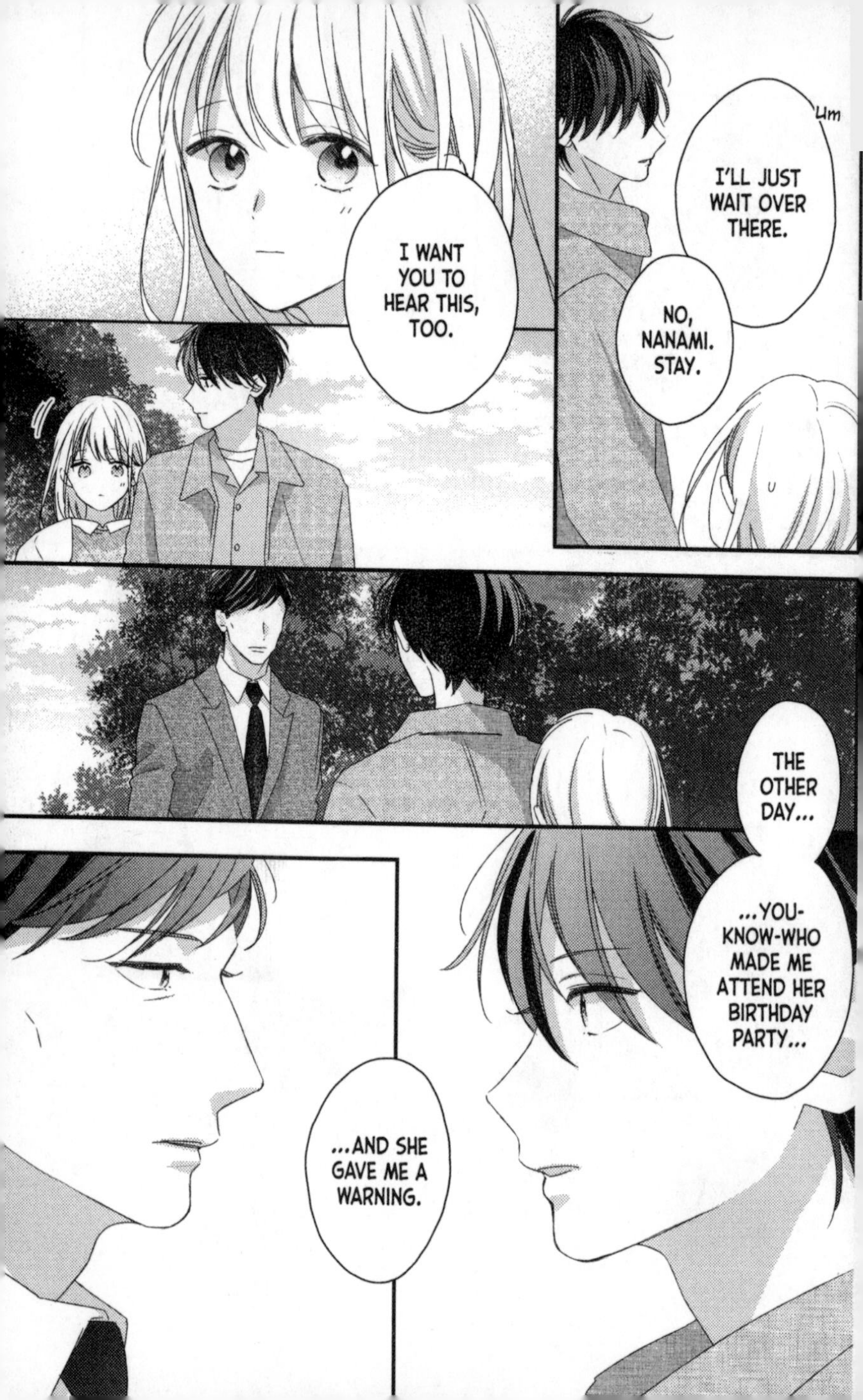
Um
I'LL JUST WAIT OVER THERE.
NO, NANAMI. STAY.
I WANT YOU TO HEAR THIS, TOO.
THE OTHER DAY...
...YOU-KNOW-WHO MADE ME ATTEND HER BIRTHDAY PARTY...
...AND SHE GAVE ME A WARNING.

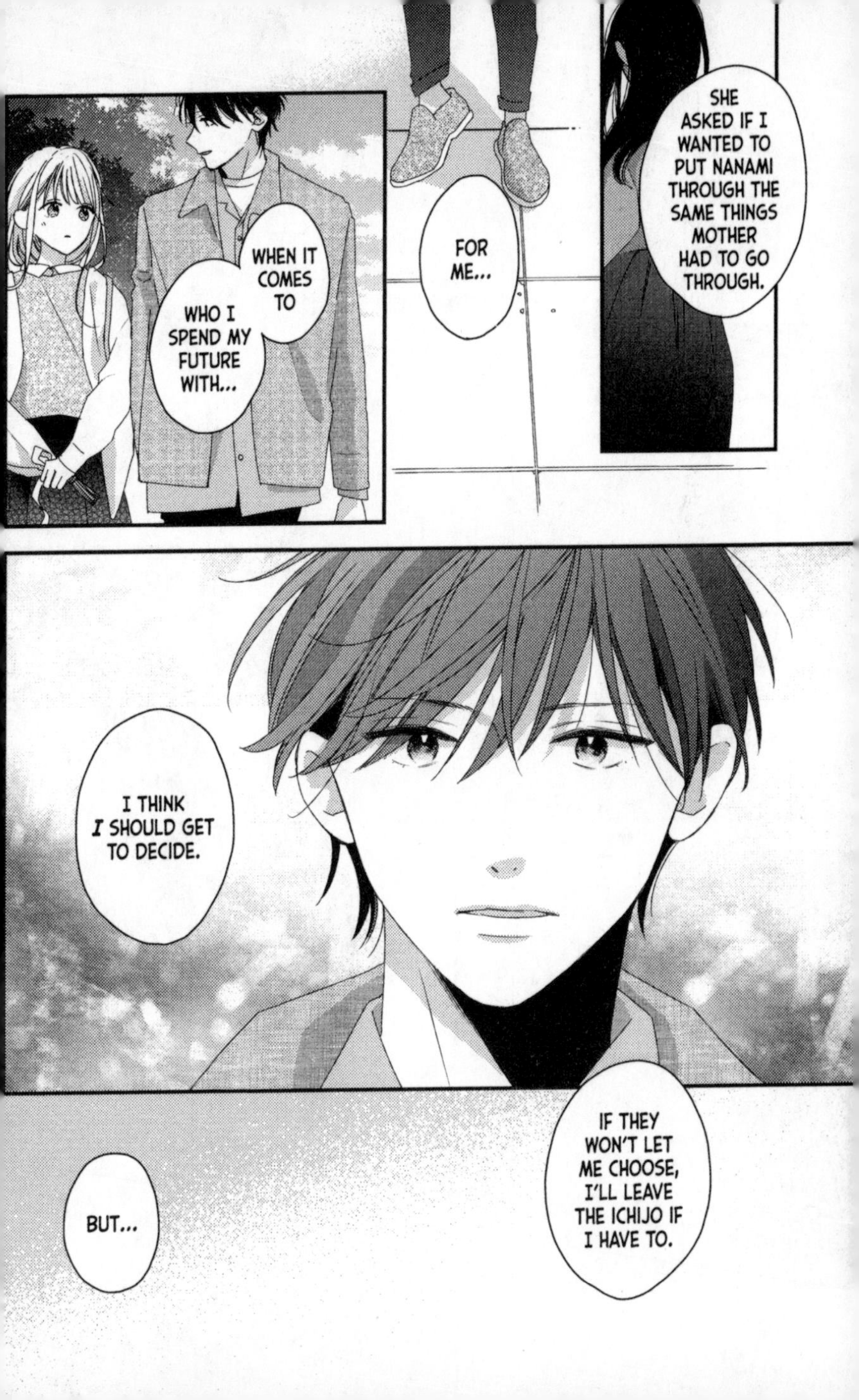
SHE ASKED IF I WANTED TO PUT NANAMI THROUGH THE SAME THINGS MOTHER HAD TO GO THROUGH.
FOR ME...
WHEN IT COMES TO
WHO I SPEND MY FUTURE WITH...
I THINK *I* SHOULD GET TO DECIDE.
IF THEY WON'T LET ME CHOOSE, I'LL LEAVE THE ICHIJO IF I HAVE TO.
BUT...

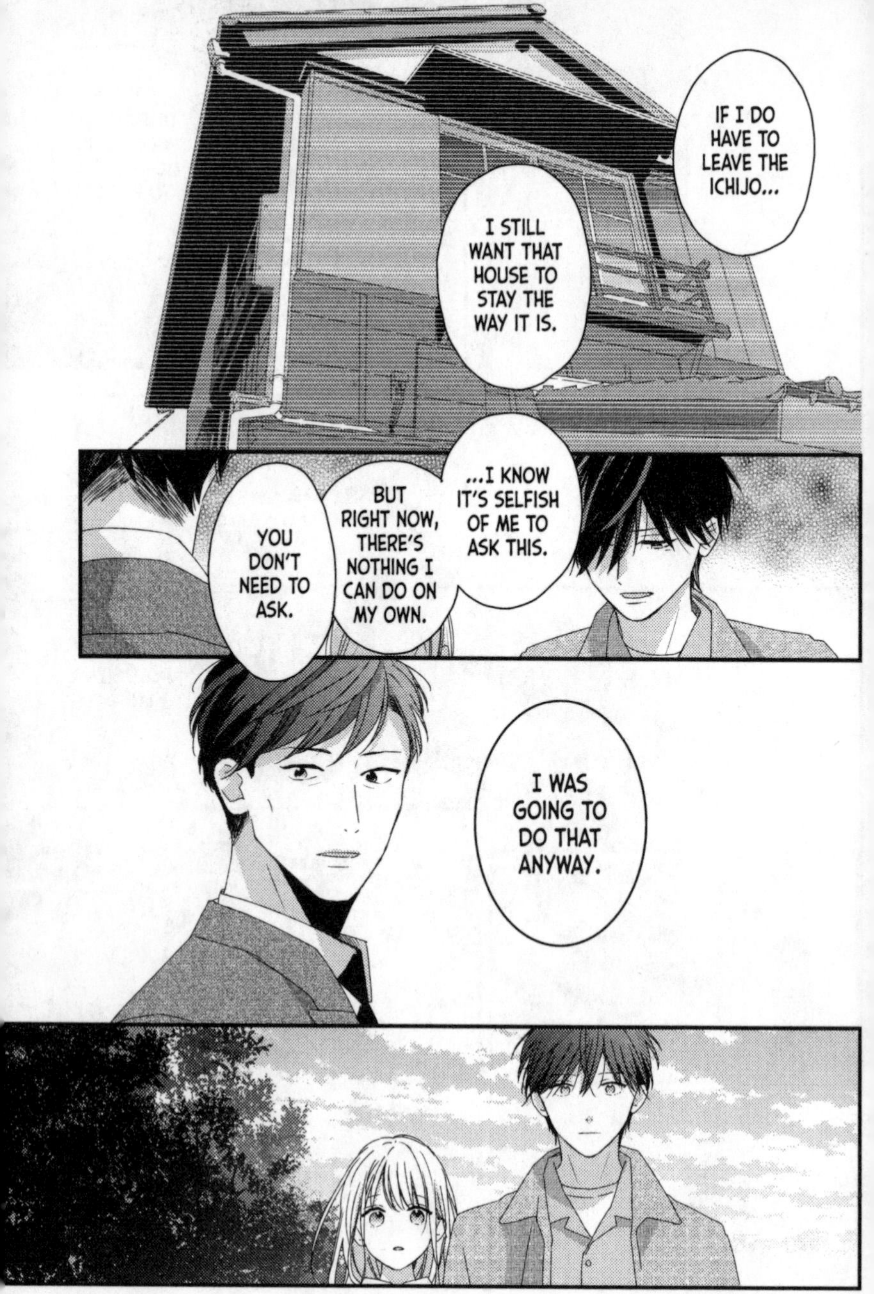
IF I DO HAVE TO LEAVE THE ICHIJO...
I STILL WANT THAT HOUSE TO STAY THE WAY IT IS.
...I KNOW IT'S SELFISH OF ME TO ASK THIS.
BUT RIGHT NOW, THERE'S NOTHING I CAN DO ON MY OWN.
YOU DON'T NEED TO ASK.
I WAS GOING TO DO THAT ANYWAY.

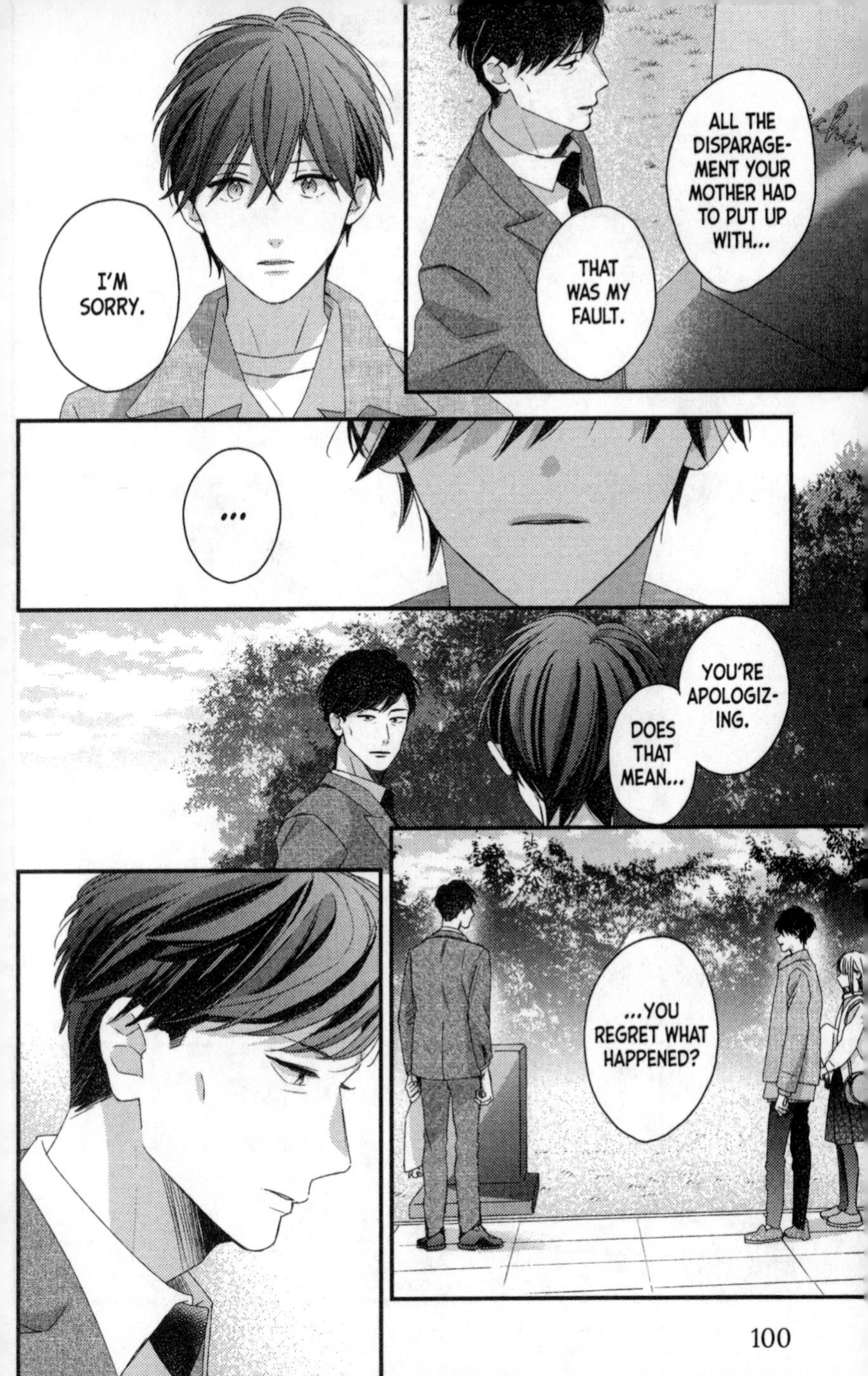
ALL THE DISPARAGE-MENT YOUR MOTHER HAD TO PUT UP WITH...
THAT WAS MY FAULT.
I'M SORRY.
...
YOU'RE APOLOGIZ-ING.
DOES THAT MEAN...
...YOU REGRET WHAT HAPPENED?

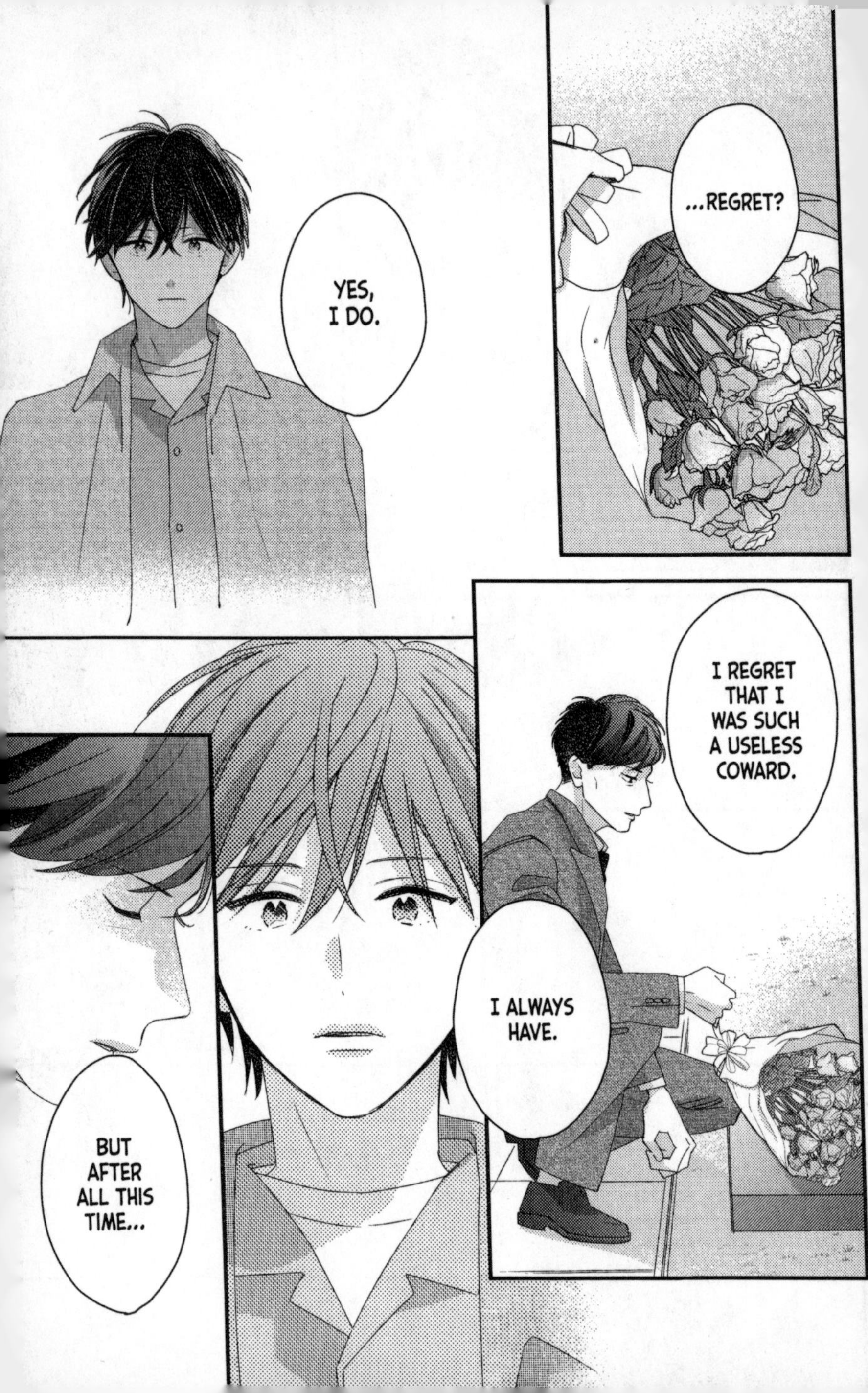
...REGRET?
YES, I DO.
I REGRET THAT I WAS SUCH A USELESS COWARD.
I ALWAYS HAVE.
BUT AFTER ALL THIS TIME...

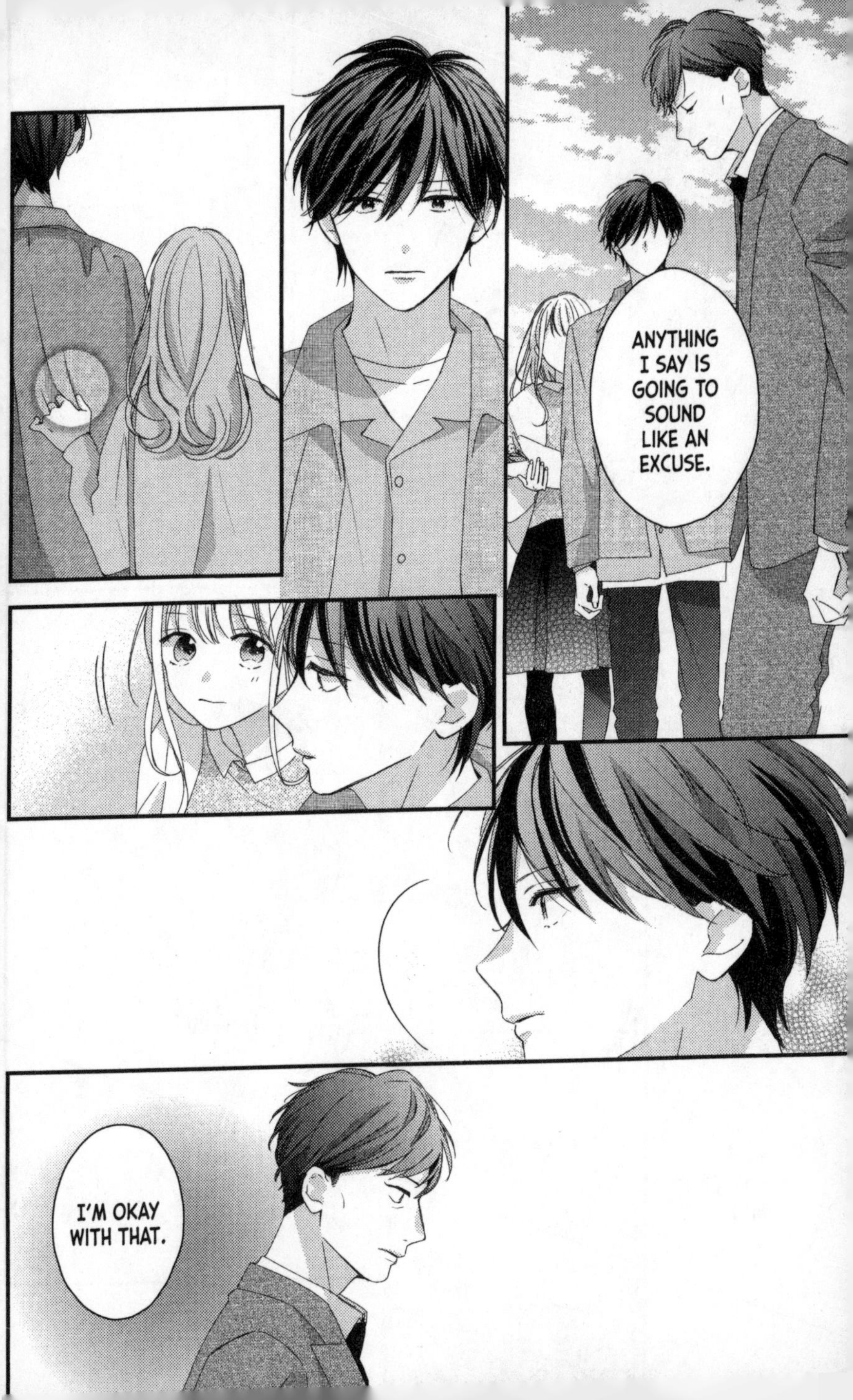
ANYTHING I SAY IS GOING TO SOUND LIKE AN EXCUSE.
I'M OKAY WITH THAT.

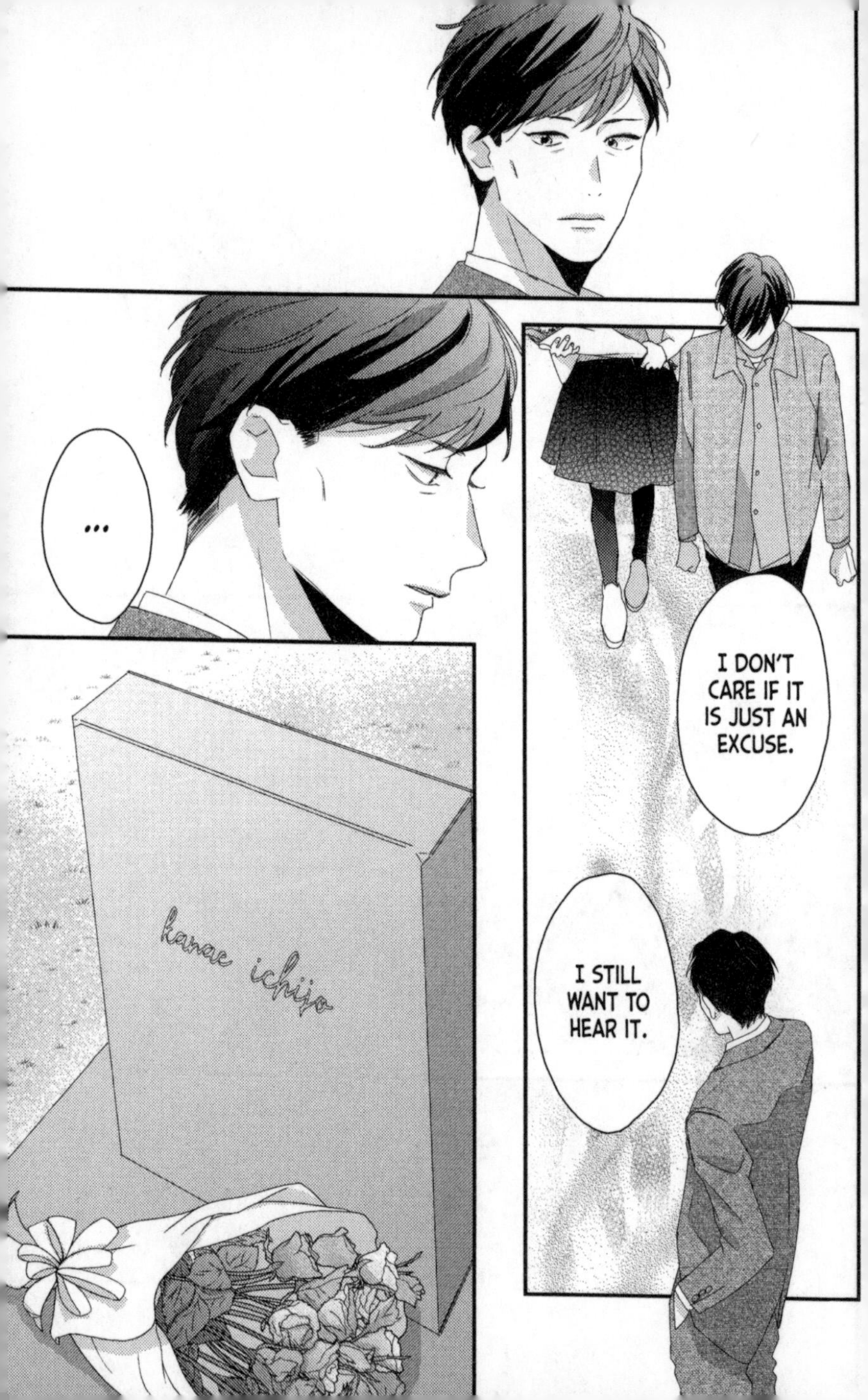
I DON'T CARE IF IT IS JUST AN EXCUSE.
I STILL WANT TO HEAR IT.
...
kanae ichijo

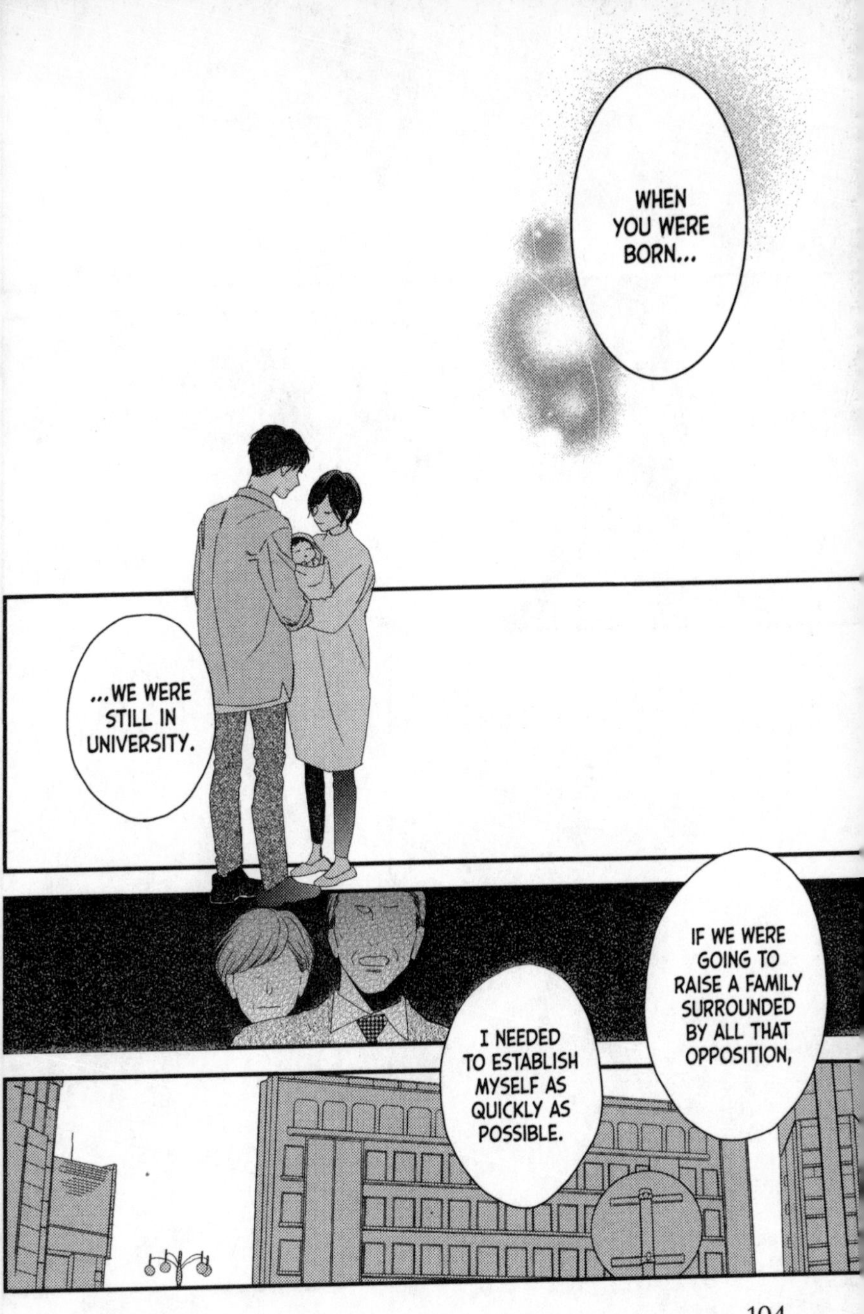
WHEN YOU WERE BORN...
...WE WERE STILL IN UNIVERSITY.
IF WE WERE GOING TO RAISE A FAMILY SURROUNDED BY ALL THAT OPPOSITION,
I NEEDED TO ESTABLISH MYSELF AS QUICKLY AS POSSIBLE.

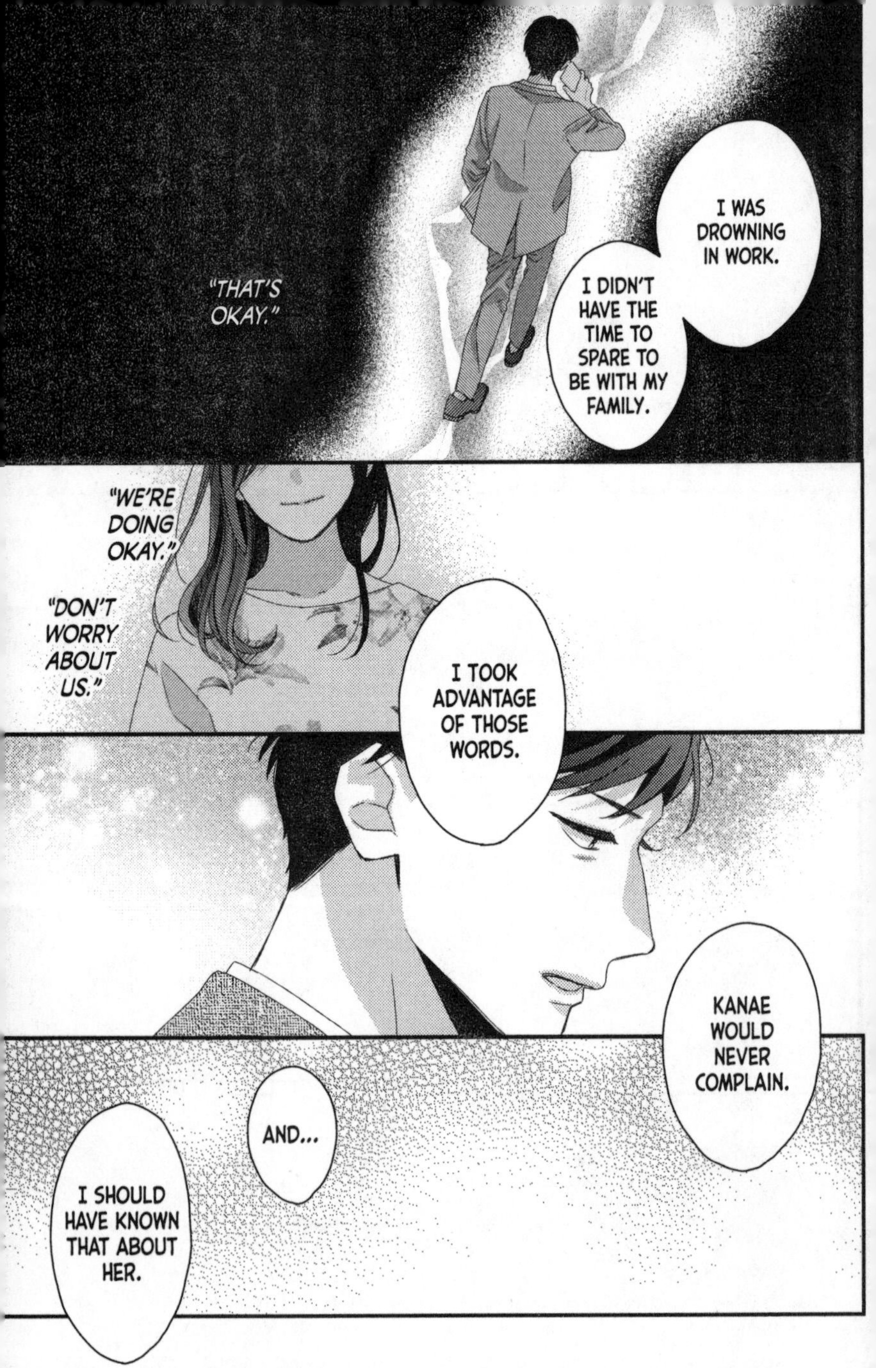
I WAS DROWNING IN WORK.
I DIDN'T HAVE THE TIME TO SPARE TO BE WITH MY FAMILY.
"THAT'S OKAY."
"WE'RE DOING OKAY."
"DON'T WORRY ABOUT US."
I TOOK ADVANTAGE OF THOSE WORDS.
KANAE WOULD NEVER COMPLAIN.
AND...
I SHOULD HAVE KNOWN THAT ABOUT HER.

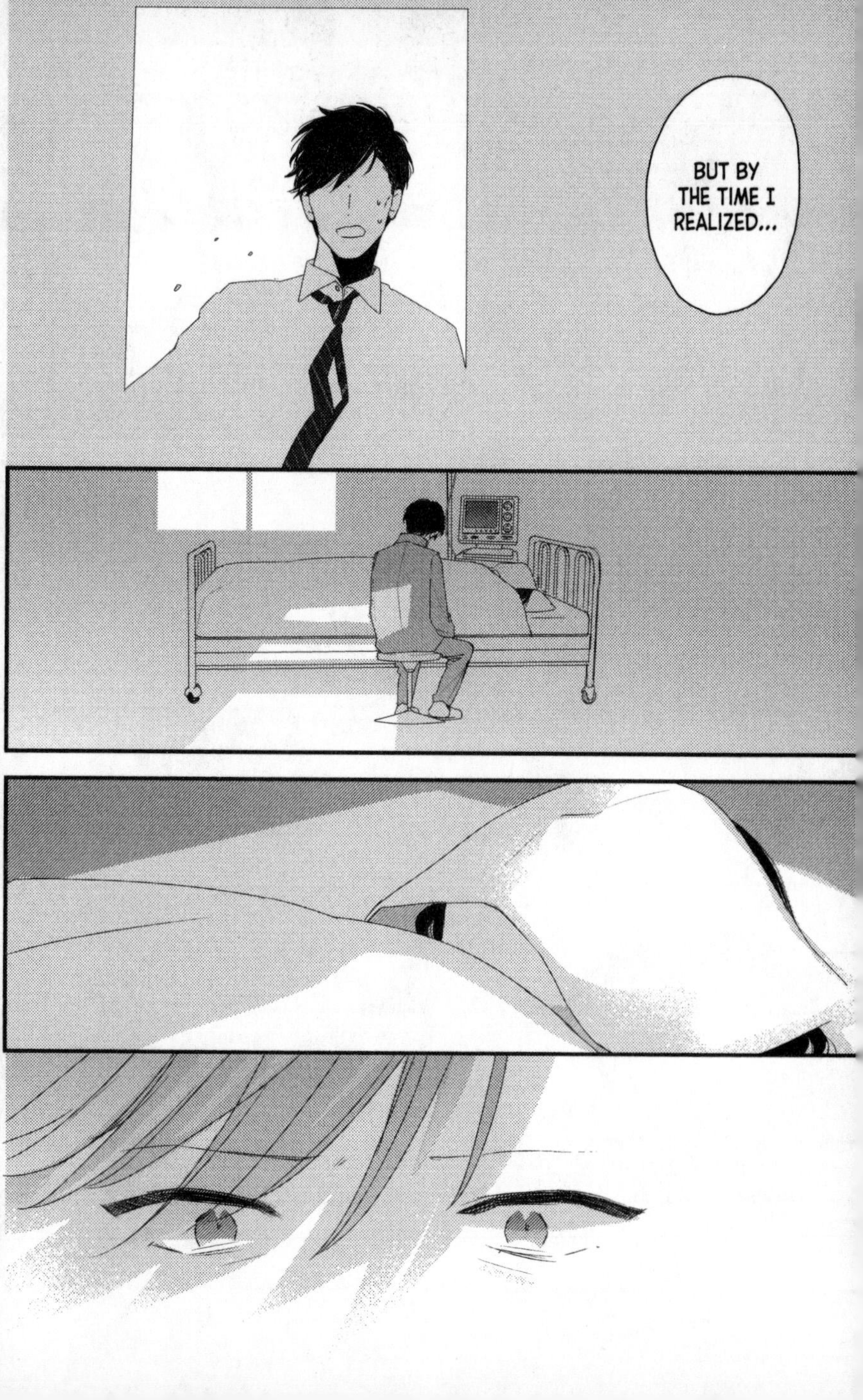
BUT BY THE TIME I REALIZED...

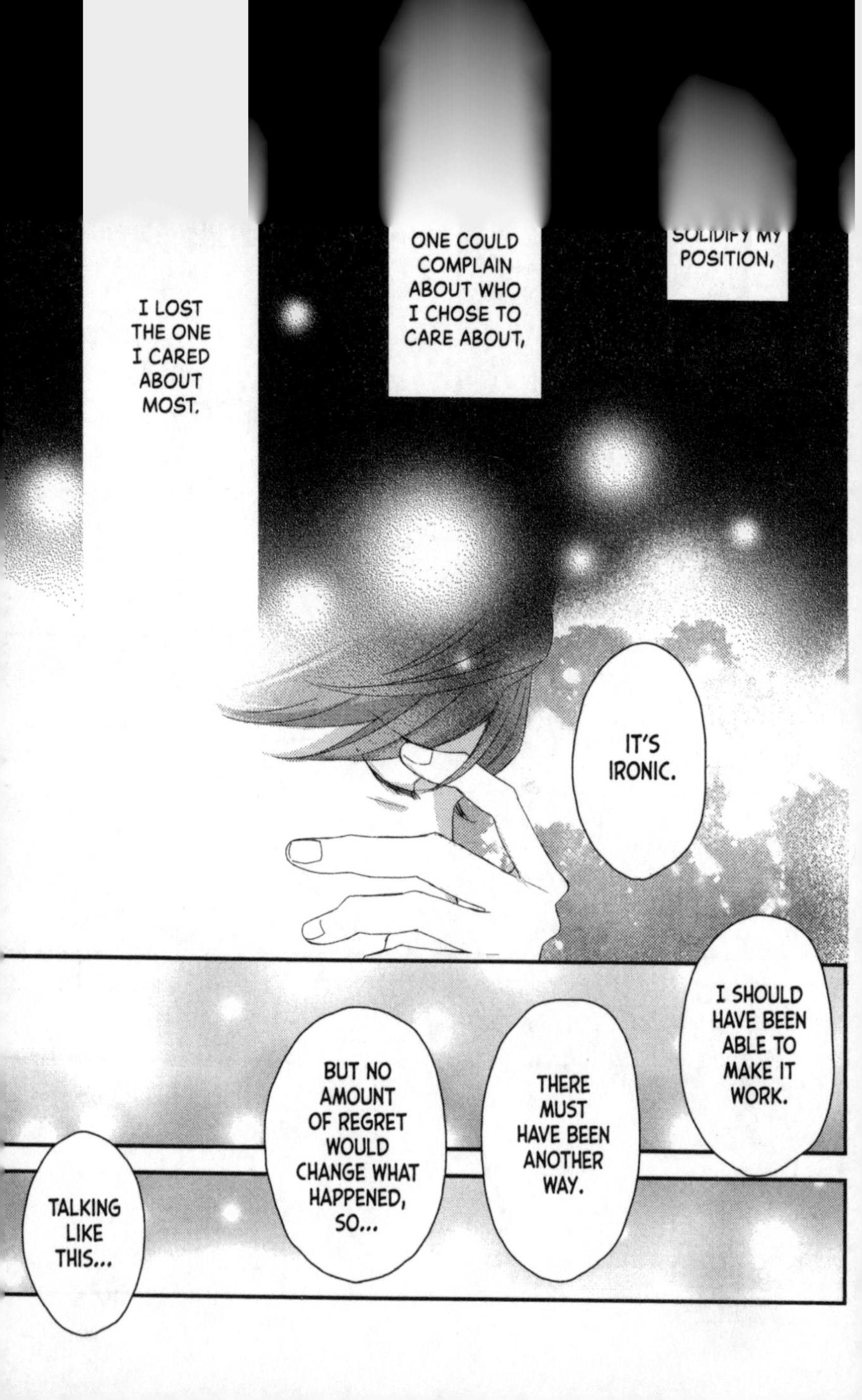
SOLIDIFY MY POSITION,
ONE COULD COMPLAIN ABOUT WHO I CHOSE TO CARE ABOUT,
I LOST THE ONE I CARED ABOUT MOST.
IT'S IRONIC.
I SHOULD HAVE BEEN ABLE TO MAKE IT WORK.
THERE MUST HAVE BEEN ANOTHER WAY.
BUT NO AMOUNT OF REGRET WOULD CHANGE WHAT HAPPENED, SO...
TALKING LIKE THIS...

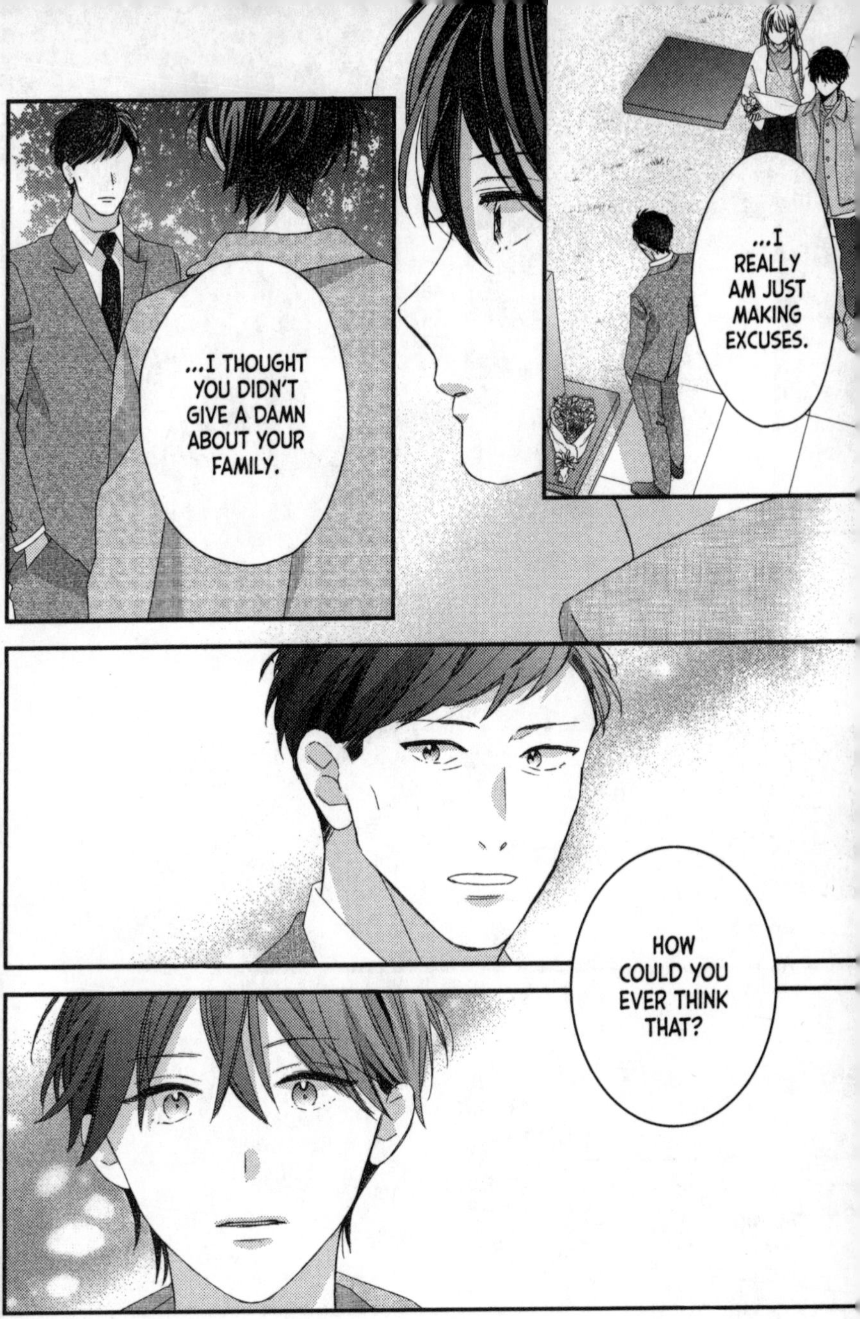
...I REALLY AM JUST MAKING EXCUSES.
...I THOUGHT YOU DIDN'T GIVE A DAMN ABOUT YOUR FAMILY.
HOW COULD YOU EVER THINK THAT?

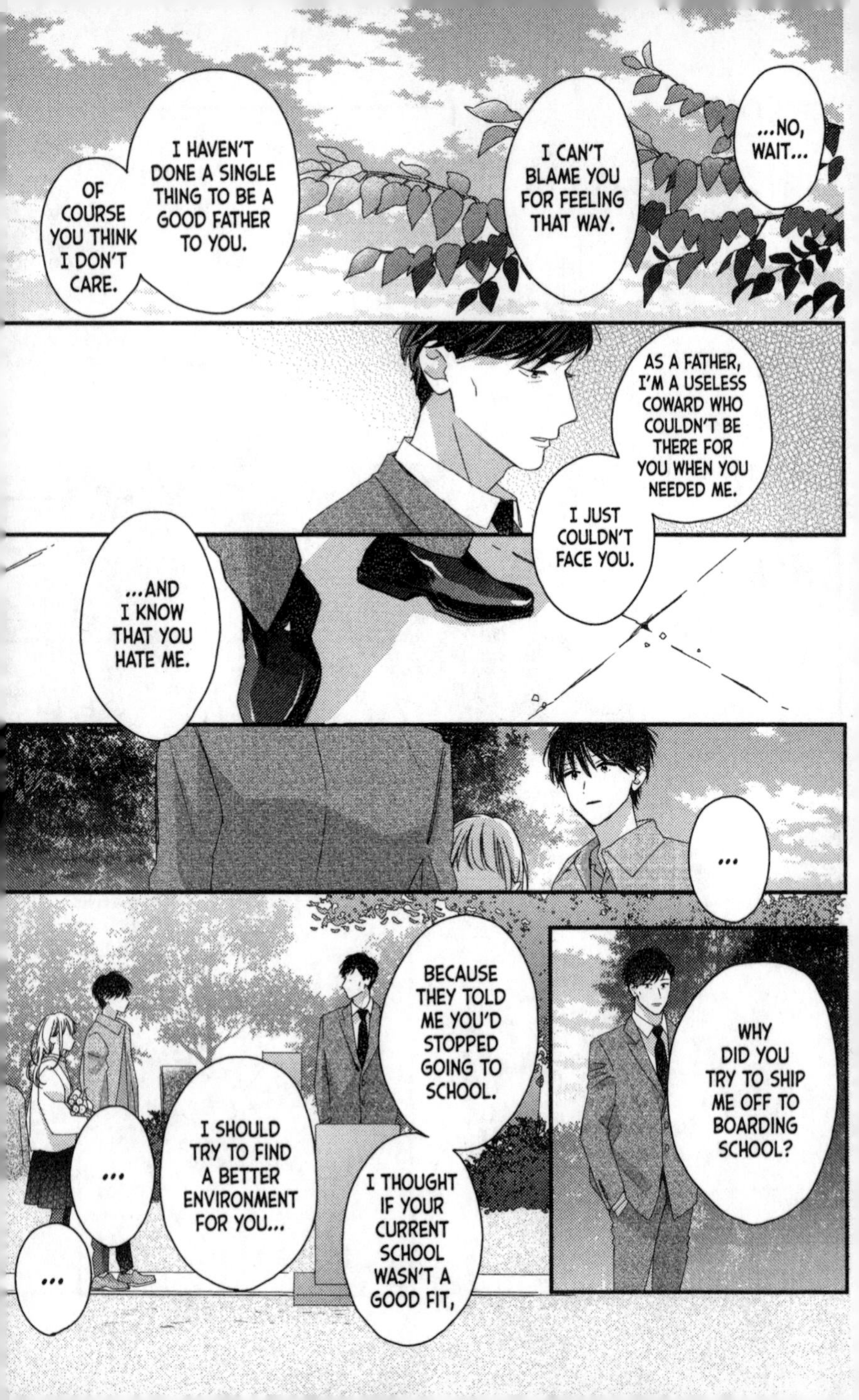
...NO, WAIT...
I CAN'T BLAME YOU FOR FEELING THAT WAY.
I HAVEN'T DONE A SINGLE THING TO BE A GOOD FATHER TO YOU.
OF COURSE YOU THINK I DON'T CARE.
AS A FATHER, I'M A USELESS COWARD WHO COULDN'T BE THERE FOR YOU WHEN YOU NEEDED ME.
I JUST COULDN'T FACE YOU.
...AND I KNOW THAT YOU HATE ME.
...
WHY DID YOU TRY TO SHIP ME OFF TO BOARDING SCHOOL?
BECAUSE THEY TOLD ME YOU'D STOPPED GOING TO SCHOOL.
I THOUGHT IF YOUR CURRENT SCHOOL WASN'T A GOOD FIT,
I SHOULD TRY TO FIND A BETTER ENVIRONMENT FOR YOU...
...
...

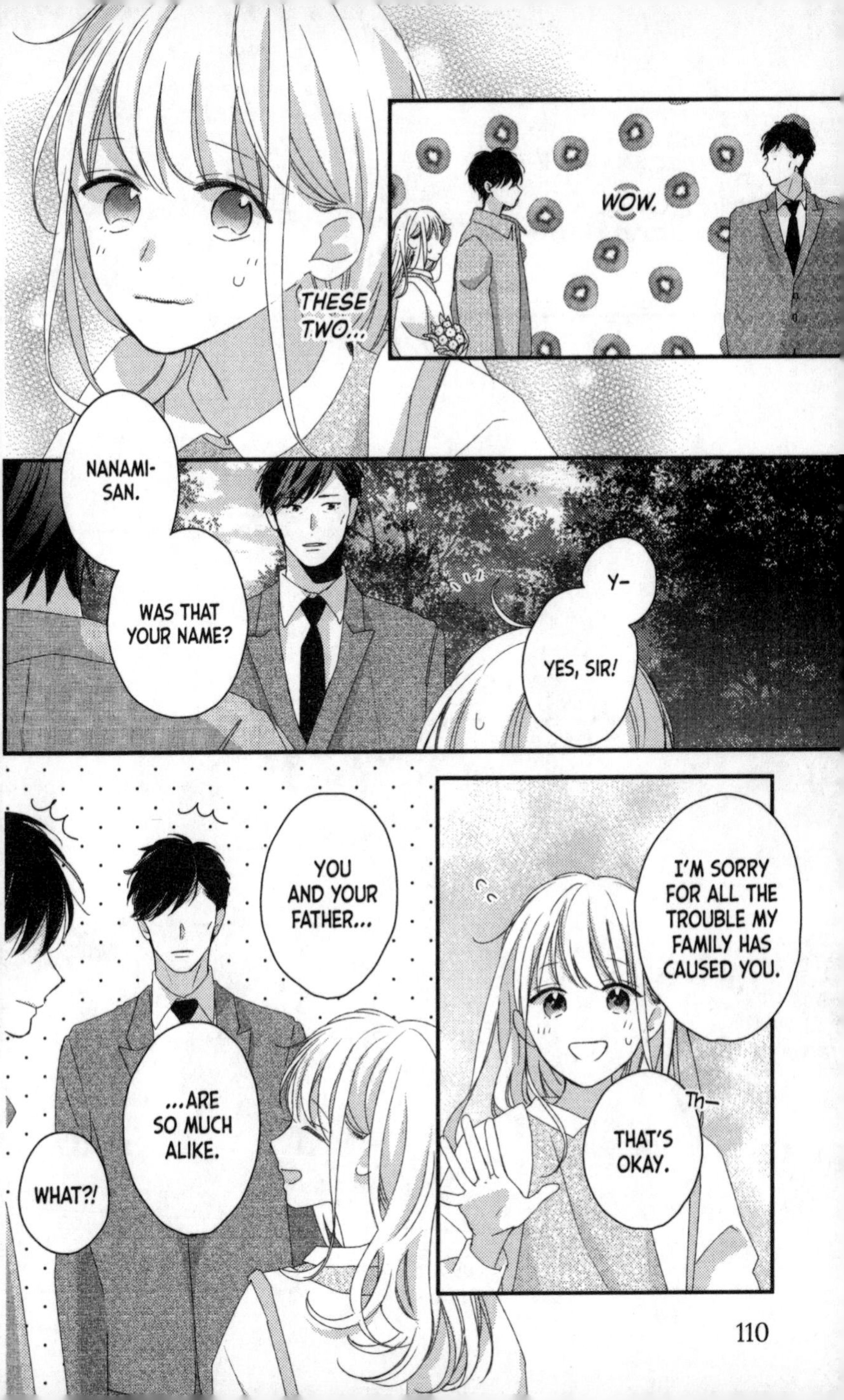
WOW.
THESE TWO...
NANAMI-SAN.
WAS THAT YOUR NAME?
Y-
YES, SIR!
I'M SORRY FOR ALL THE TROUBLE MY FAMILY HAS CAUSED YOU.
Th-
THAT'S OKAY.
YOU AND YOUR FATHER...
...ARE SO MUCH ALIKE.
WHAT?!

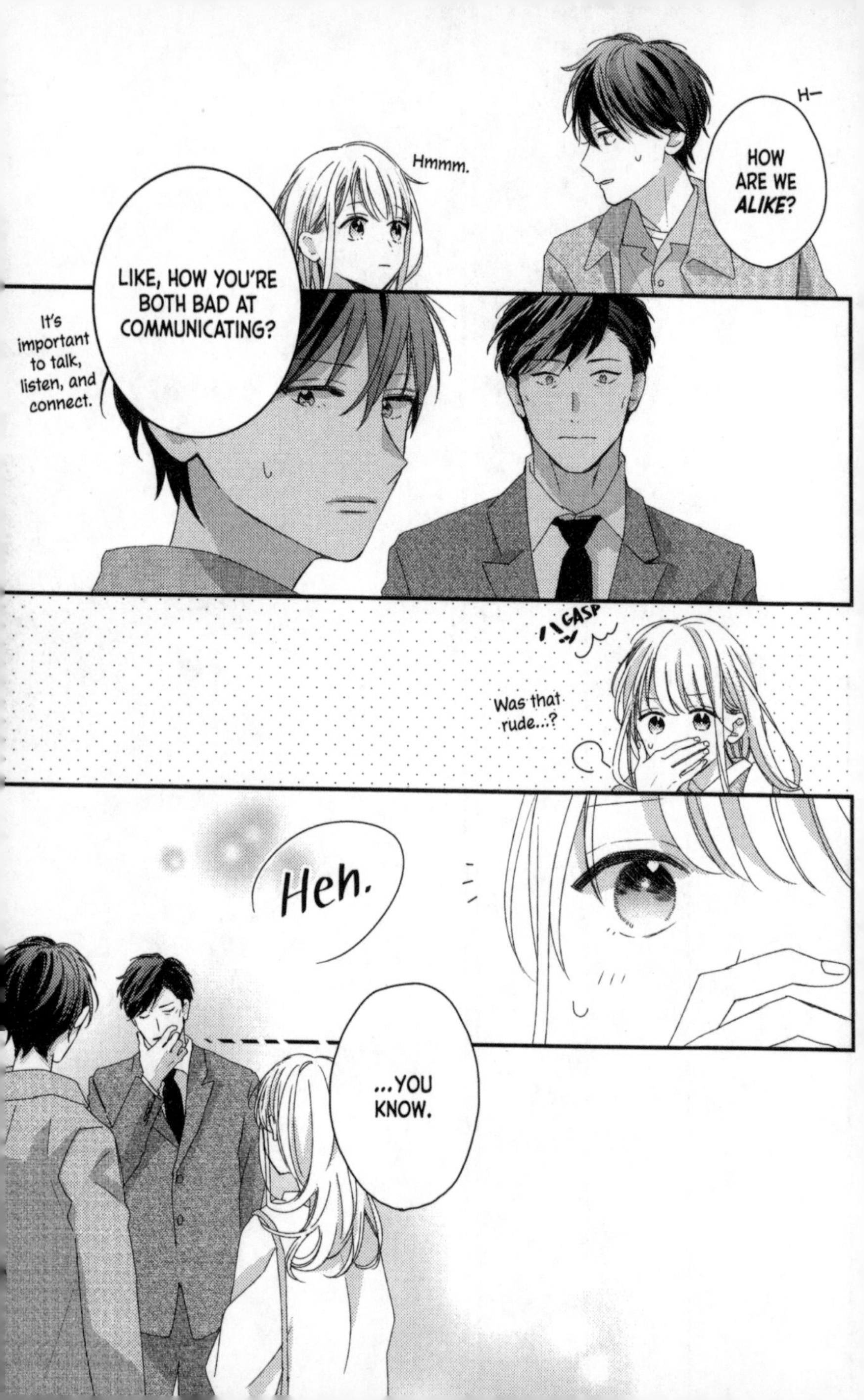
H—
HOW ARE WE ALIKE?
Hmmm.
LIKE, HOW YOU'RE BOTH BAD AT COMMUNICATING?
It's important to talk, listen, and connect.
GASP
Was that rude...?
Heh.
...YOU KNOW.

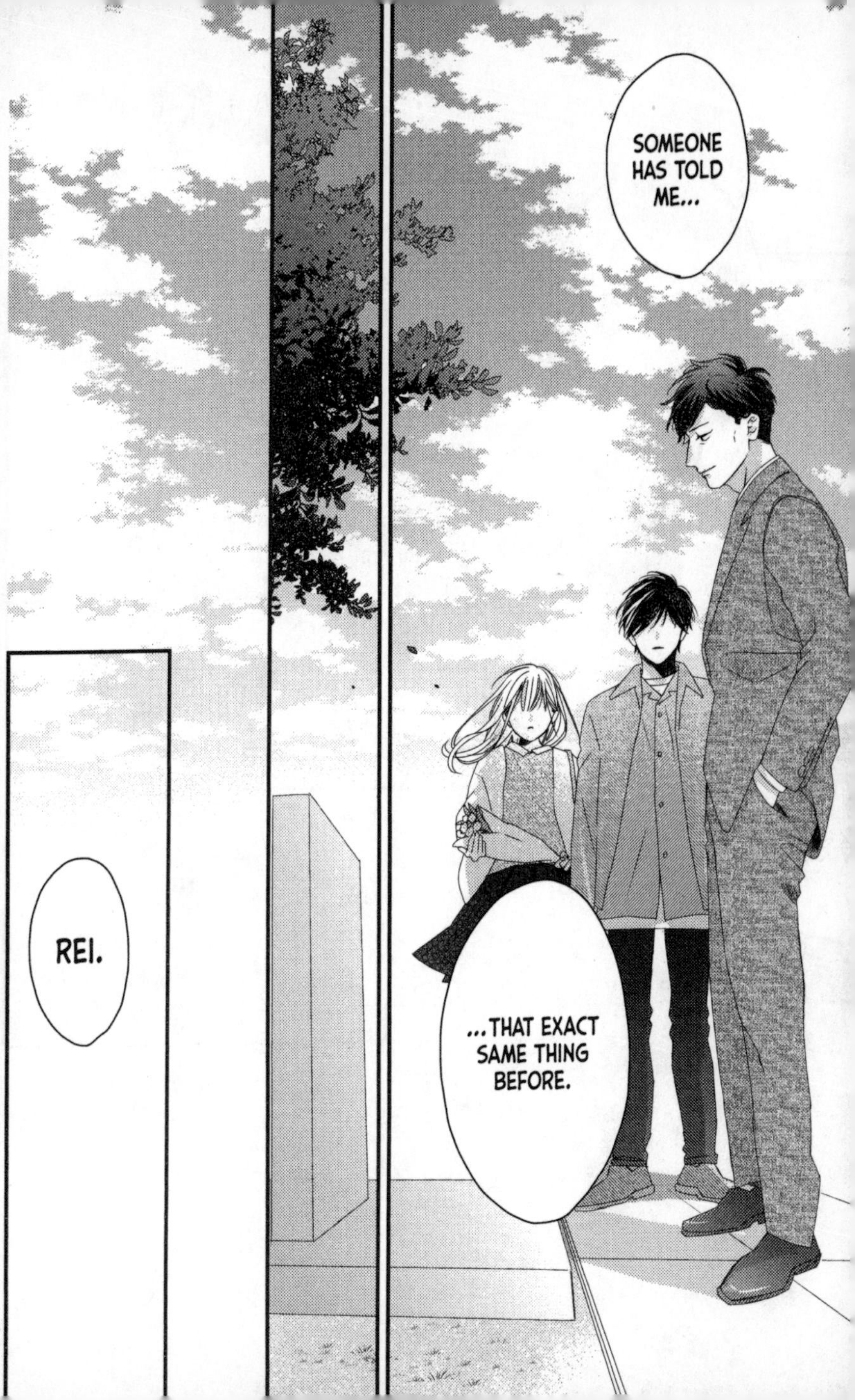
SOMEONE HAS TOLD ME...
...THAT EXACT SAME THING BEFORE.
REI.

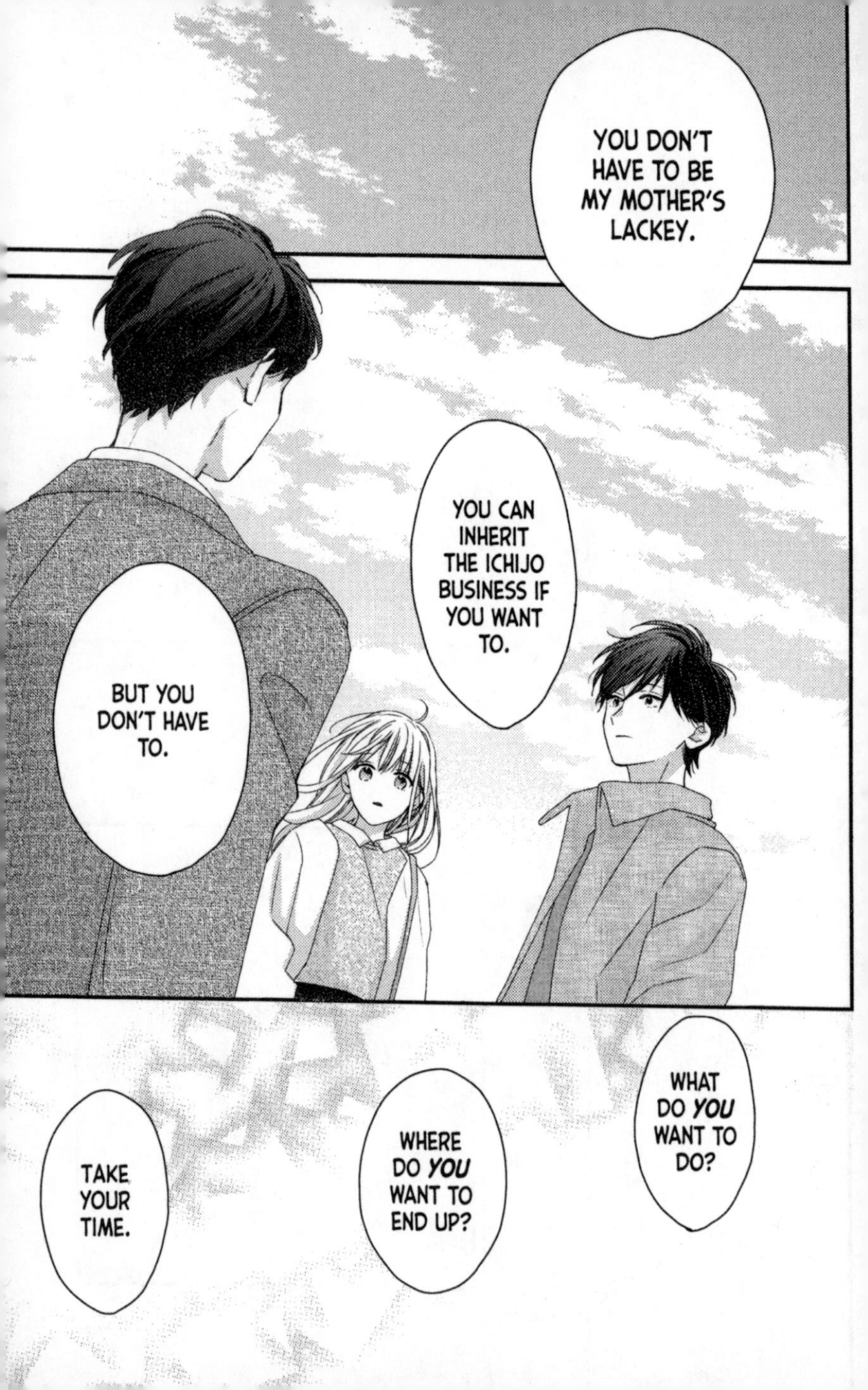
YOU DON'T HAVE TO BE MY MOTHER'S LACKEY.
YOU CAN INHERIT THE ICHIJO BUSINESS IF YOU WANT TO.
BUT YOU DON'T HAVE TO.
WHAT DO *YOU* WANT TO DO?
WHERE DO *YOU* WANT TO END UP?
TAKE YOUR TIME.

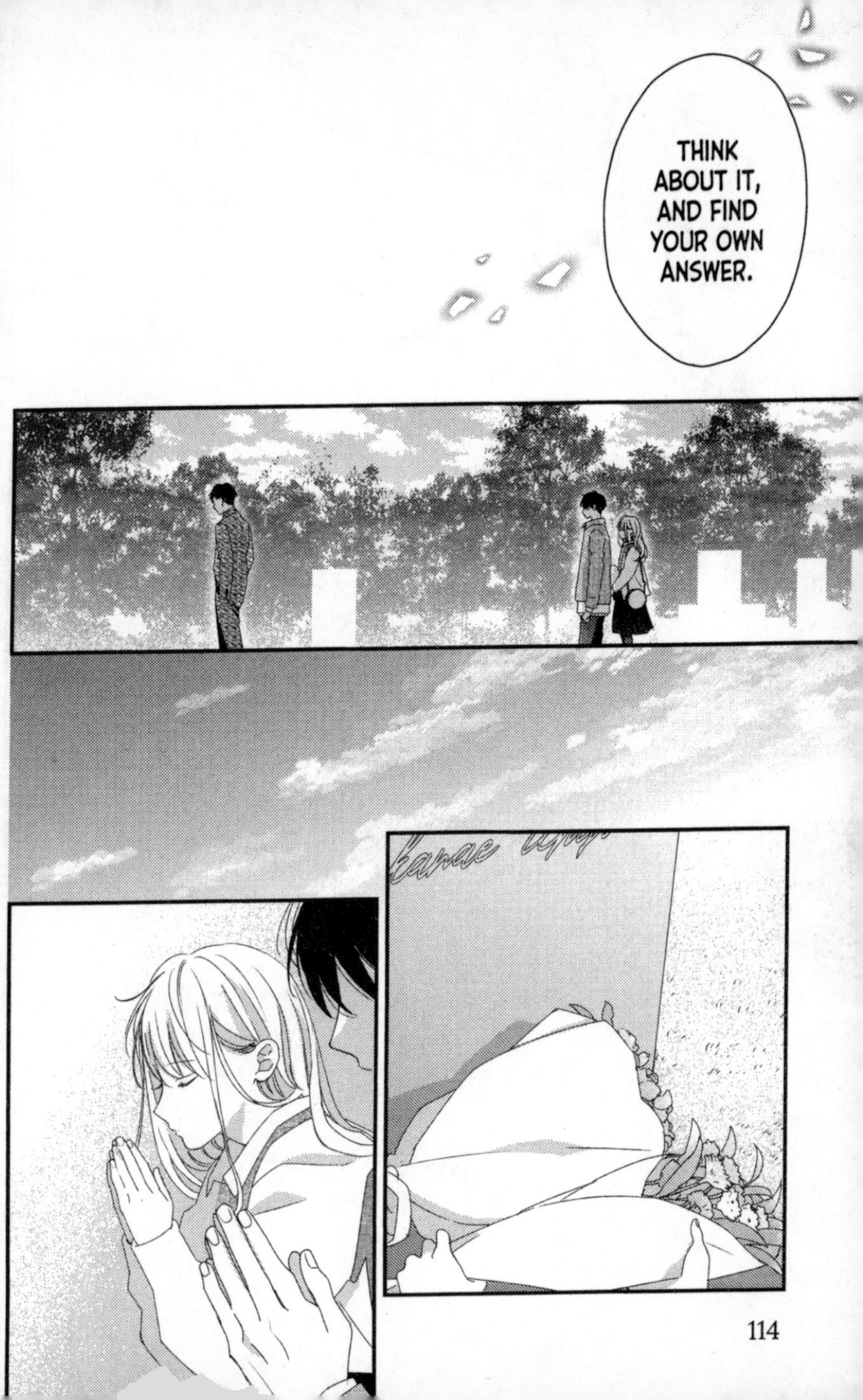
THINK ABOUT IT, AND FIND YOUR OWN ANSWER.

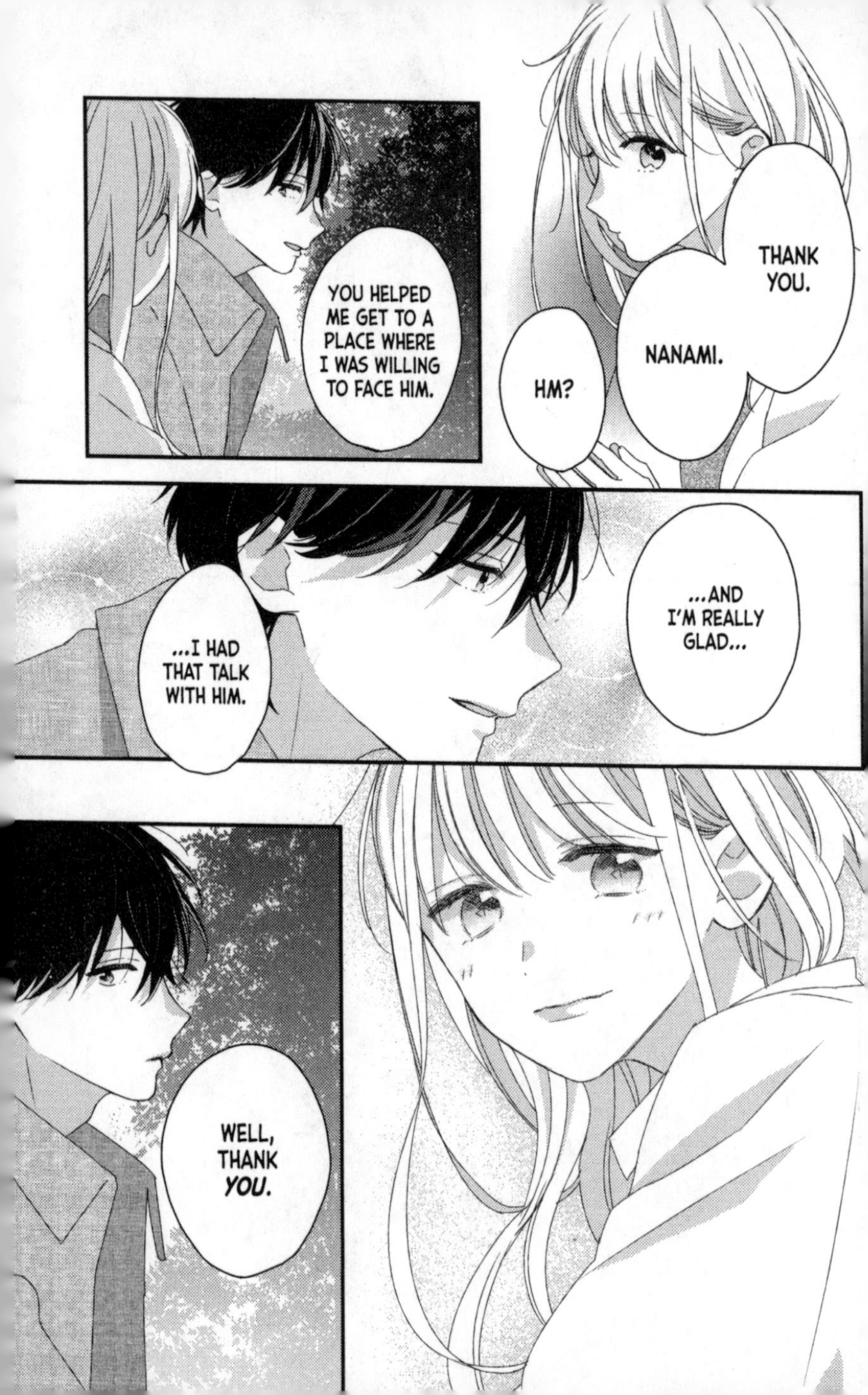
THANK YOU.
NANAMI.
HM?
YOU HELPED ME GET TO A PLACE WHERE I WAS WILLING TO FACE HIM.
...AND I'M REALLY GLAD...
...I HAD THAT TALK WITH HIM.
WELL, THANK *YOU*.

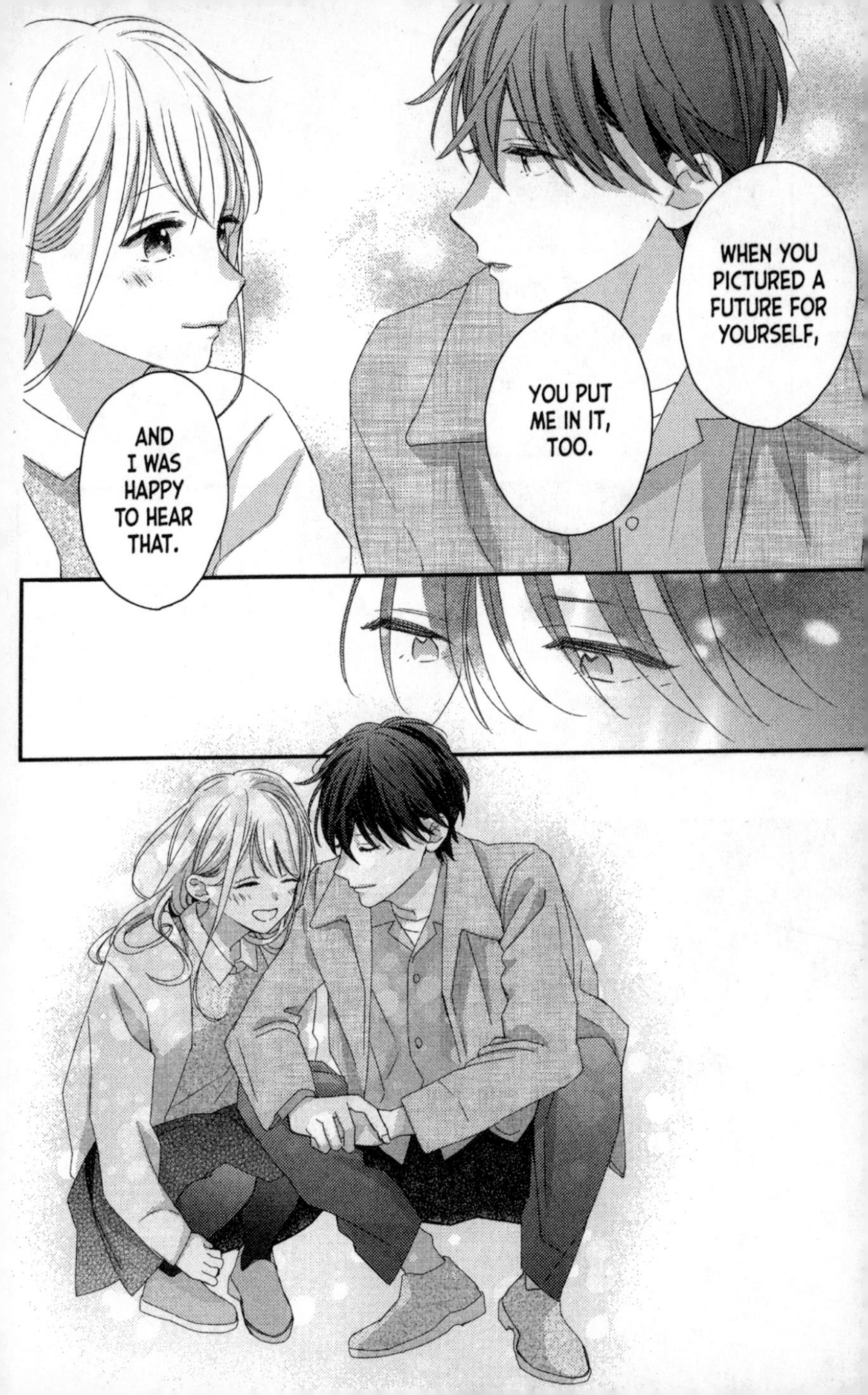
WHEN YOU PICTURED A FUTURE FOR YOURSELF,
YOU PUT ME IN IT, TOO.
AND I WAS HAPPY TO HEAR THAT.

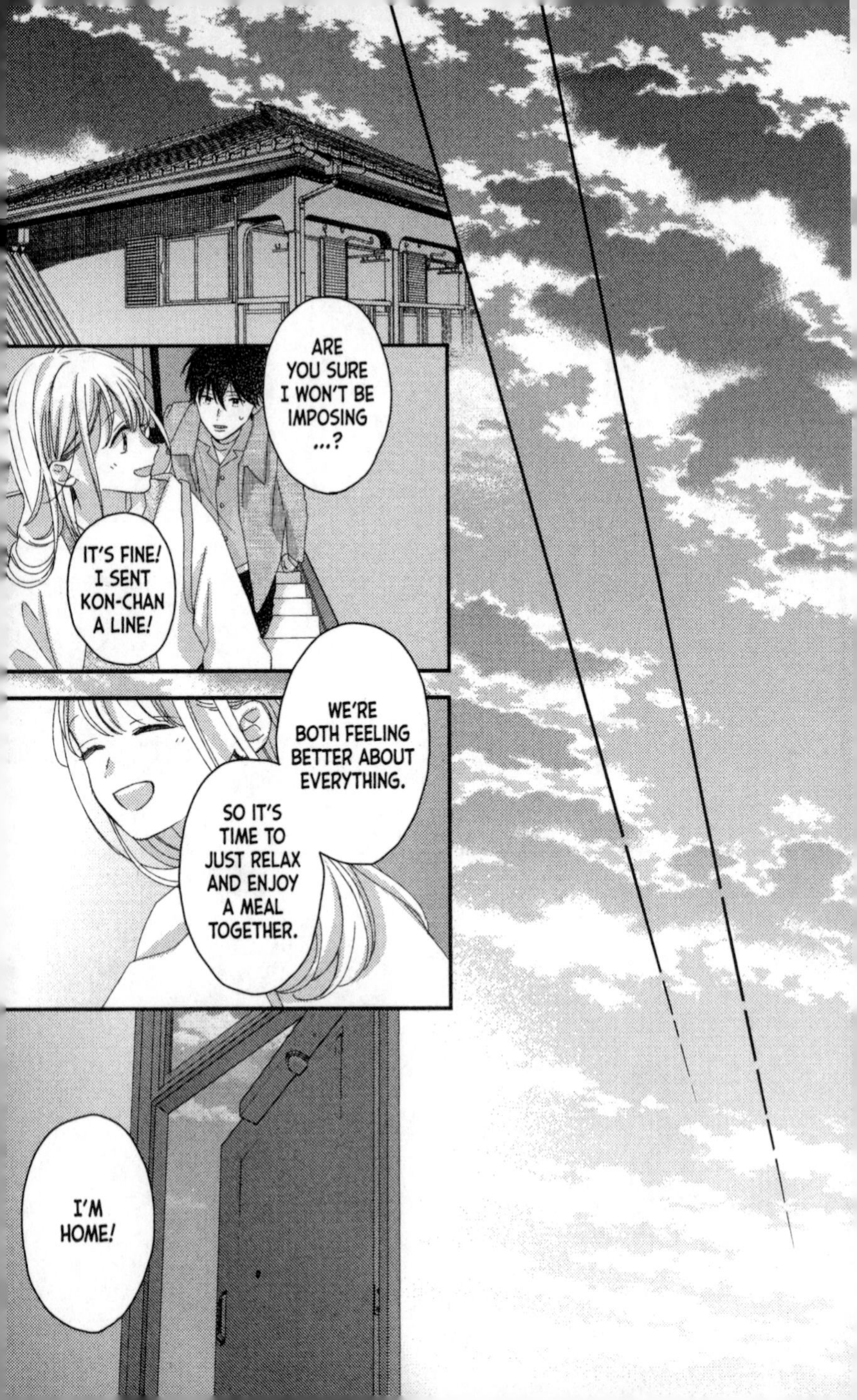
ARE YOU SURE I WON'T BE IMPOSING ...?
IT'S FINE! I SENT KON-CHAN A LINE!
WE'RE BOTH FEELING BETTER ABOUT EVERYTHING.
SO IT'S TIME TO JUST RELAX AND ENJOY A MEAL TOGETHER.
I'M HOME!

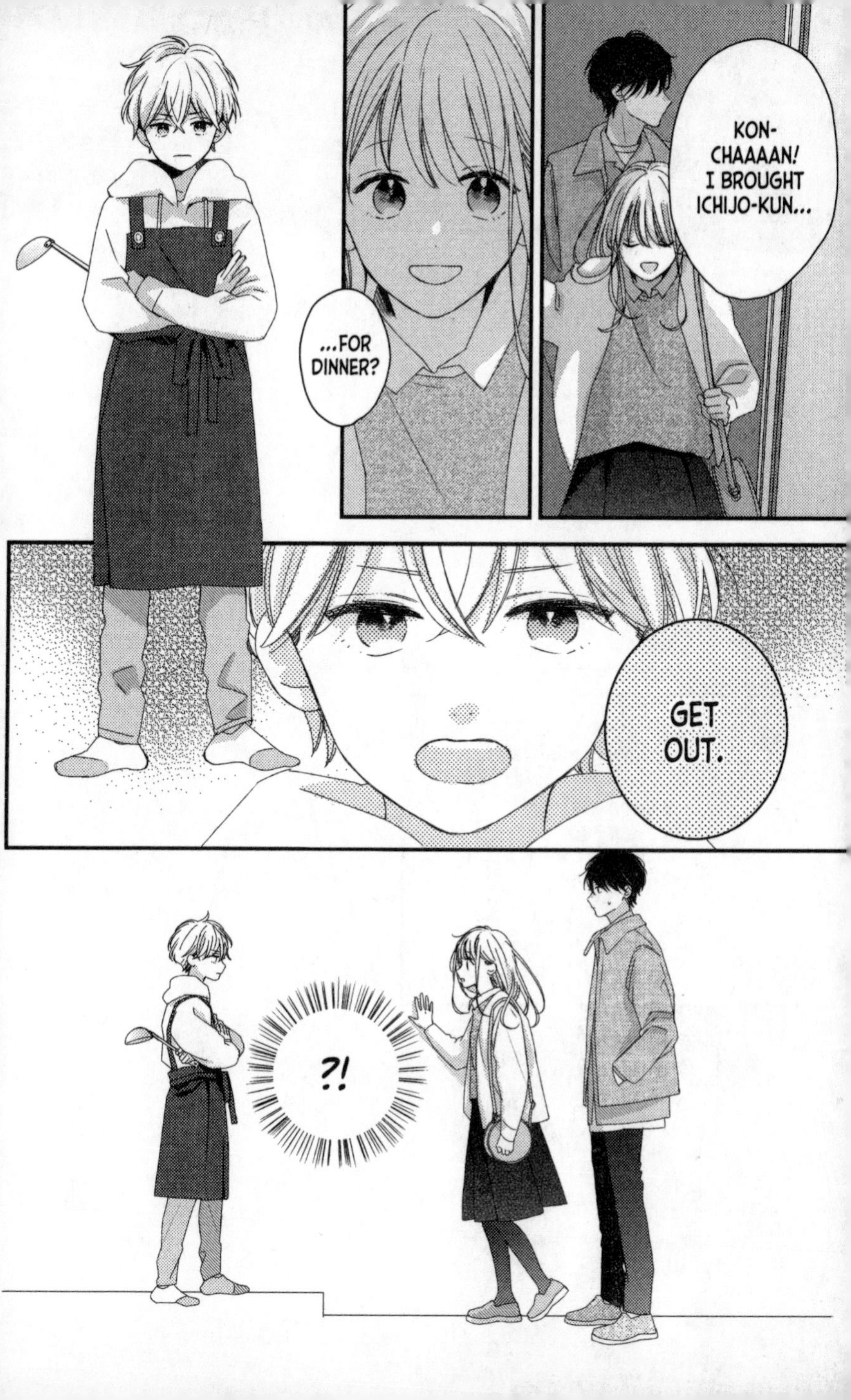
KON-CHAAAAN! I BROUGHT ICHIJO-KUN...
...FOR DINNER?
GET OUT.
?!

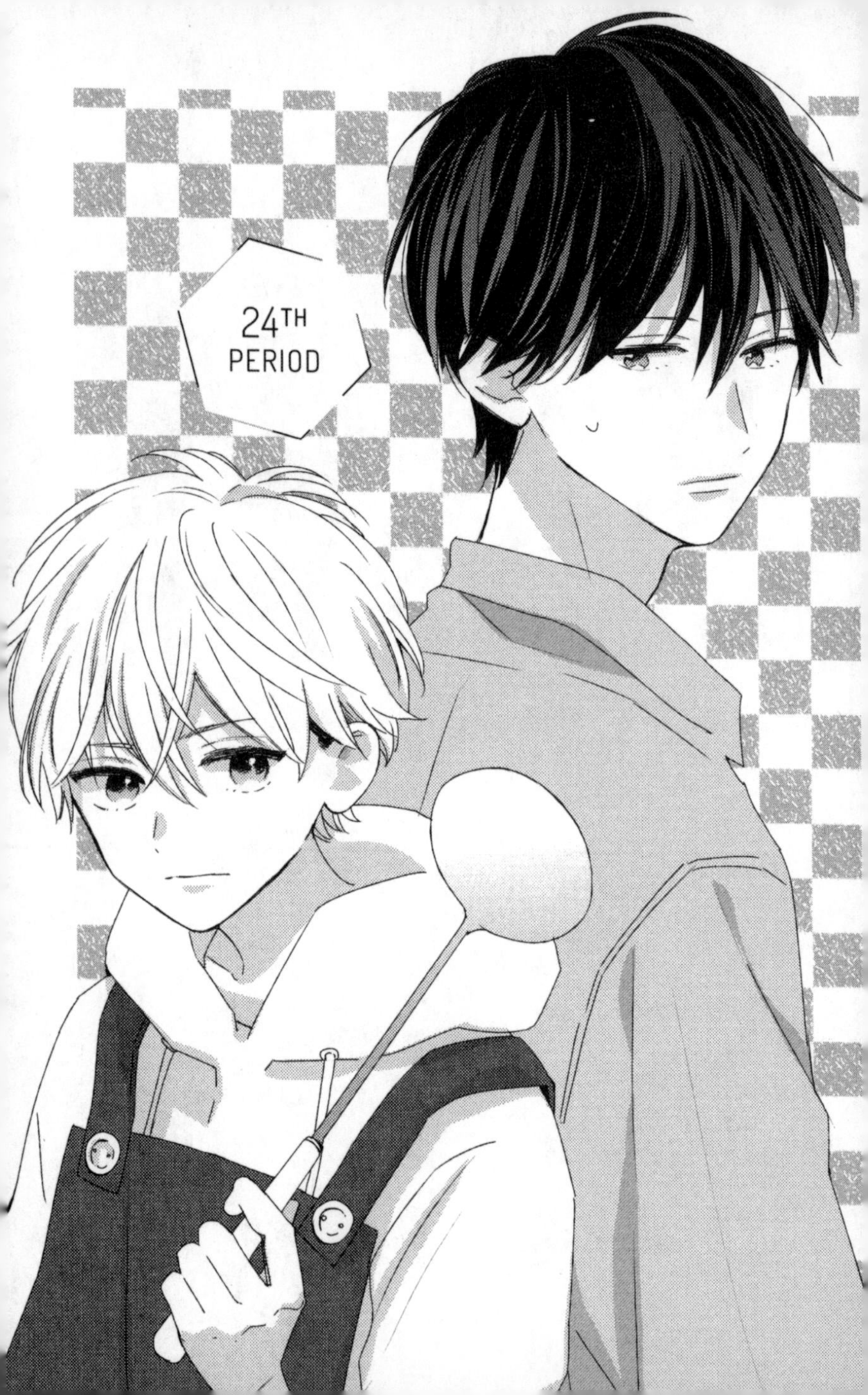
24TH PERIOD

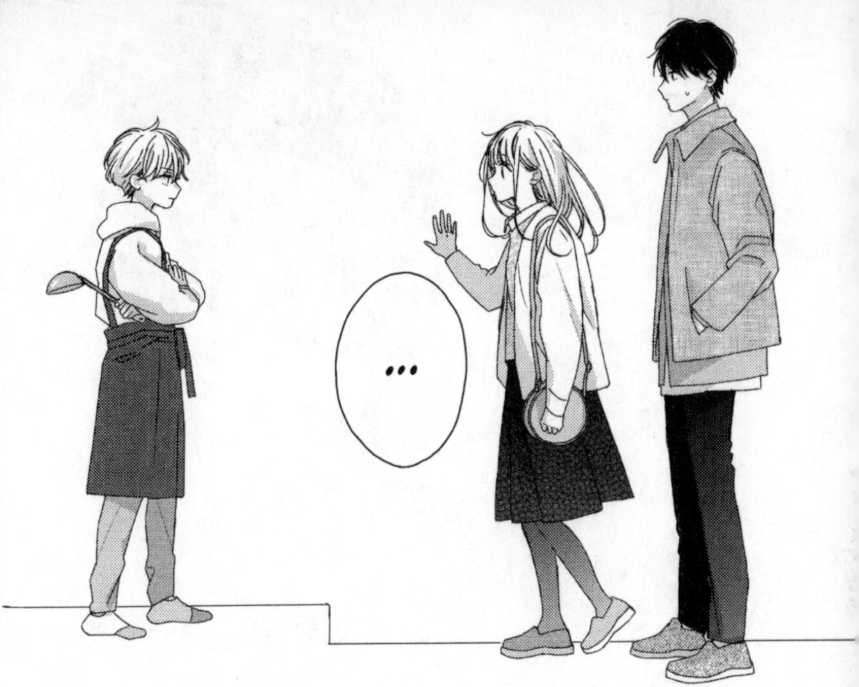
...

Special Thanks

AKI NISHIHIRO-CHAN

FRIENDS, FAMILY

MY EDITOR

EVERYONE AT THE DESSERT EDITORIAL DEPARTMENT

ARCO INC.

EVERYONE WHO WAS INVOLVED IN THE CREATION AND SELLING OF THIS WORK.

I HOPE WE MEET AGAIN
IN THE NEXT VOLUME!

PLEASE CHECK IT OUT! 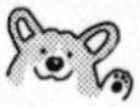

野切耀子

YOKO NOGIRI

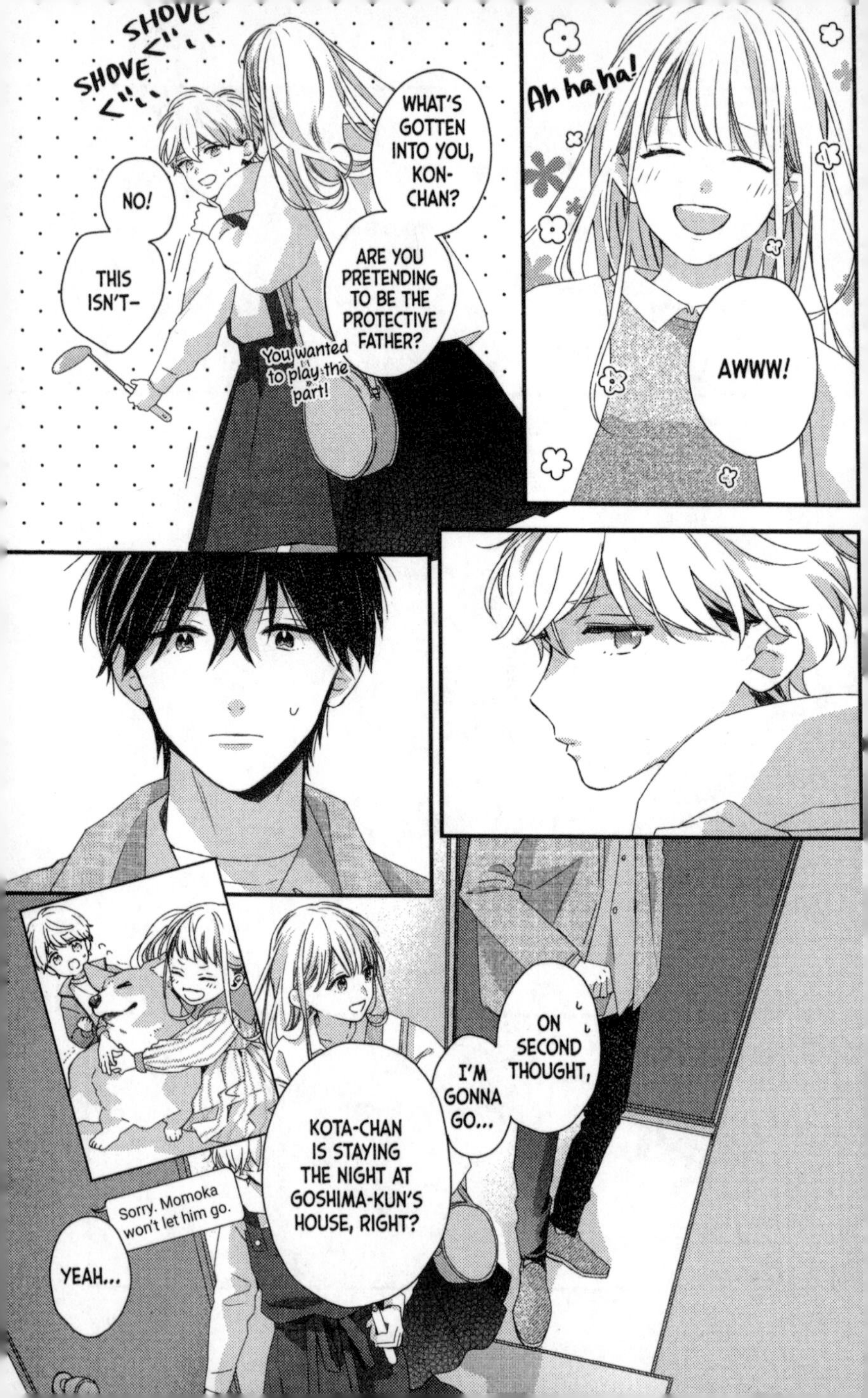
Ah ha ha!
AWWW!
SHOVE
SHOVE
WHAT'S GOTTEN INTO YOU, KON-CHAN?
ARE YOU PRETENDING TO BE THE PROTECTIVE FATHER?
You wanted to play the part!
NO!
THIS ISN'T–
ON SECOND THOUGHT,
I'M GONNA GO...
KOTA-CHAN IS STAYING THE NIGHT AT GOSHIMA-KUN'S HOUSE, RIGHT?
Sorry. Momoka won't let him go.
YEAH...

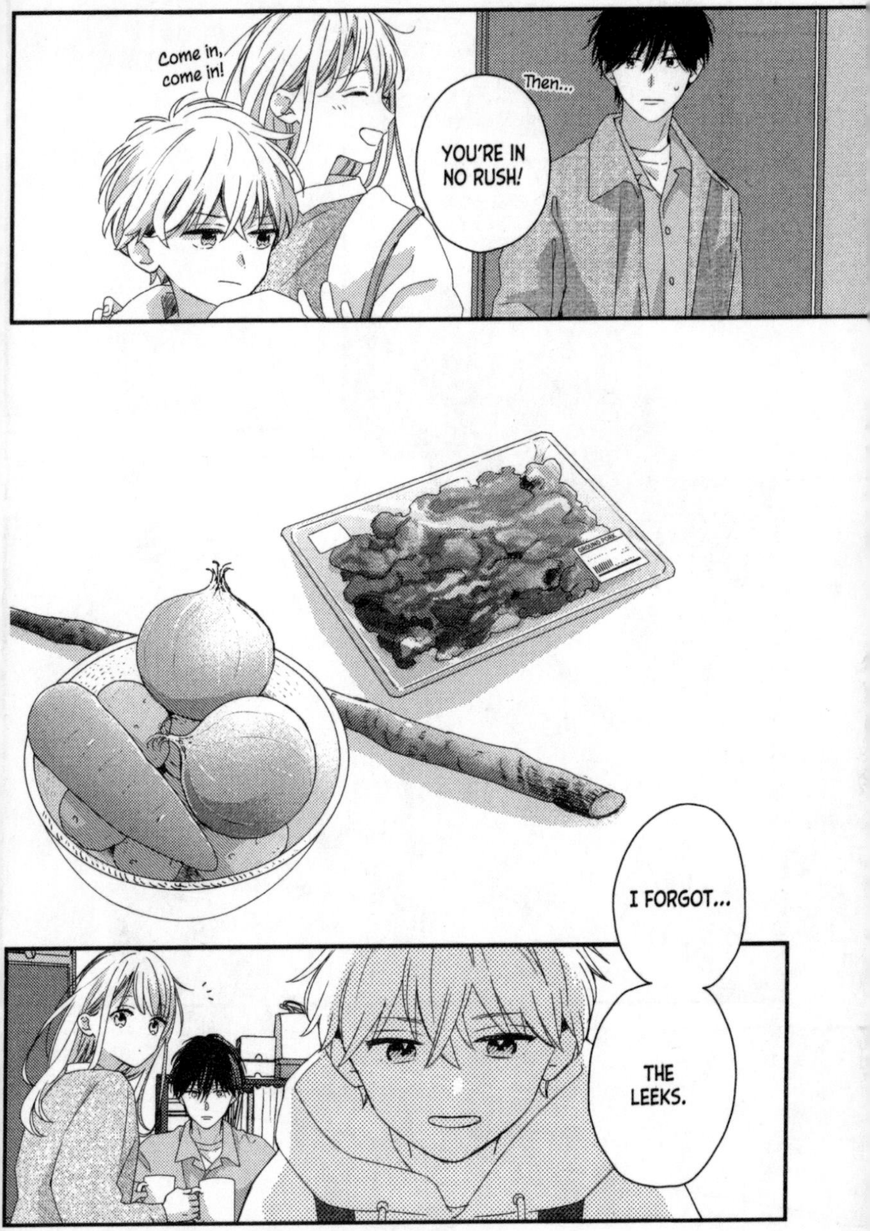

Then...
YOU'RE IN NO RUSH!
Come in, come in!
I FORGOT...
THE LEEKS.

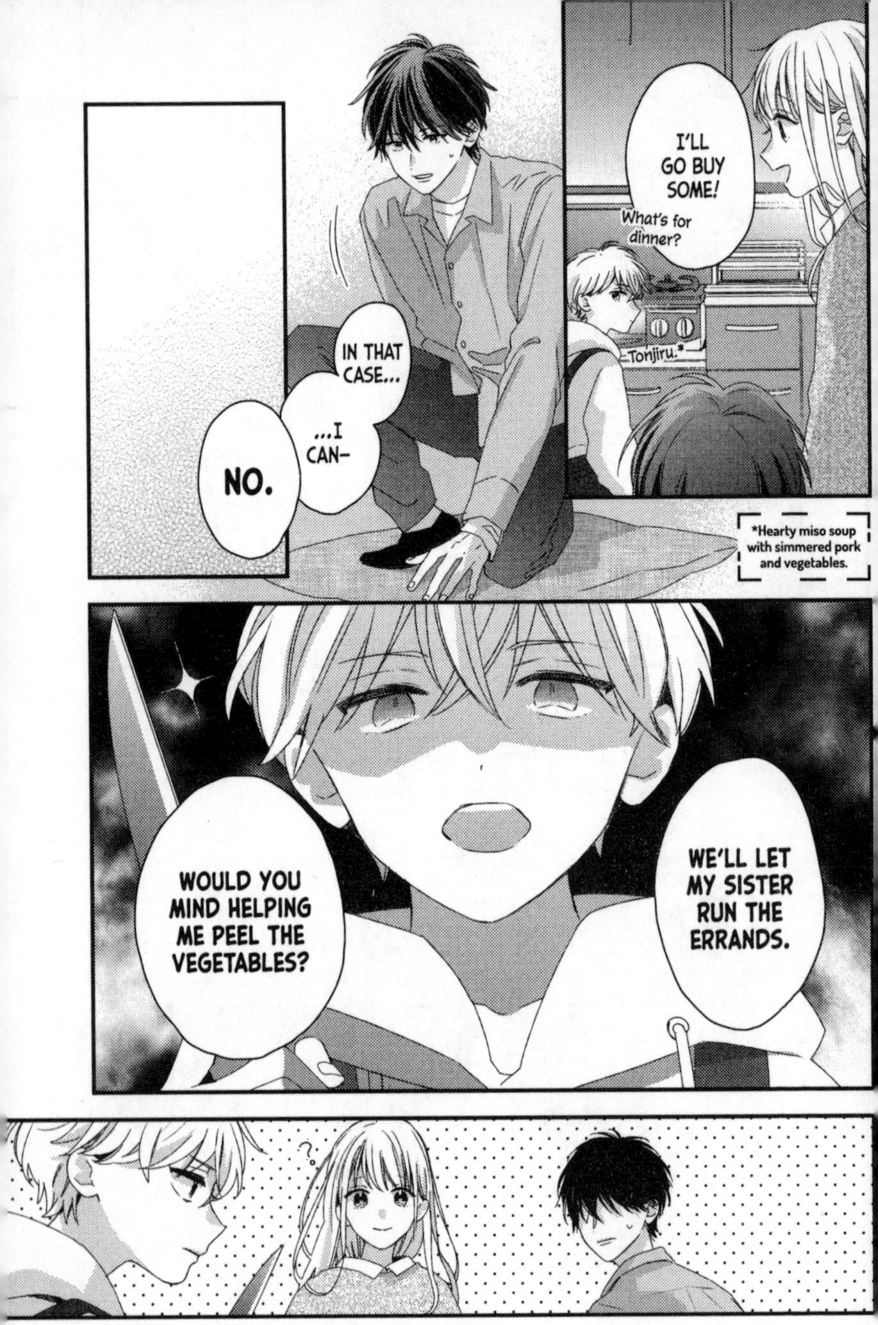
I'LL GO BUY SOME!
What's for dinner?
Tonjiru.*
IN THAT CASE...
...I CAN–
NO.
*Hearty miso soup with simmered pork and vegetables.
WE'LL LET MY SISTER RUN THE ERRANDS.
WOULD YOU MIND HELPING ME PEEL THE VEGETABLES?

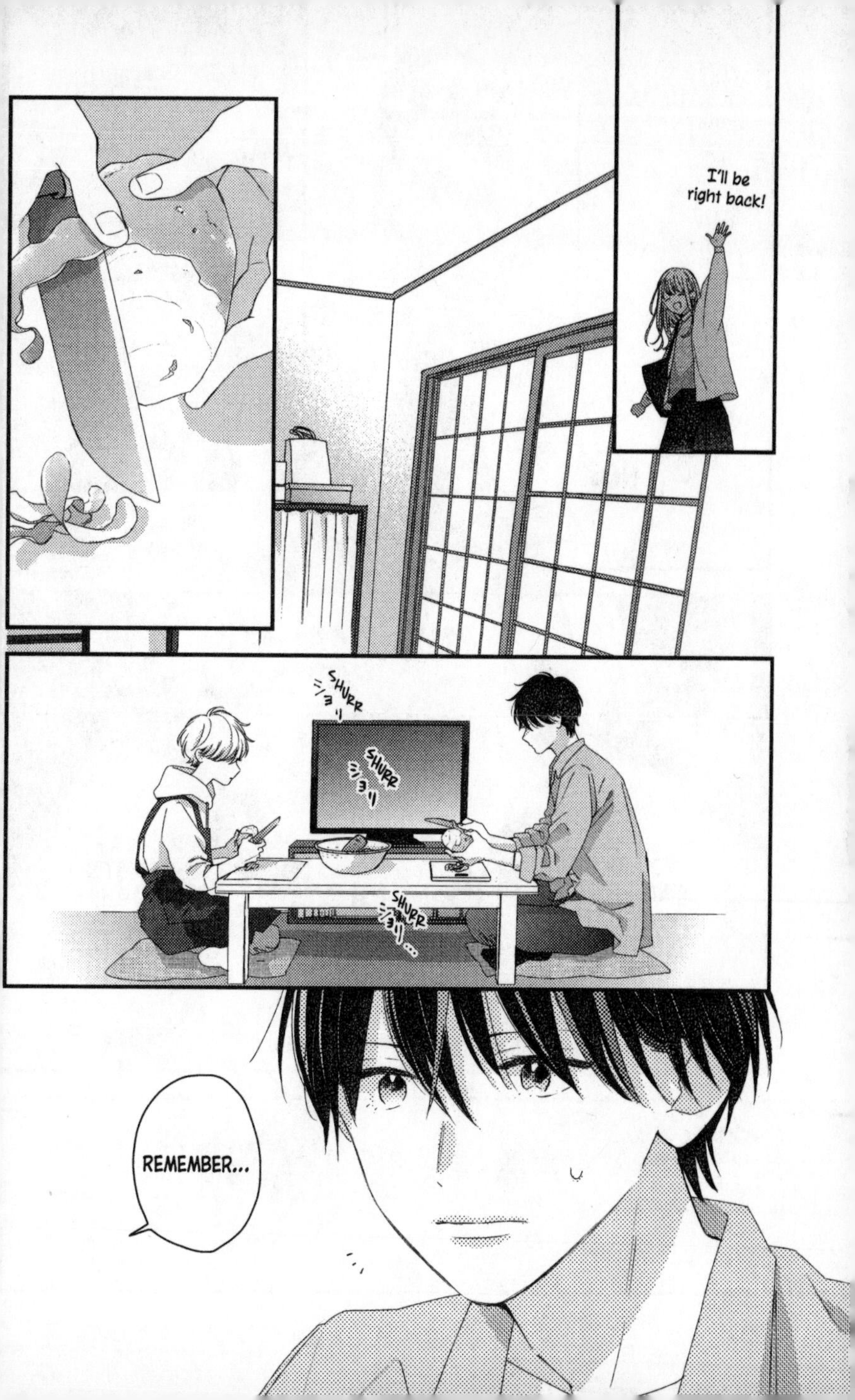
I'll be right back!
SHURR
シュリ
SHURR
シュリ
SHURR
シュリ…
REMEMBER...

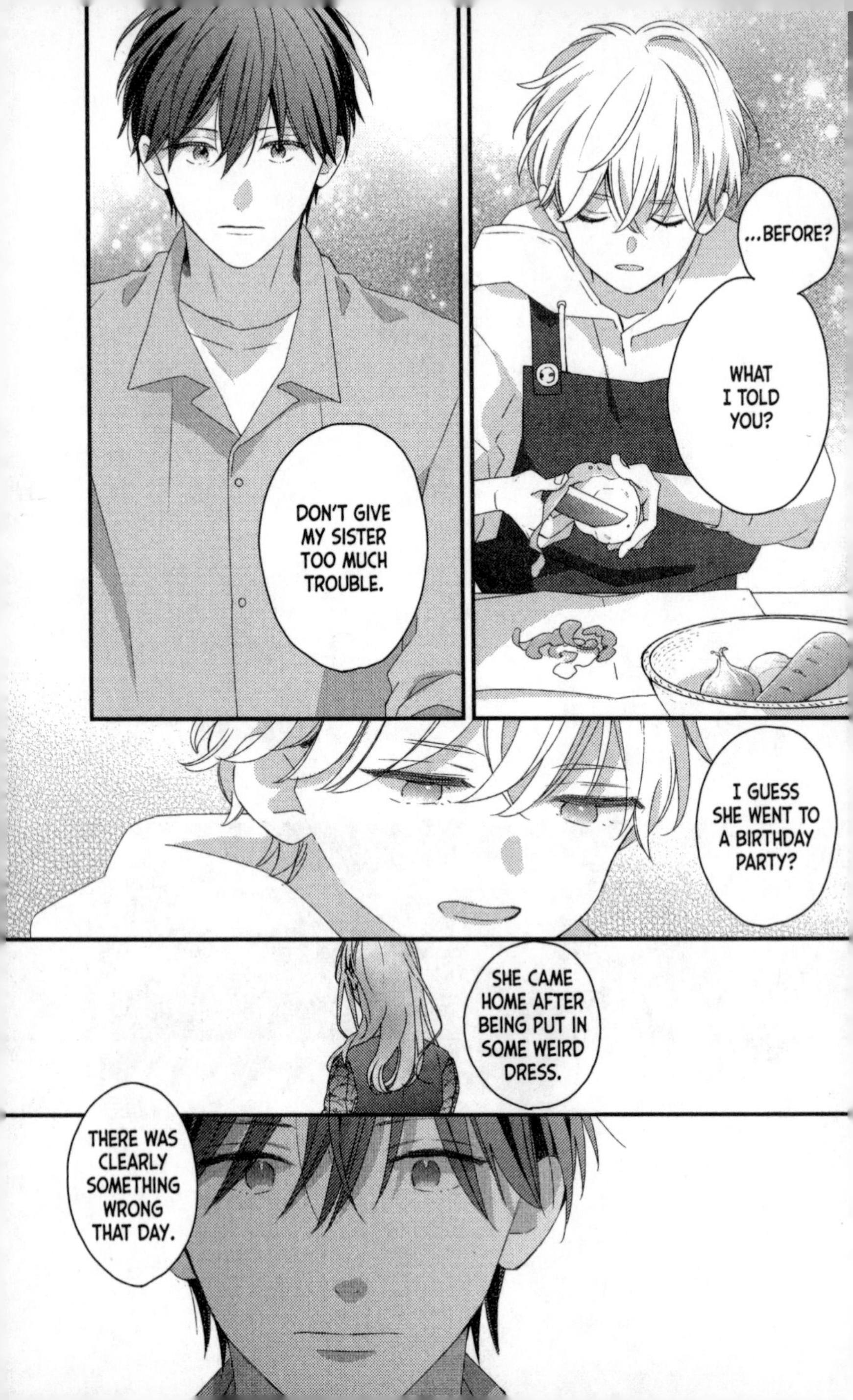
...BEFORE?
WHAT I TOLD YOU?
DON'T GIVE MY SISTER TOO MUCH TROUBLE.
I GUESS SHE WENT TO A BIRTHDAY PARTY?
SHE CAME HOME AFTER BEING PUT IN SOME WEIRD DRESS.
THERE WAS CLEARLY SOMETHING WRONG THAT DAY.

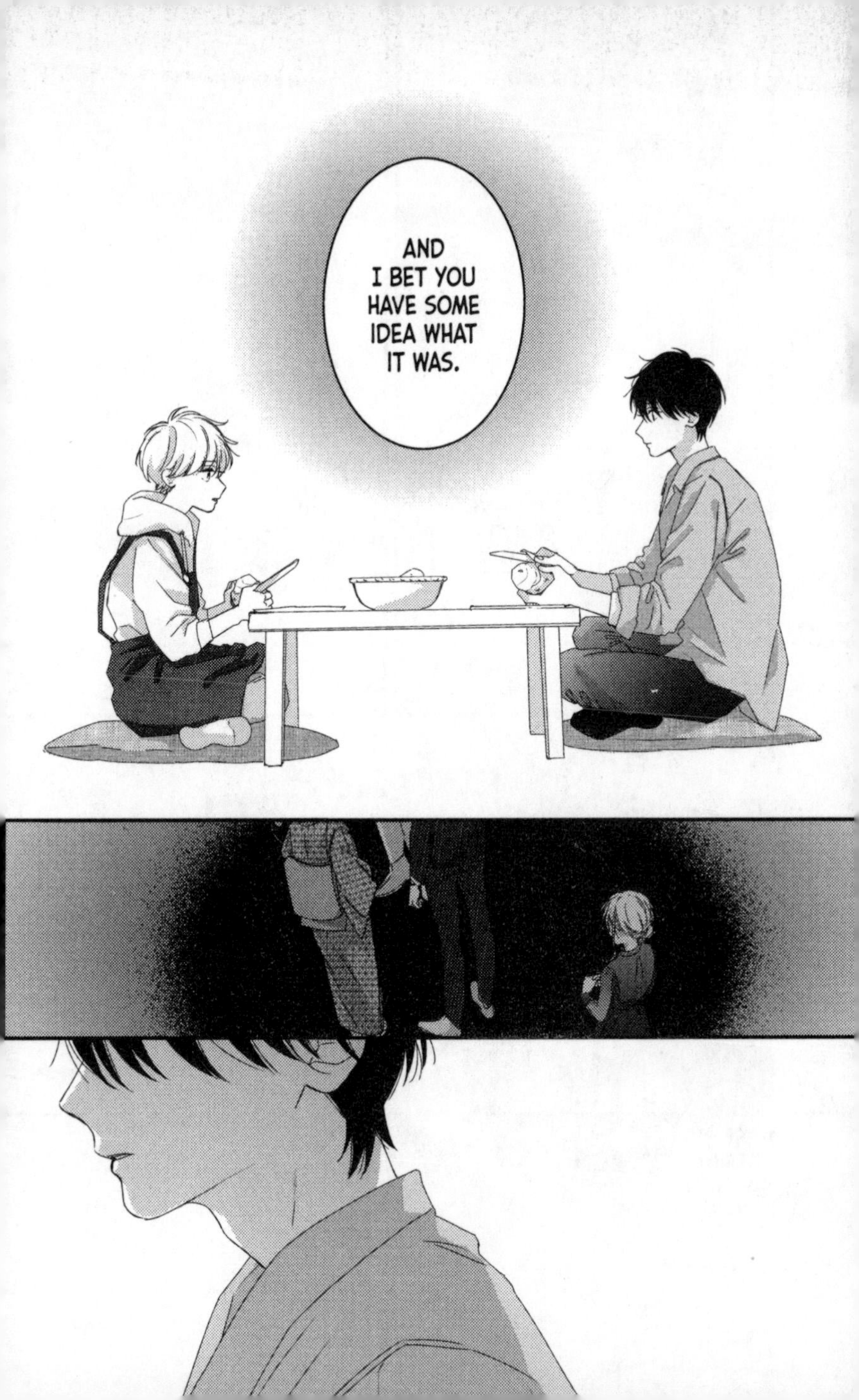
AND I BET YOU HAVE SOME IDEA WHAT IT WAS.

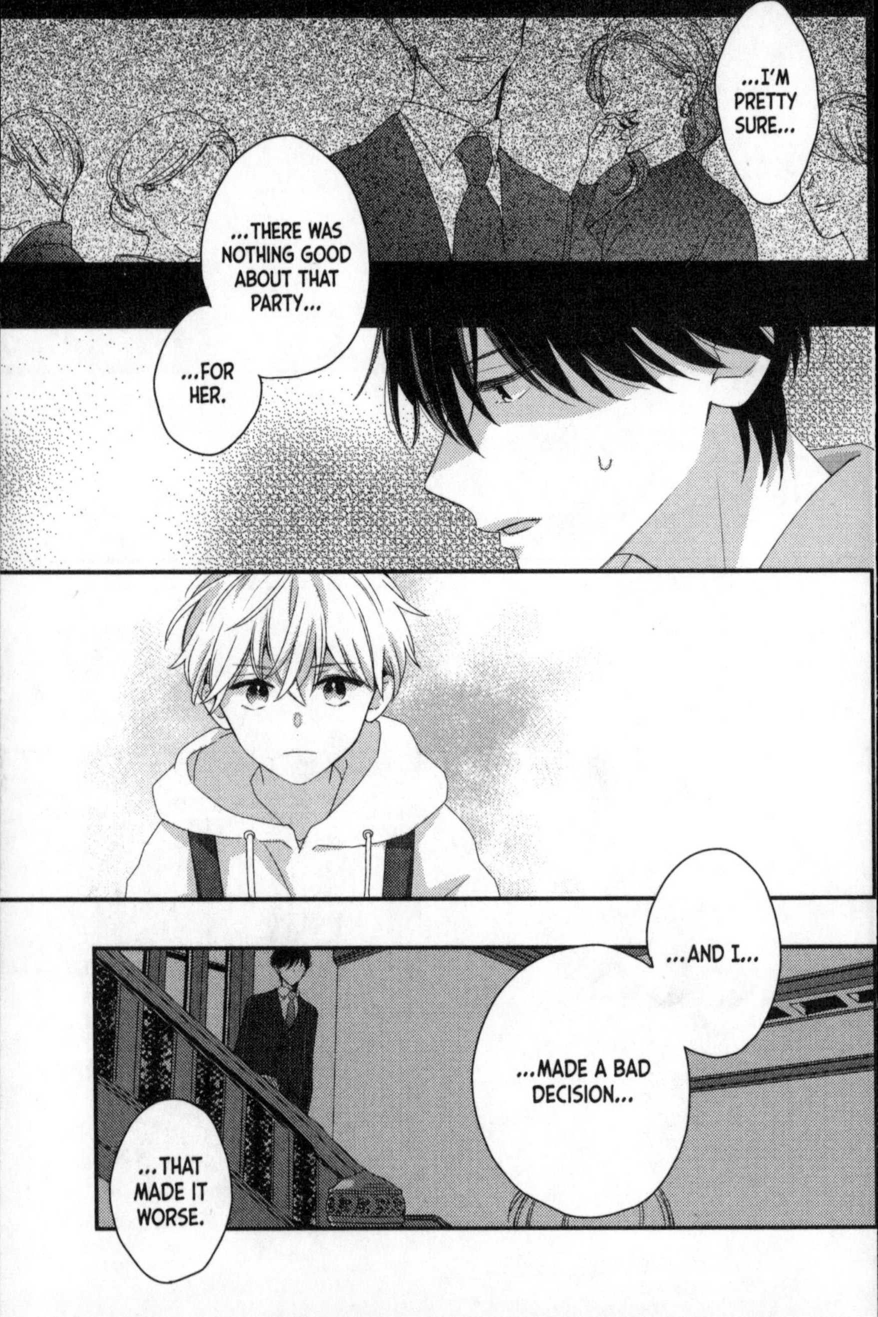
...I'M PRETTY SURE...
...THERE WAS NOTHING GOOD ABOUT THAT PARTY...
...FOR HER.
...AND I...
...MADE A BAD DECISION...
...THAT MADE IT WORSE.

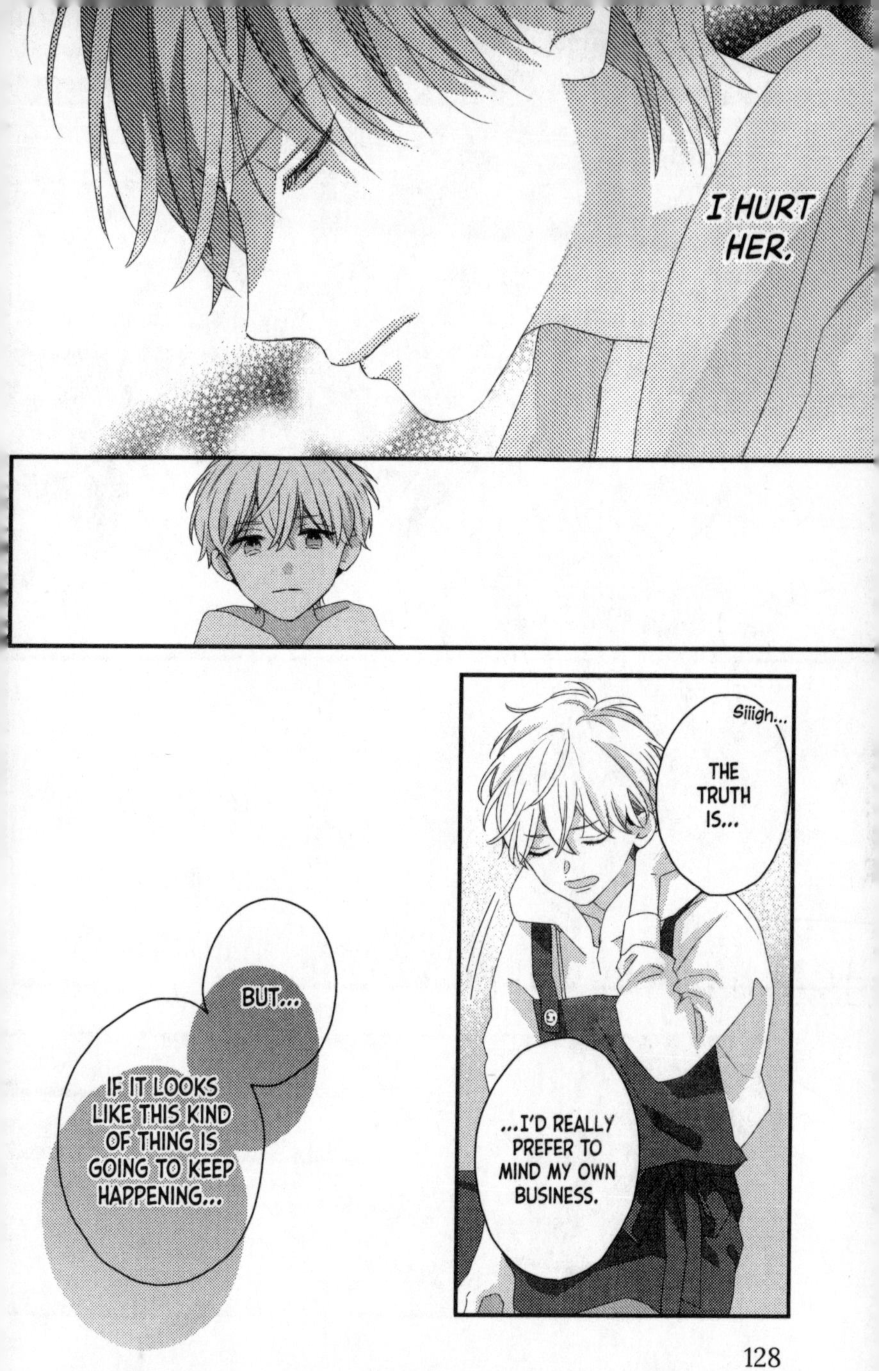
I HURT HER.
Siiigh...
THE TRUTH IS...
...I'D REALLY PREFER TO MIND MY OWN BUSINESS.
BUT...
IF IT LOOKS LIKE THIS KIND OF THING IS GOING TO KEEP HAPPENING...

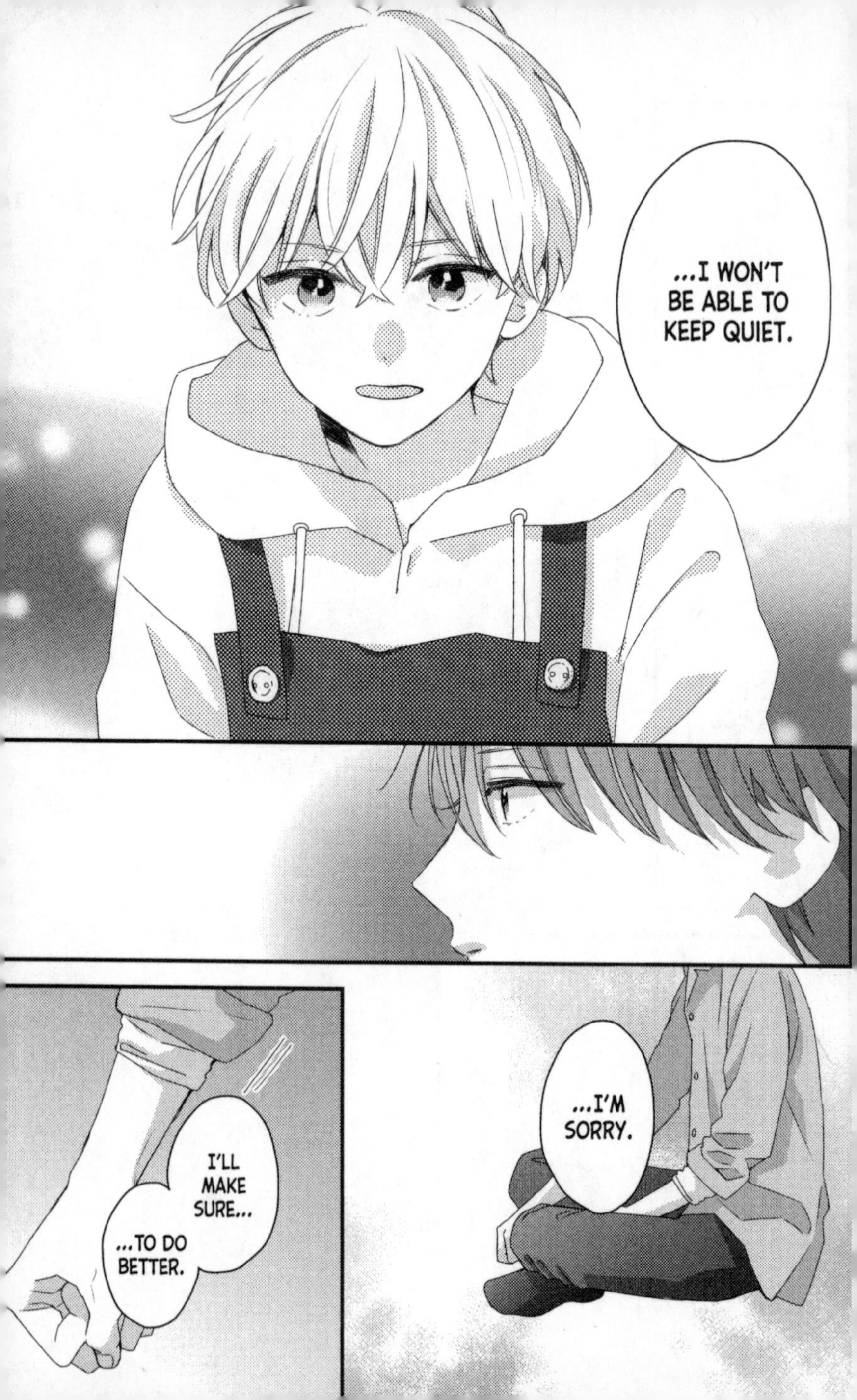
...I WON'T BE ABLE TO KEEP QUIET.
...I'M SORRY.
I'LL MAKE SURE...
...TO DO BETTER.

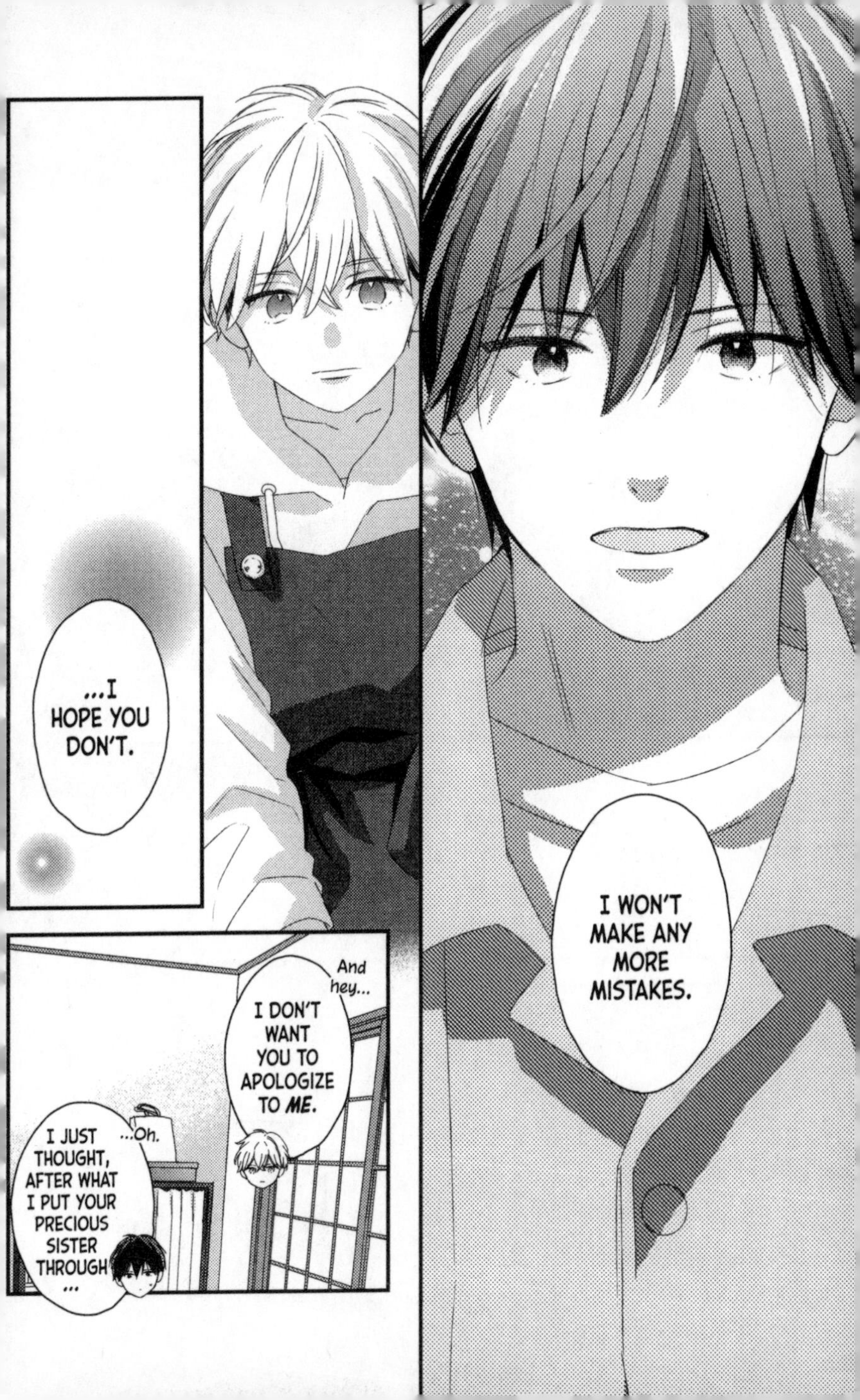
I WON'T MAKE ANY MORE MISTAKES.
...I HOPE YOU DON'T.
And hey...
I DON'T WANT YOU TO APOLOGIZE TO *ME*.
...Oh.
I JUST THOUGHT, AFTER WHAT I PUT YOUR PRECIOUS SISTER THROUGH...

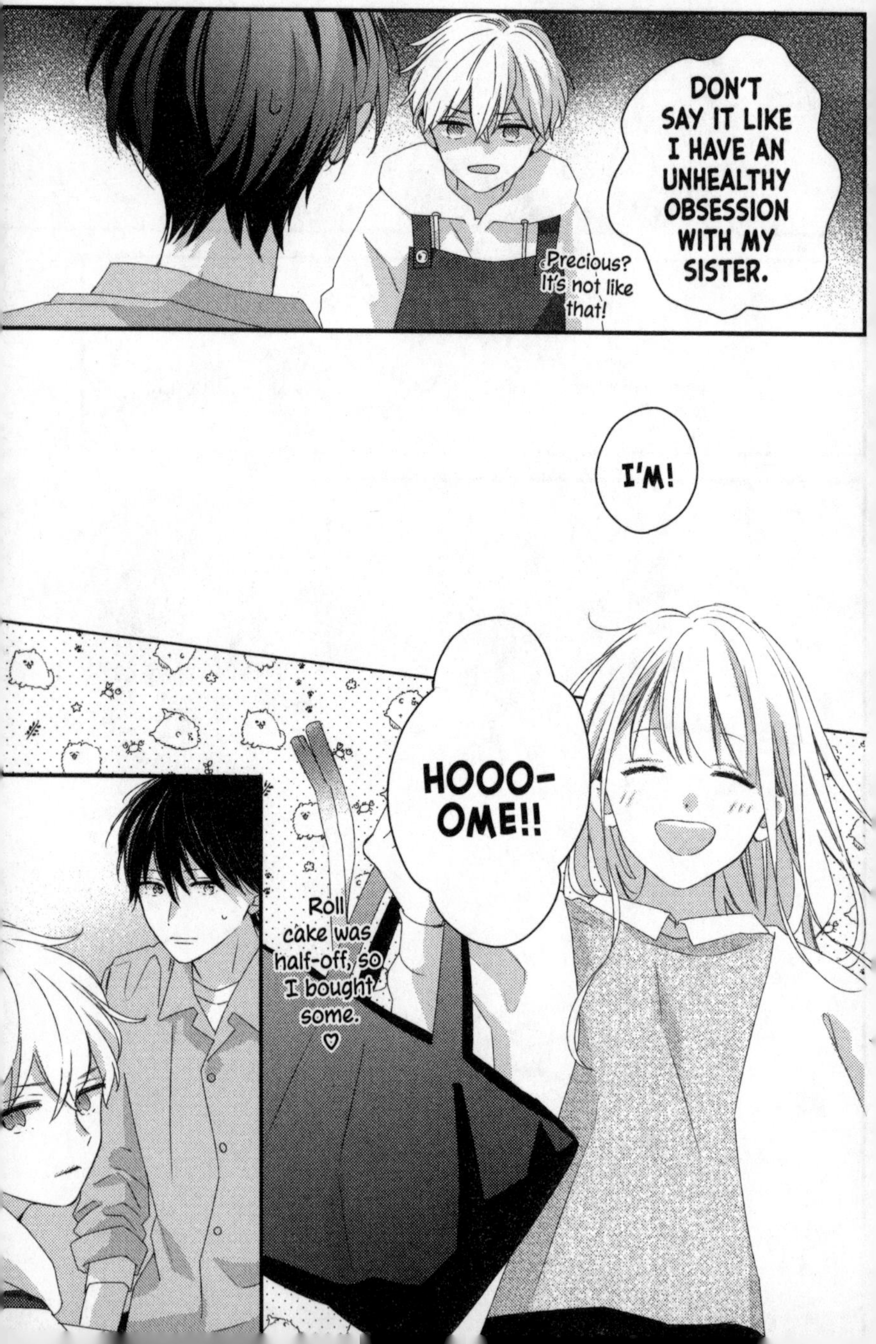
DON'T SAY IT LIKE I HAVE AN UNHEALTHY OBSESSION WITH MY SISTER.
Precious? It's not like that!
I'M!
HOOOO-OME!!
Roll cake was half-off, so I bought some. ♡

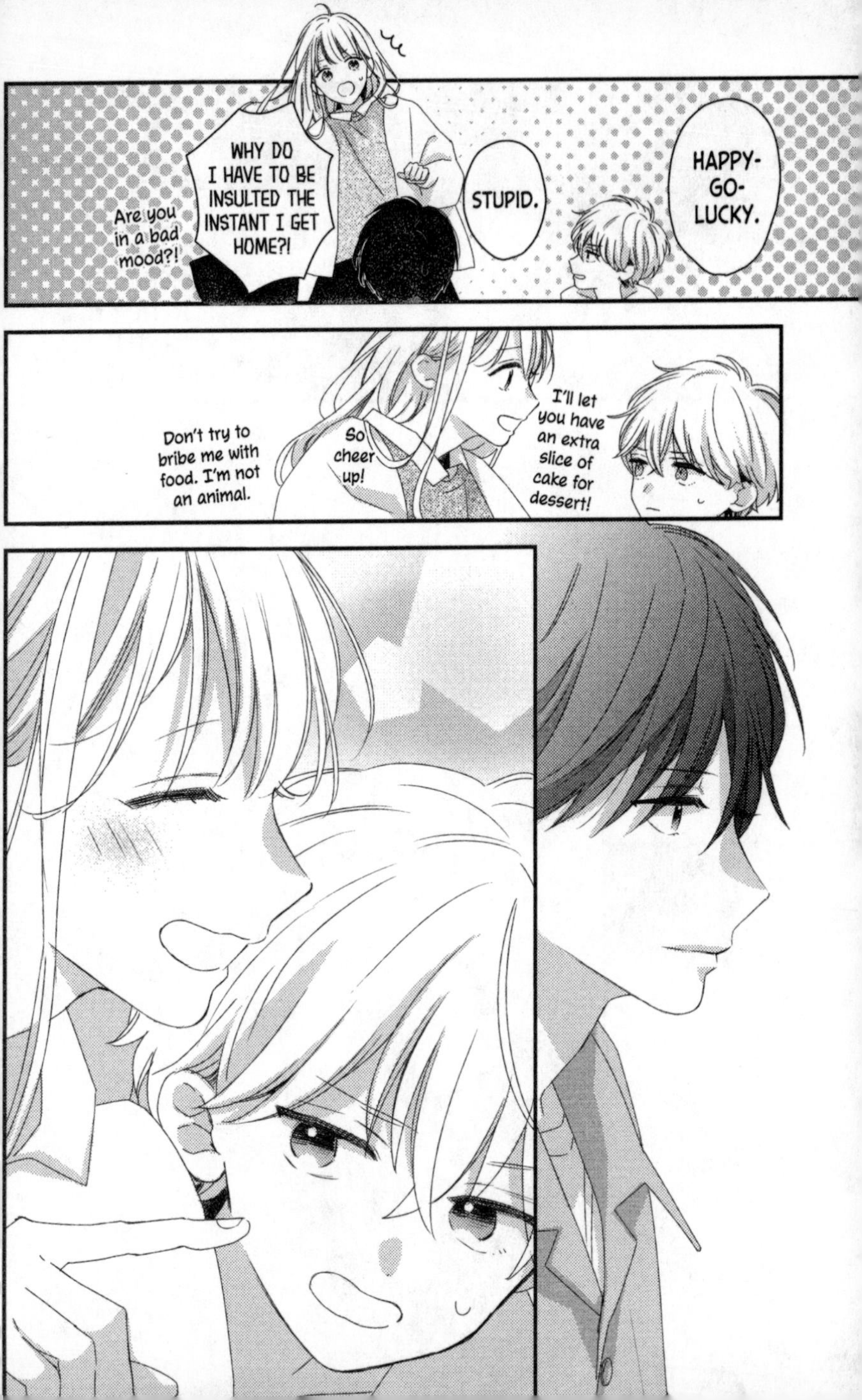
HAPPY-GO-LUCKY.
STUPID.
WHY DO I HAVE TO BE INSULTED THE INSTANT I GET HOME?!
Are you in a bad mood?!
I'll let you have an extra slice of cake for dessert!
So cheer up!
Don't try to bribe me with food. I'm not an animal.

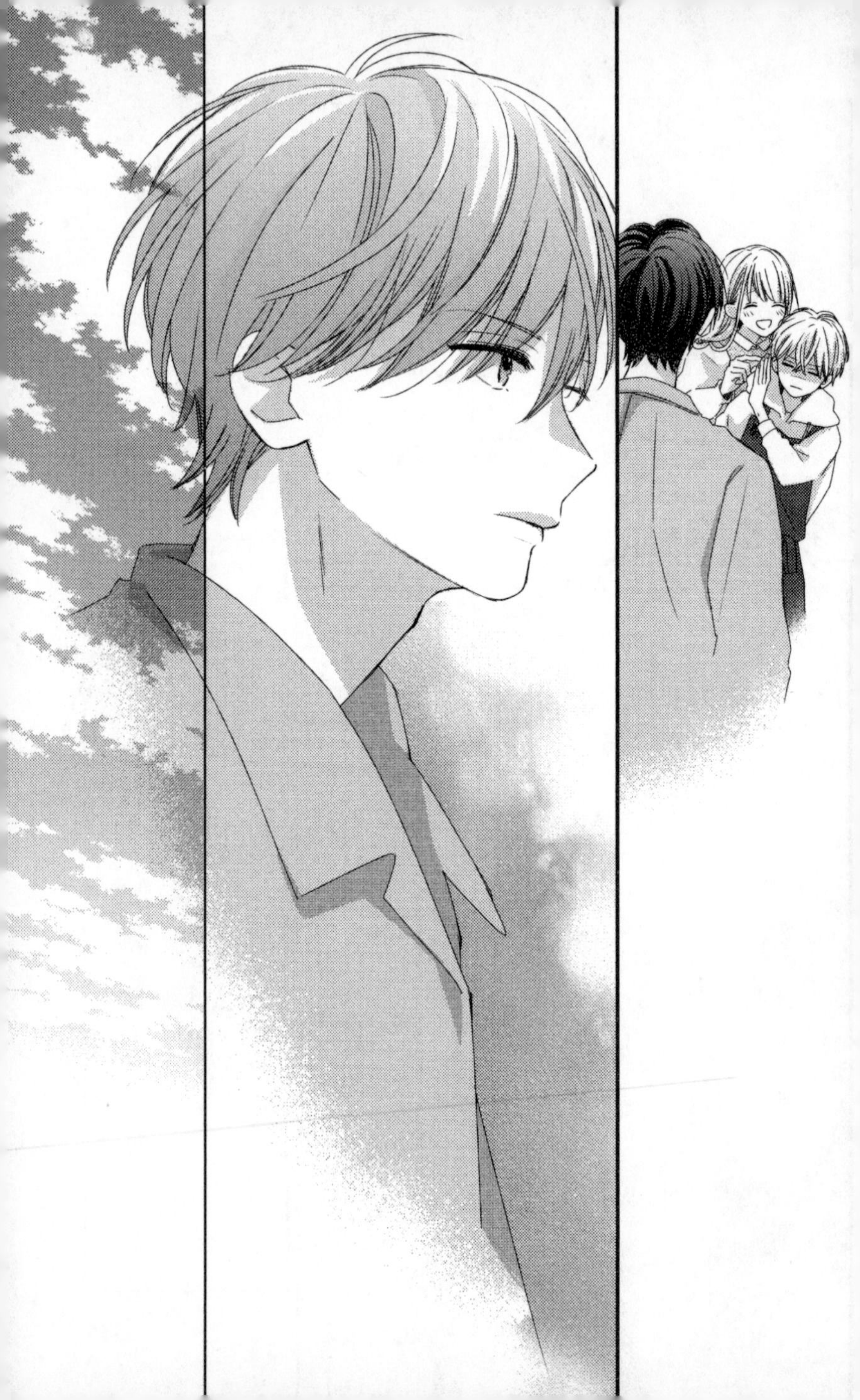

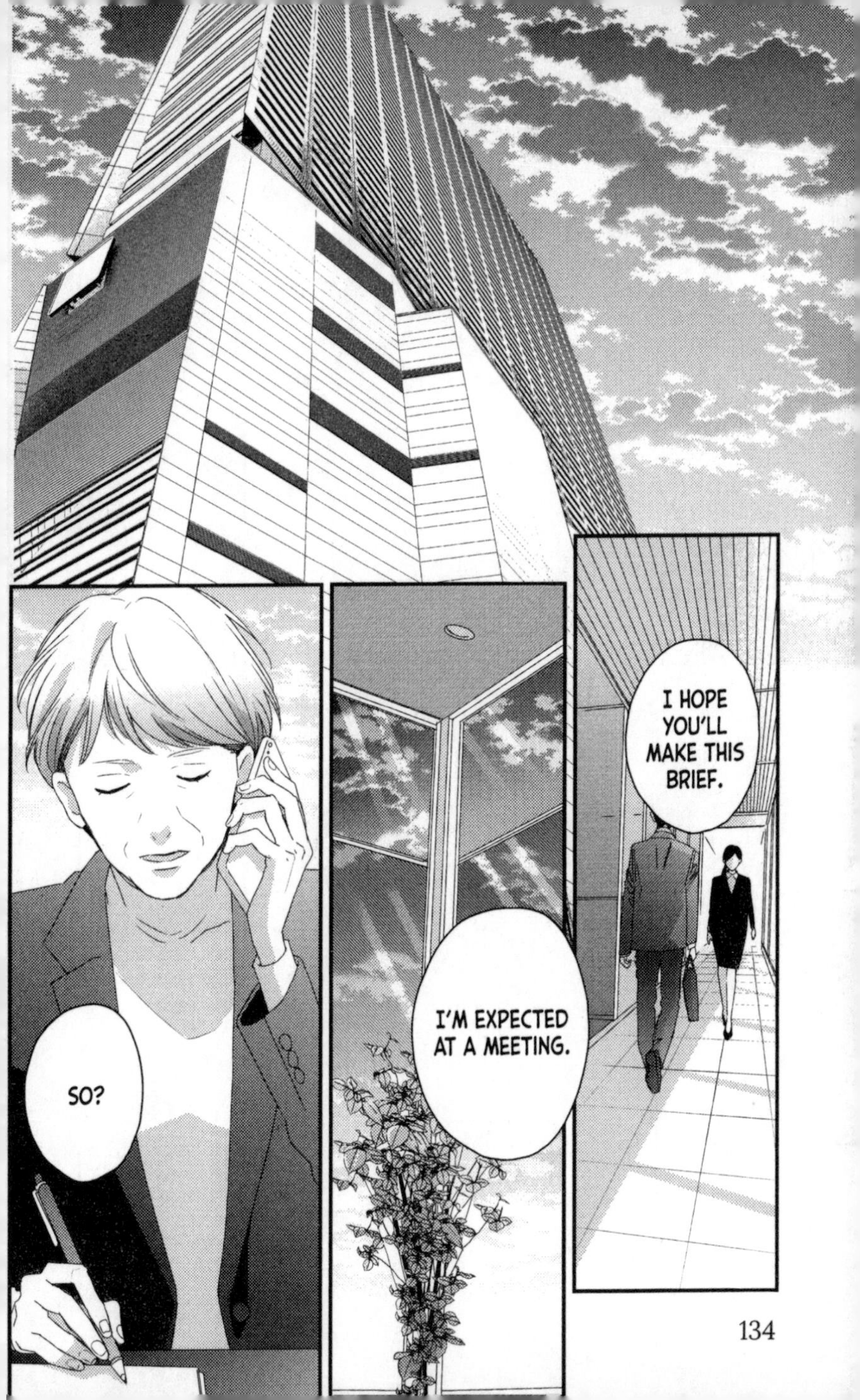
I HOPE YOU'LL MAKE THIS BRIEF.
I'M EXPECTED AT A MEETING.
SO?

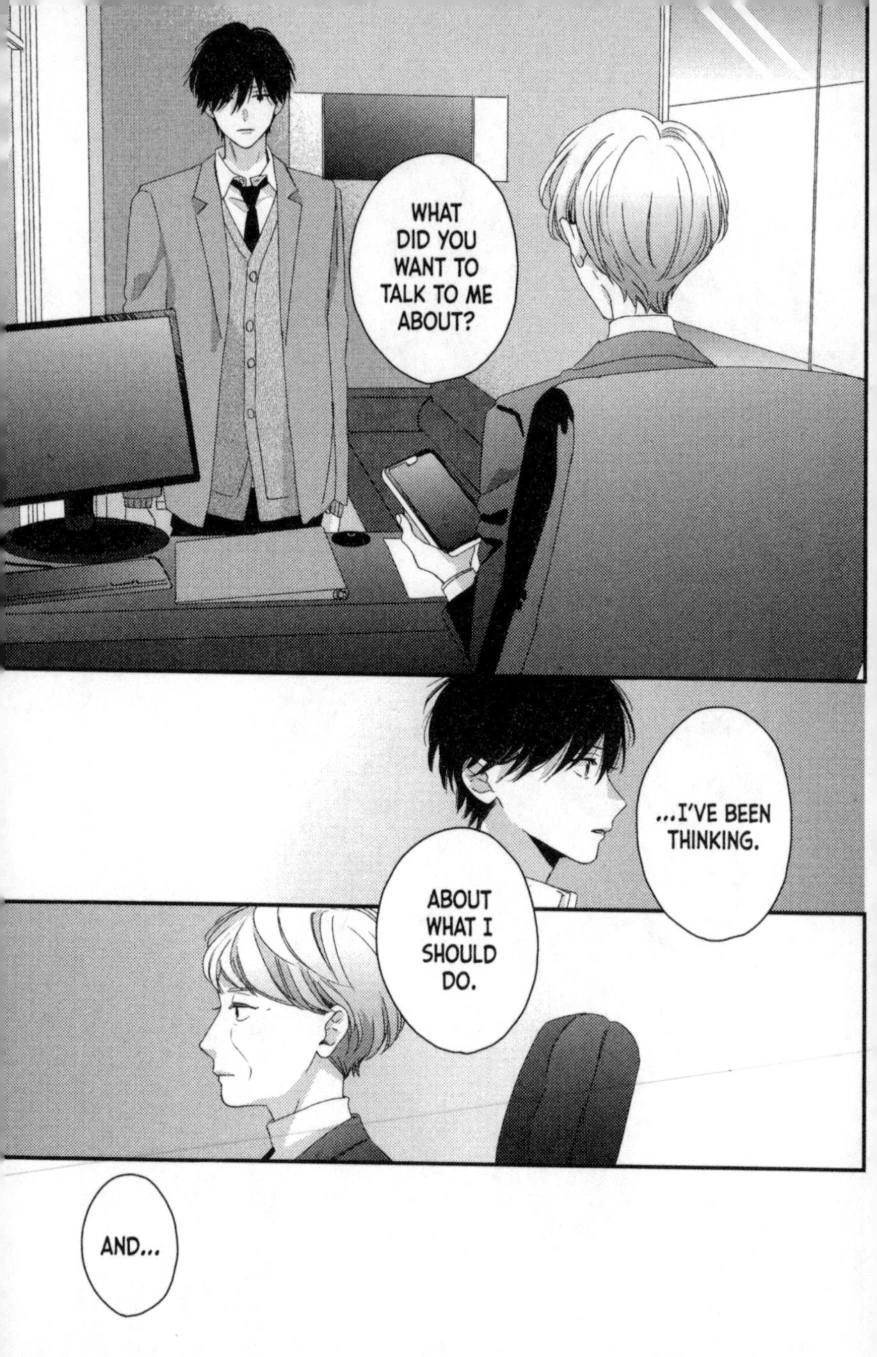
WHAT DID YOU WANT TO TALK TO ME ABOUT?
...I'VE BEEN THINKING.
ABOUT WHAT I SHOULD DO.
AND...

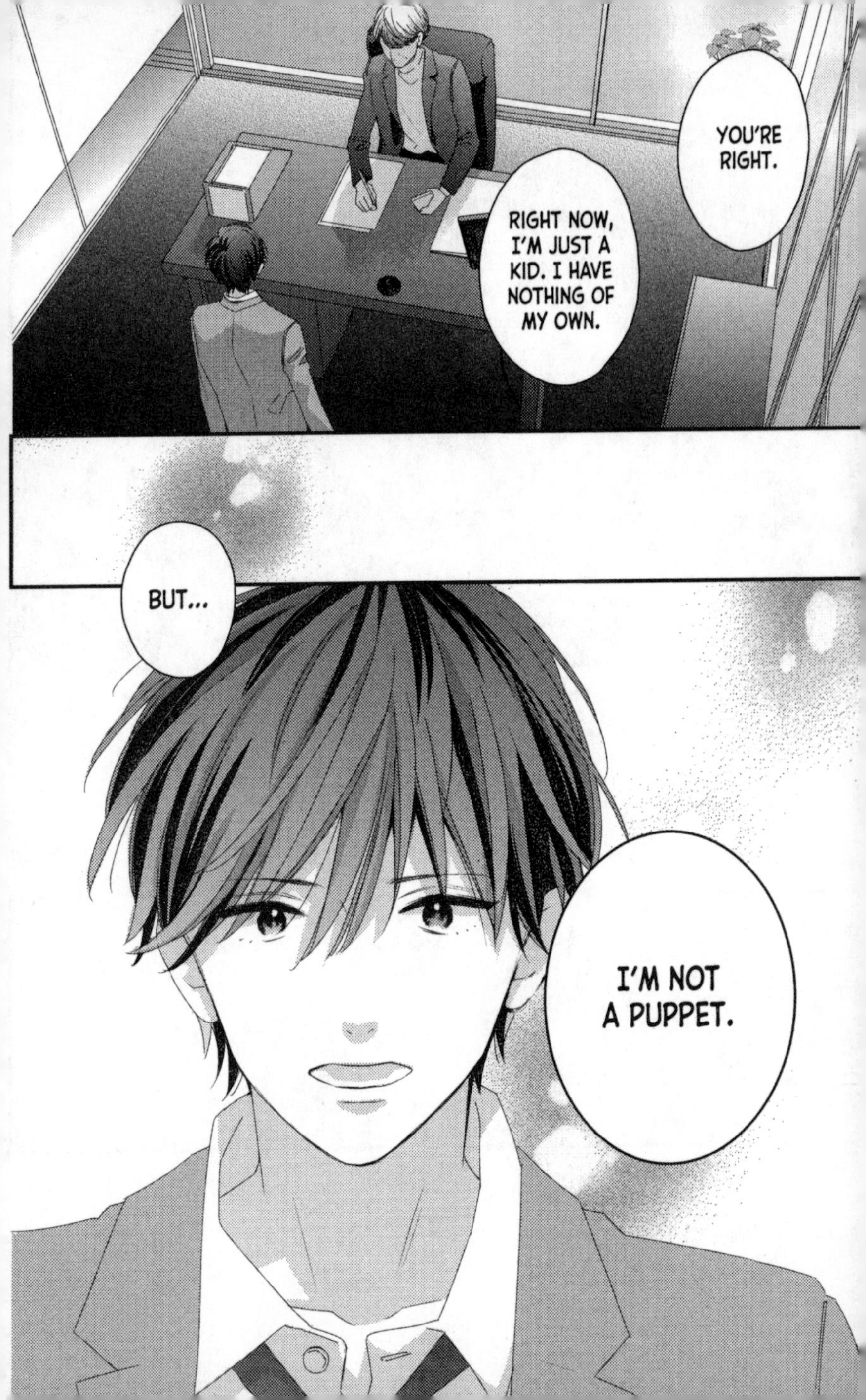
YOU'RE RIGHT.
RIGHT NOW, I'M JUST A KID. I HAVE NOTHING OF MY OWN.
BUT...
I'M NOT A PUPPET.

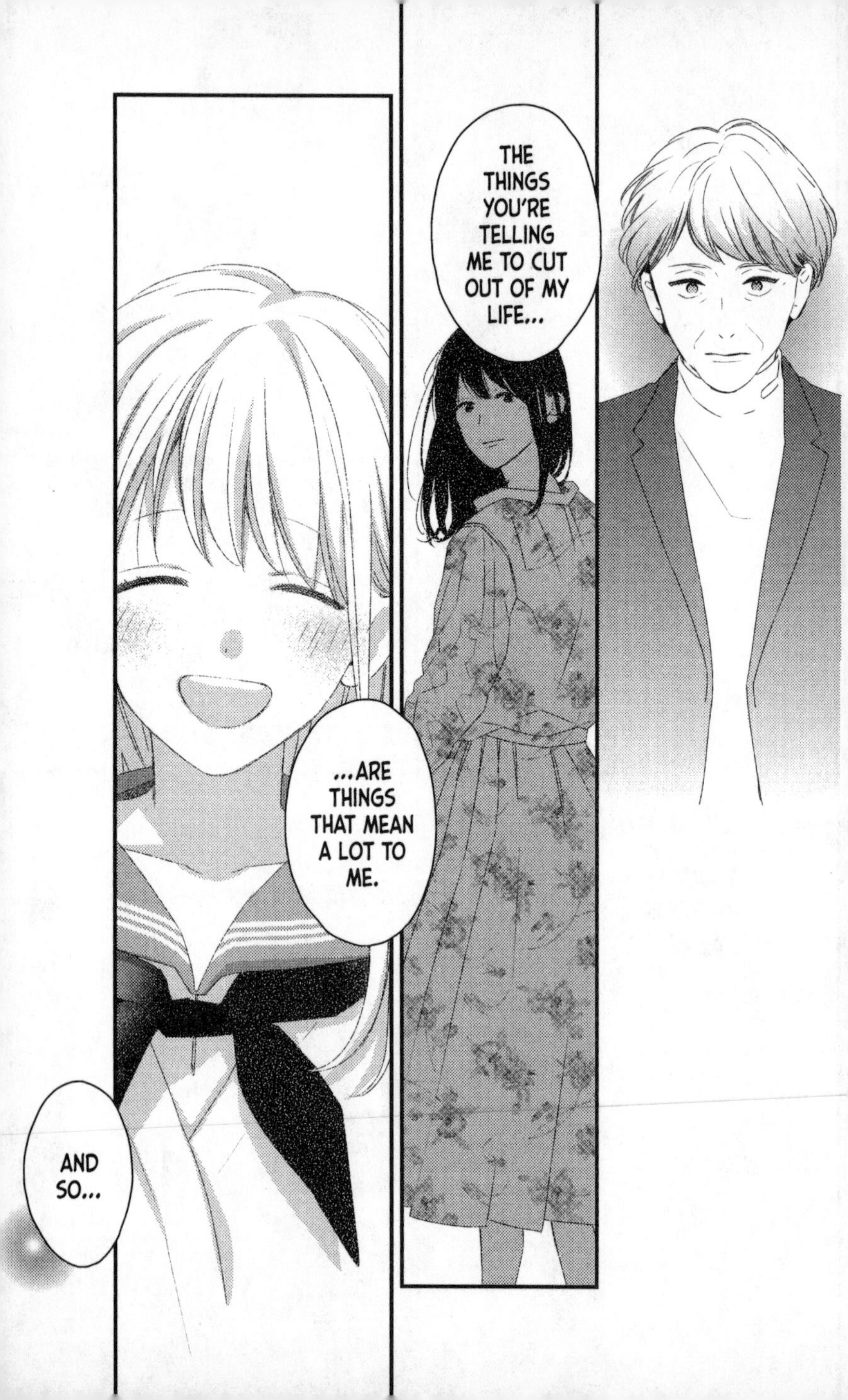
THE THINGS YOU'RE TELLING ME TO CUT OUT OF MY LIFE...
...ARE THINGS THAT MEAN A LOT TO ME.
AND SO...

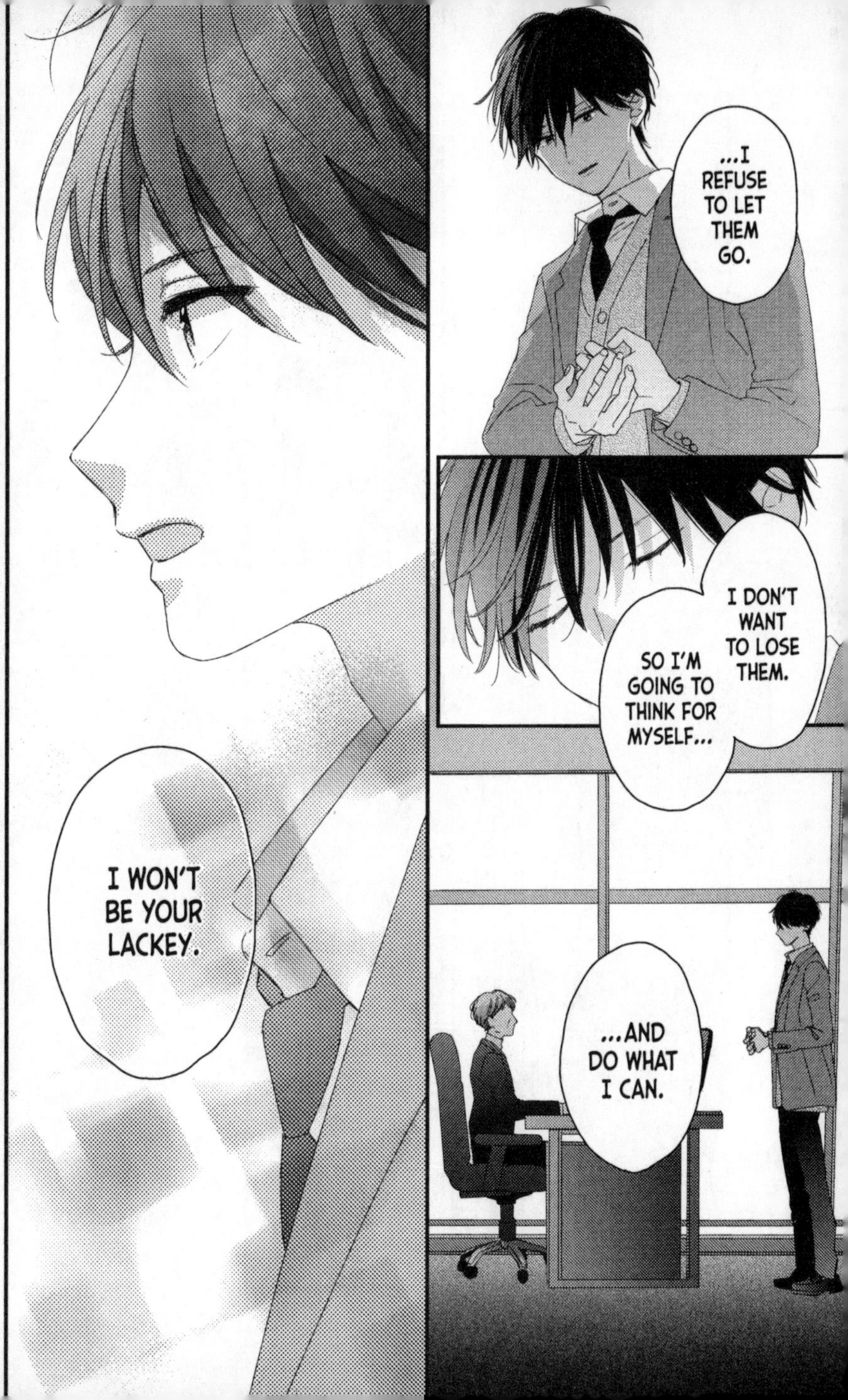
...I REFUSE TO LET THEM GO.
I DON'T WANT TO LOSE THEM.
SO I'M GOING TO THINK FOR MYSELF...
...AND DO WHAT I CAN.
I WON'T BE YOUR LACKEY.

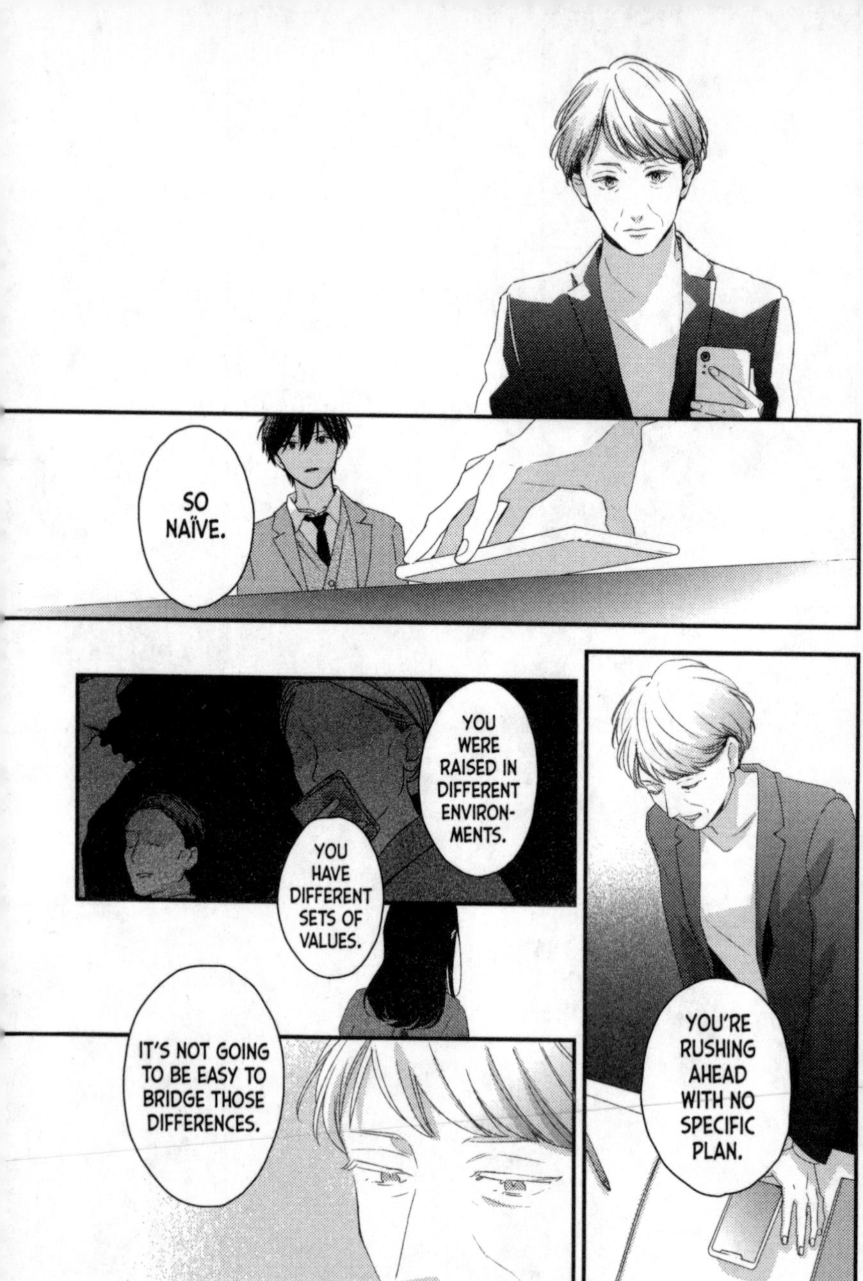
SO NAÏVE.
YOU'RE RUSHING AHEAD WITH NO SPECIFIC PLAN.
YOU WERE RAISED IN DIFFERENT ENVIRONMENTS.
YOU HAVE DIFFERENT SETS OF VALUES.
IT'S NOT GOING TO BE EASY TO BRIDGE THOSE DIFFERENCES.

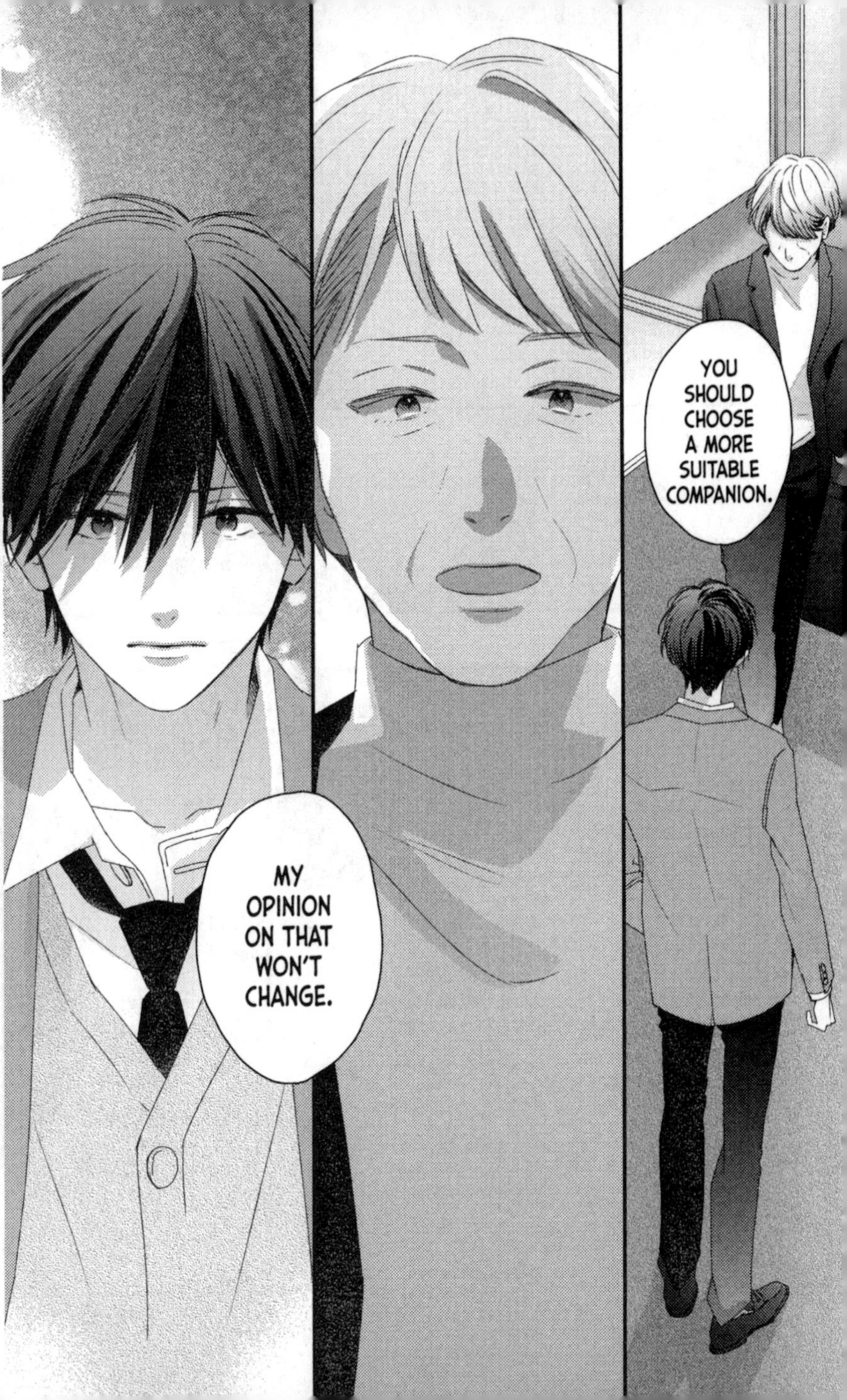
YOU SHOULD CHOOSE A MORE SUITABLE COMPANION.
MY OPINION ON THAT WON'T CHANGE.

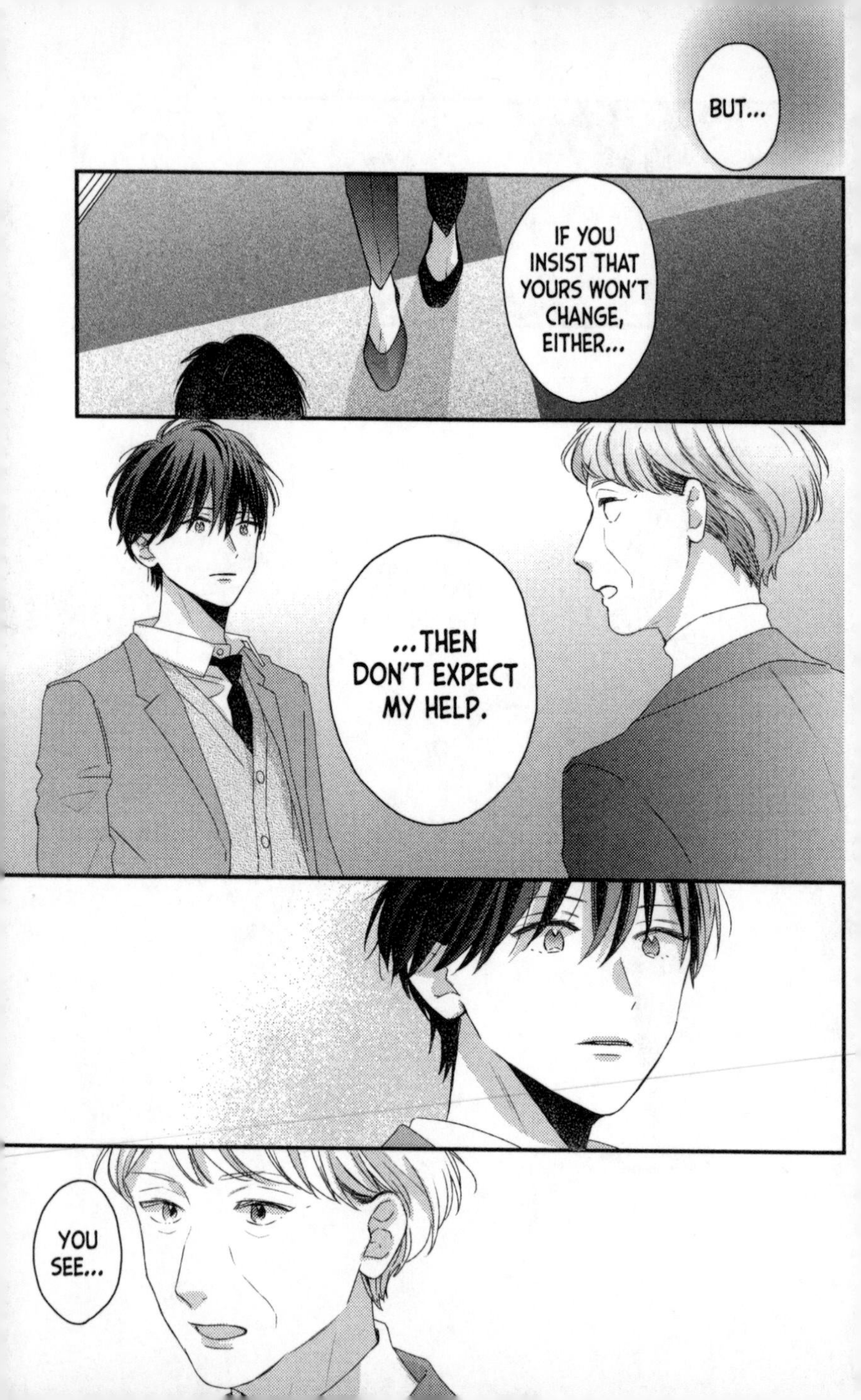
BUT...
IF YOU INSIST THAT YOURS WON'T CHANGE, EITHER...
...THEN DON'T EXPECT MY HELP.
YOU SEE...

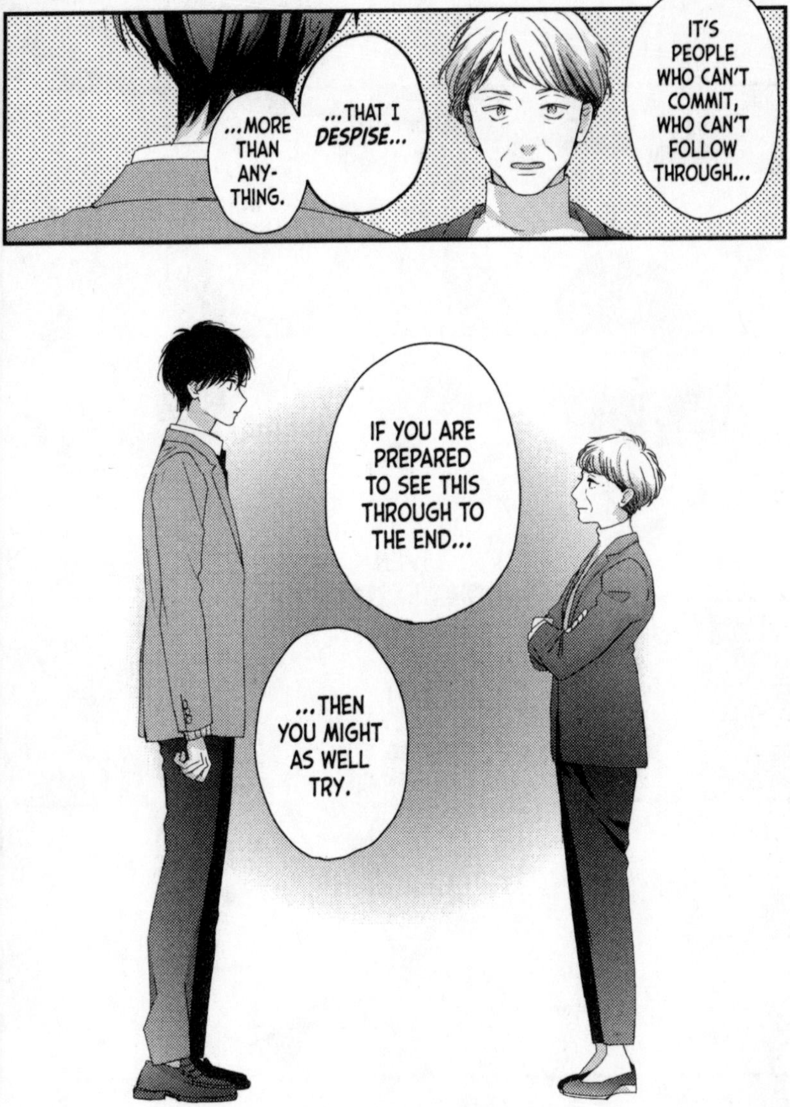
IT'S PEOPLE WHO CAN'T COMMIT, WHO CAN'T FOLLOW THROUGH...
...THAT I *DESPISE*...
...MORE THAN ANY-THING.
IF YOU ARE PREPARED TO SEE THIS THROUGH TO THE END...
...THEN YOU MIGHT AS WELL TRY.

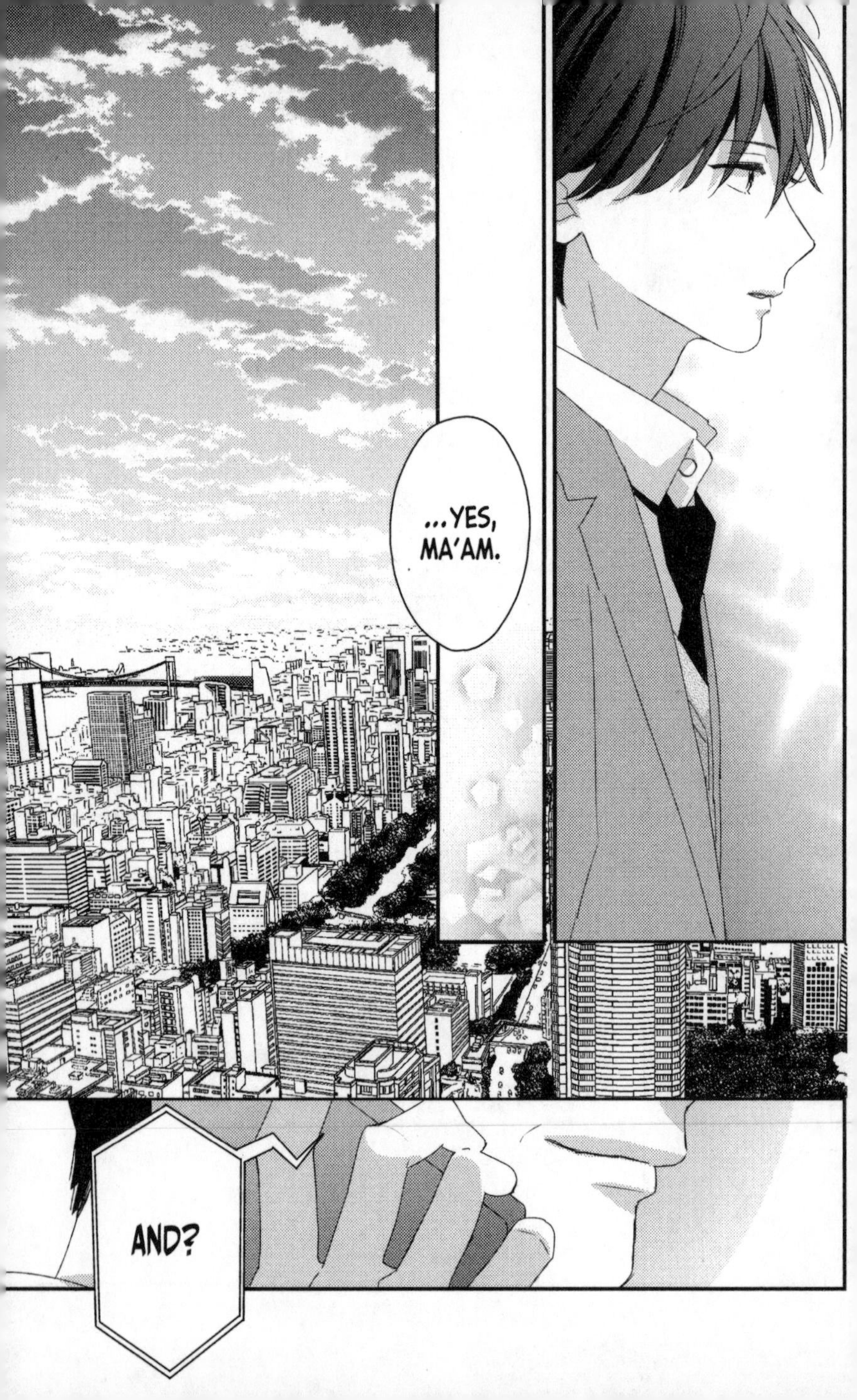
...YES, MA'AM.
AND?

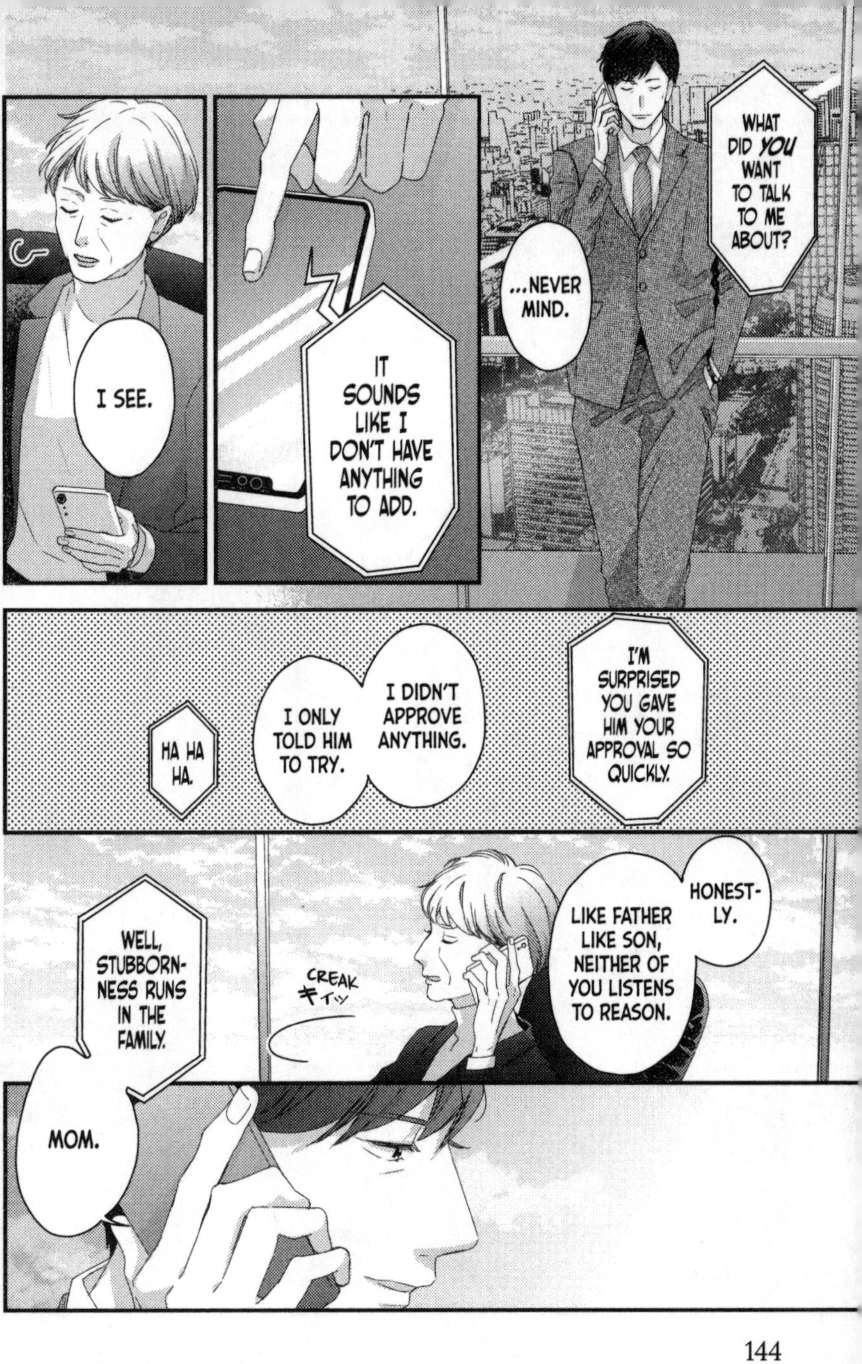
WHAT DID *YOU* WANT TO TALK TO ME ABOUT?
...NEVER MIND.
IT SOUNDS LIKE I DON'T HAVE ANYTHING TO ADD.
I SEE.
I'M SURPRISED YOU GAVE HIM YOUR APPROVAL SO QUICKLY.
I DIDN'T APPROVE ANYTHING.
I ONLY TOLD HIM TO TRY.
HA HA HA.
HONEST-LY.
LIKE FATHER LIKE SON, NEITHER OF YOU LISTENS TO REASON.
CREAK
キイッ
WELL, STUBBORN-NESS RUNS IN THE FAMILY.
MOM.

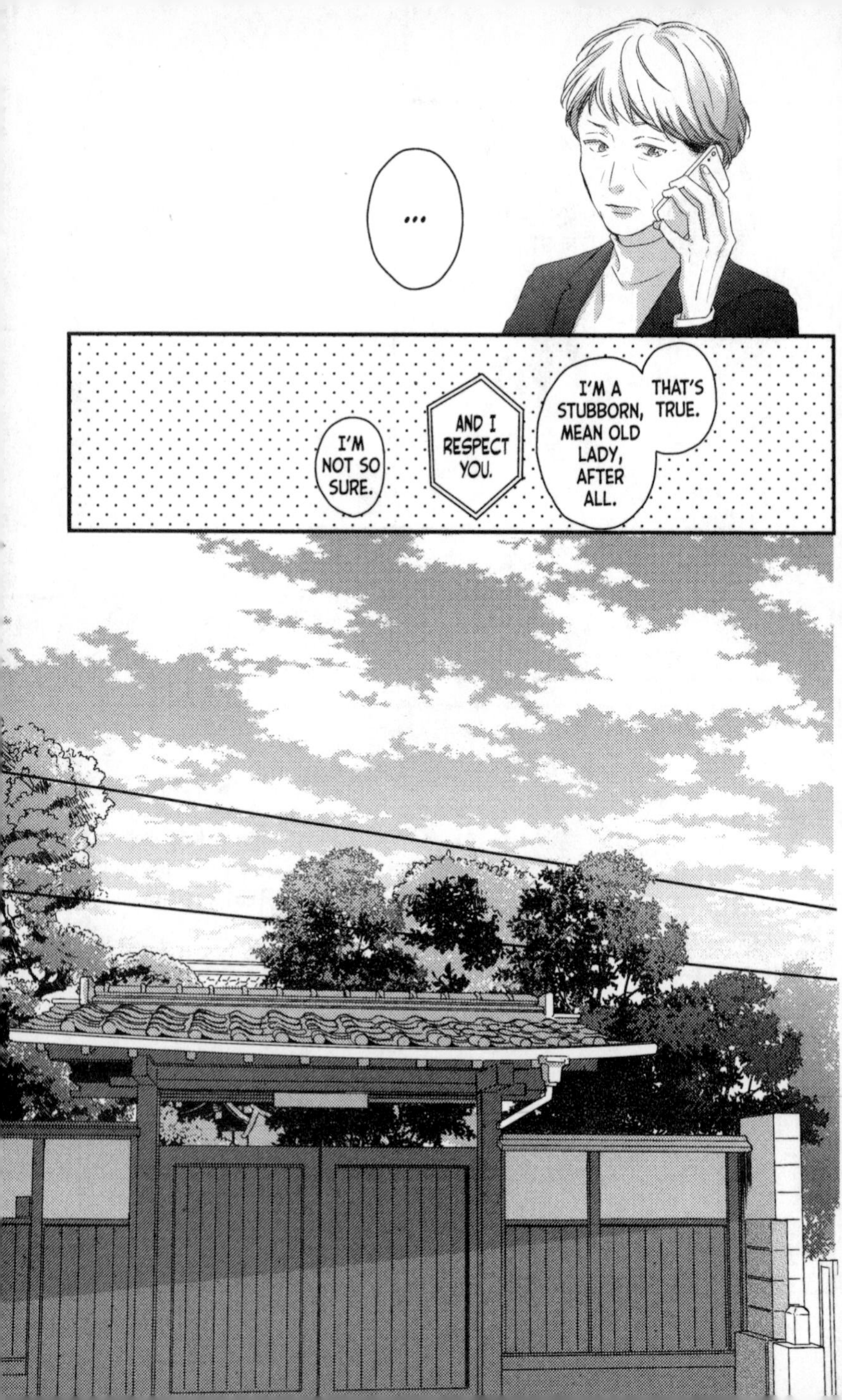
...
THAT'S TRUE.
I'M A STUBBORN, MEAN OLD LADY, AFTER ALL.
AND I RESPECT YOU.
I'M NOT SO SURE.

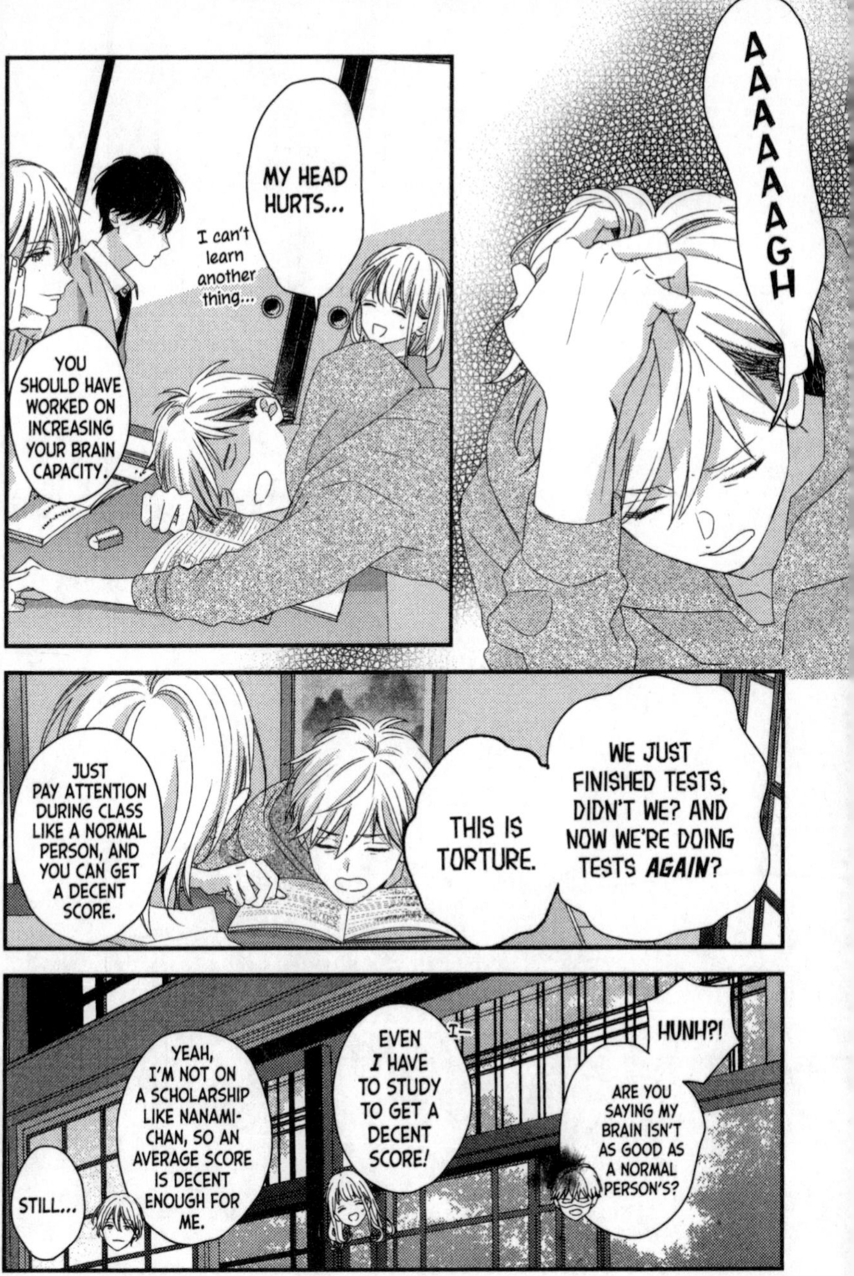
AAAAAAGH
MY HEAD HURTS...
I can't learn another thing...
YOU SHOULD HAVE WORKED ON INCREASING YOUR BRAIN CAPACITY.
WE JUST FINISHED TESTS, DIDN'T WE? AND NOW WE'RE DOING TESTS *AGAIN*?
THIS IS TORTURE.
JUST PAY ATTENTION DURING CLASS LIKE A NORMAL PERSON, AND YOU CAN GET A DECENT SCORE.
HUNH?!
ARE YOU SAYING MY BRAIN ISN'T AS GOOD AS A NORMAL PERSON'S?
I—
EVEN *I* HAVE TO STUDY TO GET A DECENT SCORE!
YEAH, I'M NOT ON A SCHOLARSHIP LIKE NANAMI-CHAN, SO AN AVERAGE SCORE IS DECENT ENOUGH FOR ME.
STILL...

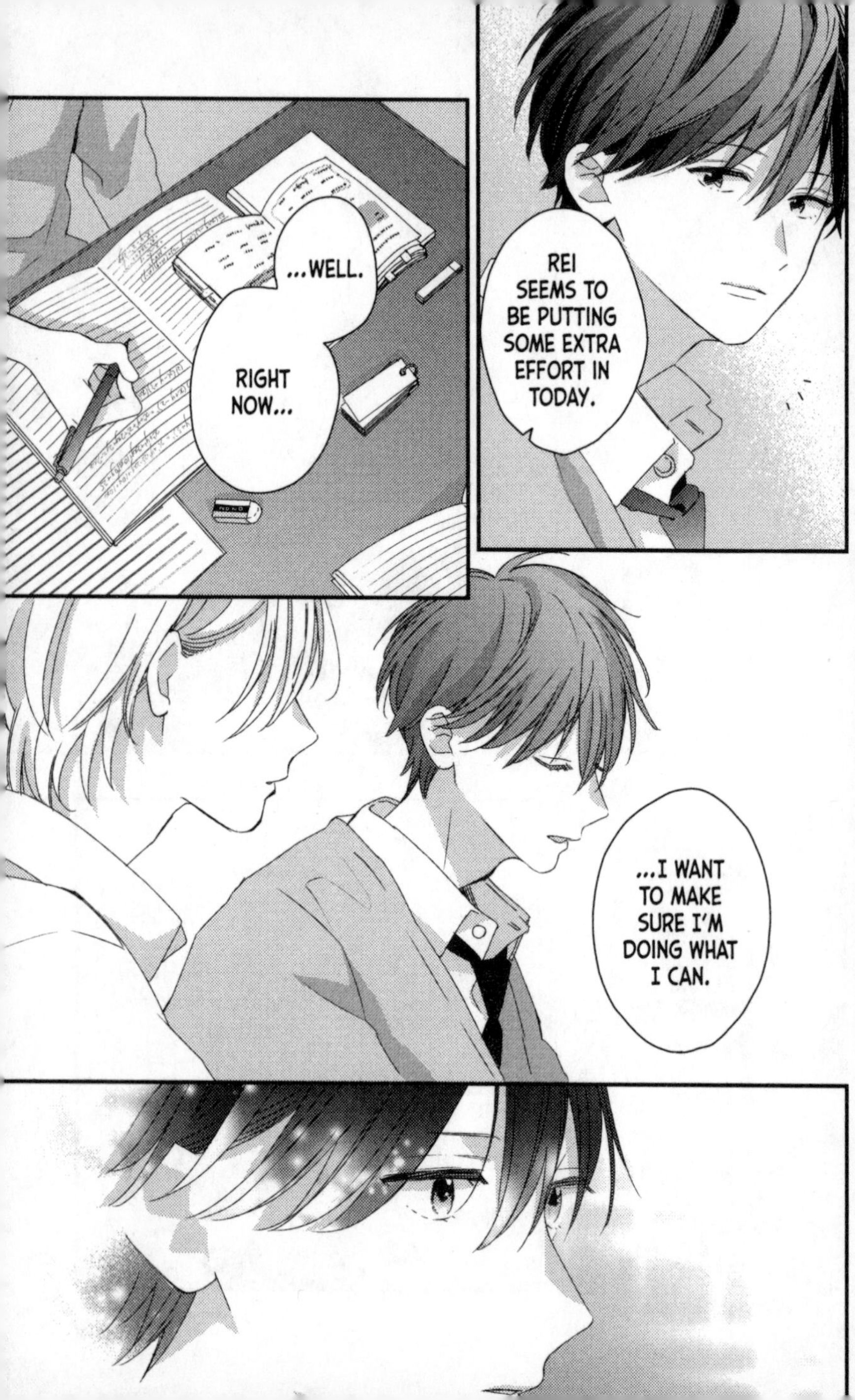
REI SEEMS TO BE PUTTING SOME EXTRA EFFORT IN TODAY.
...WELL.
RIGHT NOW...
...I WANT TO MAKE SURE I'M DOING WHAT I CAN.

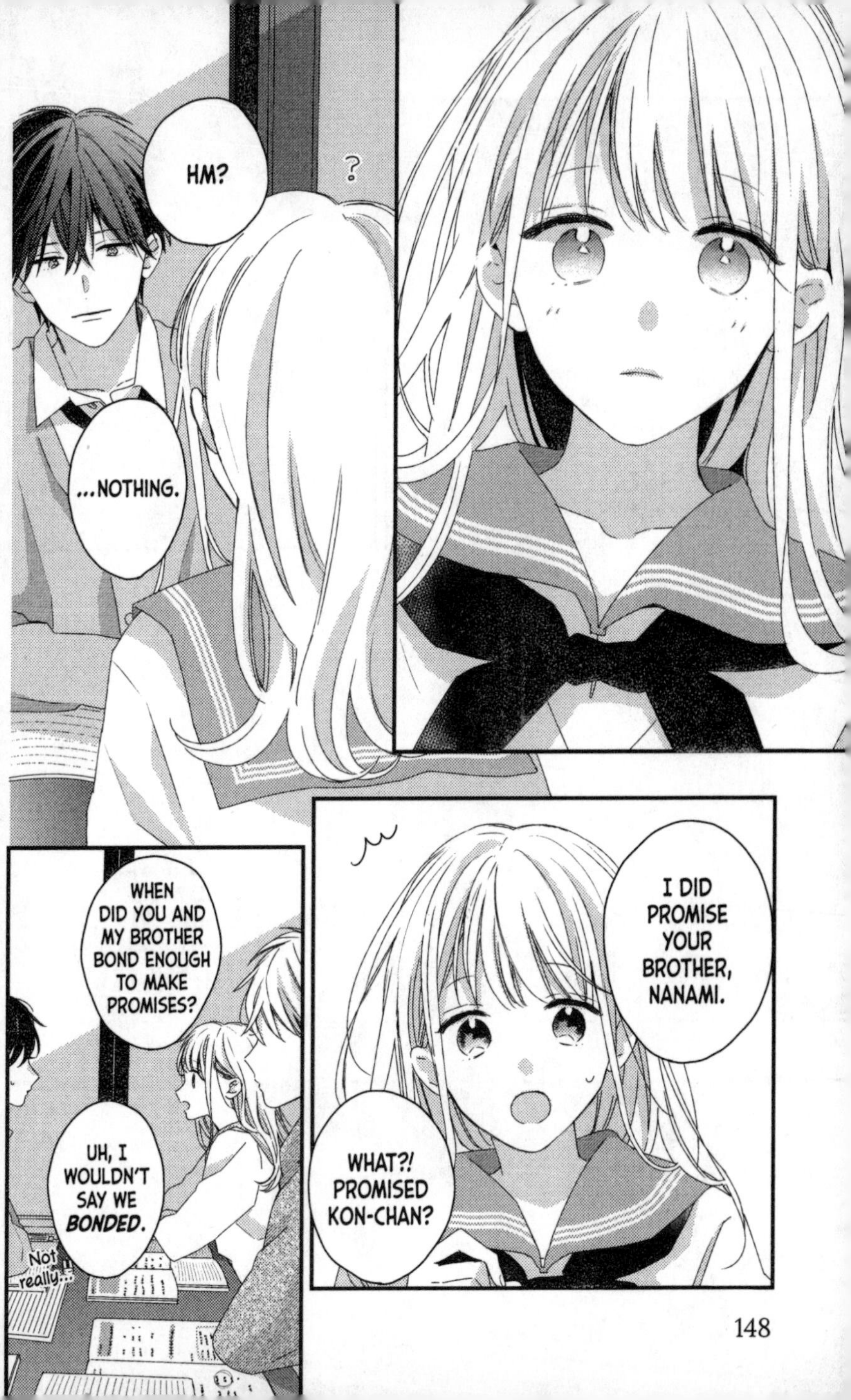
HM?
?
...NOTHING.
I DID PROMISE YOUR BROTHER, NANAMI.
WHAT?! PROMISED KON-CHAN?
WHEN DID YOU AND MY BROTHER BOND ENOUGH TO MAKE PROMISES?
UH, I WOULDN'T SAY WE *BONDED*.
Not really...

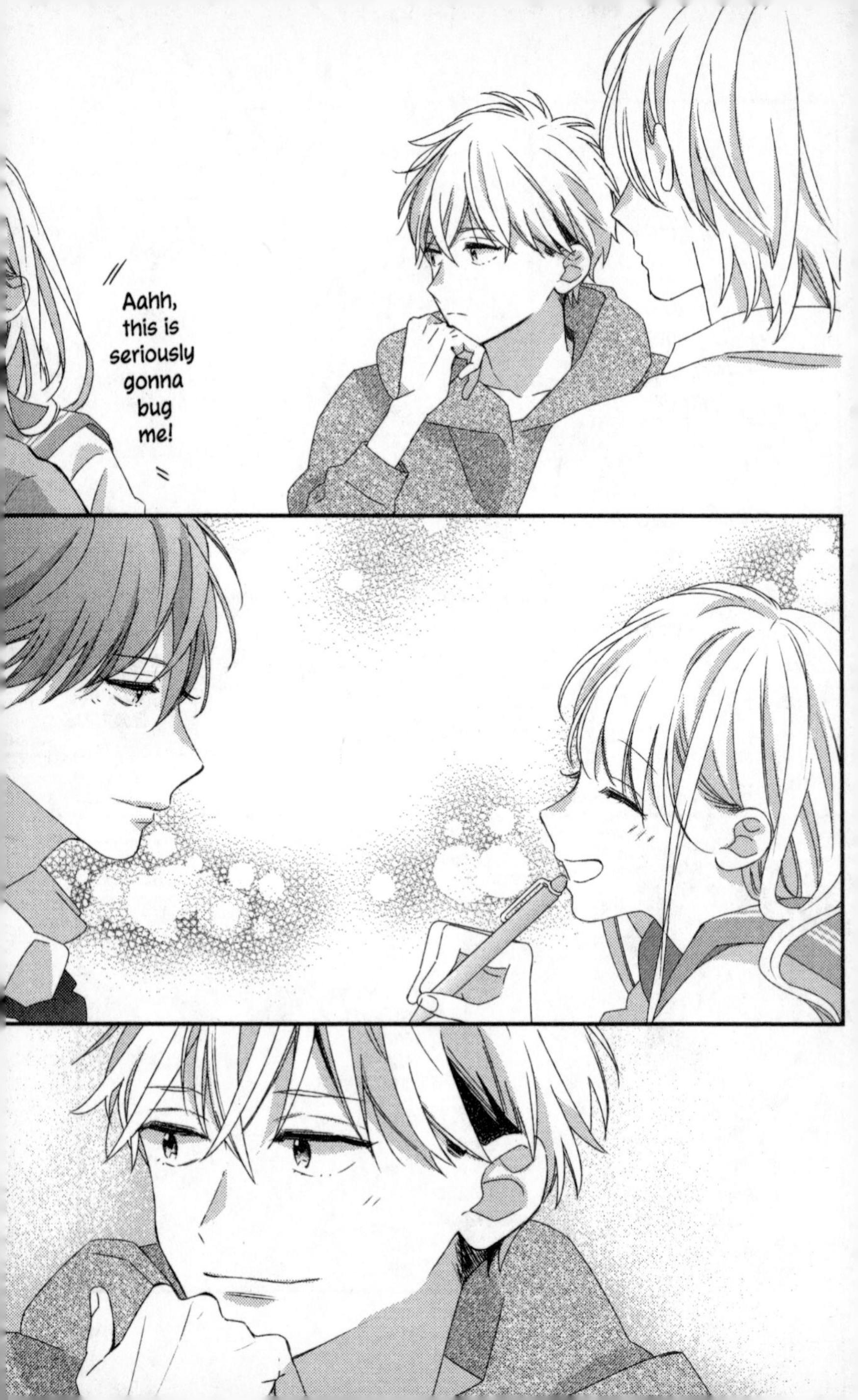
Aahh, this is seriously gonna bug me!

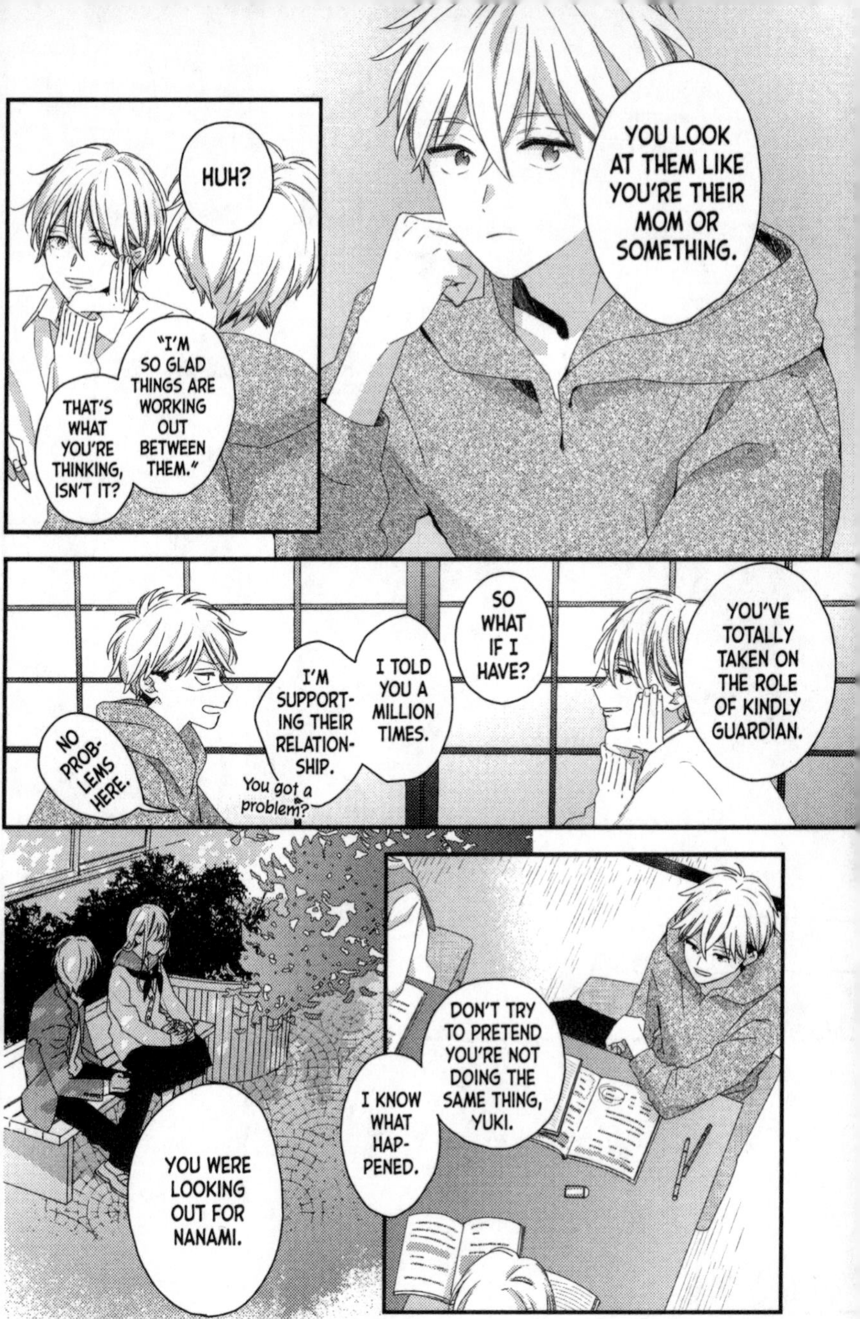
YOU LOOK AT THEM LIKE YOU'RE THEIR MOM OR SOMETHING.
HUH?
“I'M SO GLAD THINGS ARE WORKING OUT BETWEEN THEM.”
THAT'S WHAT YOU'RE THINKING, ISN'T IT?
YOU'VE TOTALLY TAKEN ON THE ROLE OF KINDLY GUARDIAN.
SO WHAT IF I HAVE?
I TOLD YOU A MILLION TIMES.
I'M SUPPORTING THEIR RELATIONSHIP.
You got a problem?
NO PROBLEMS HERE.
DON'T TRY TO PRETEND YOU'RE NOT DOING THE SAME THING, YUKI.
I KNOW WHAT HAPPENED.
YOU WERE LOOKING OUT FOR NANAMI.

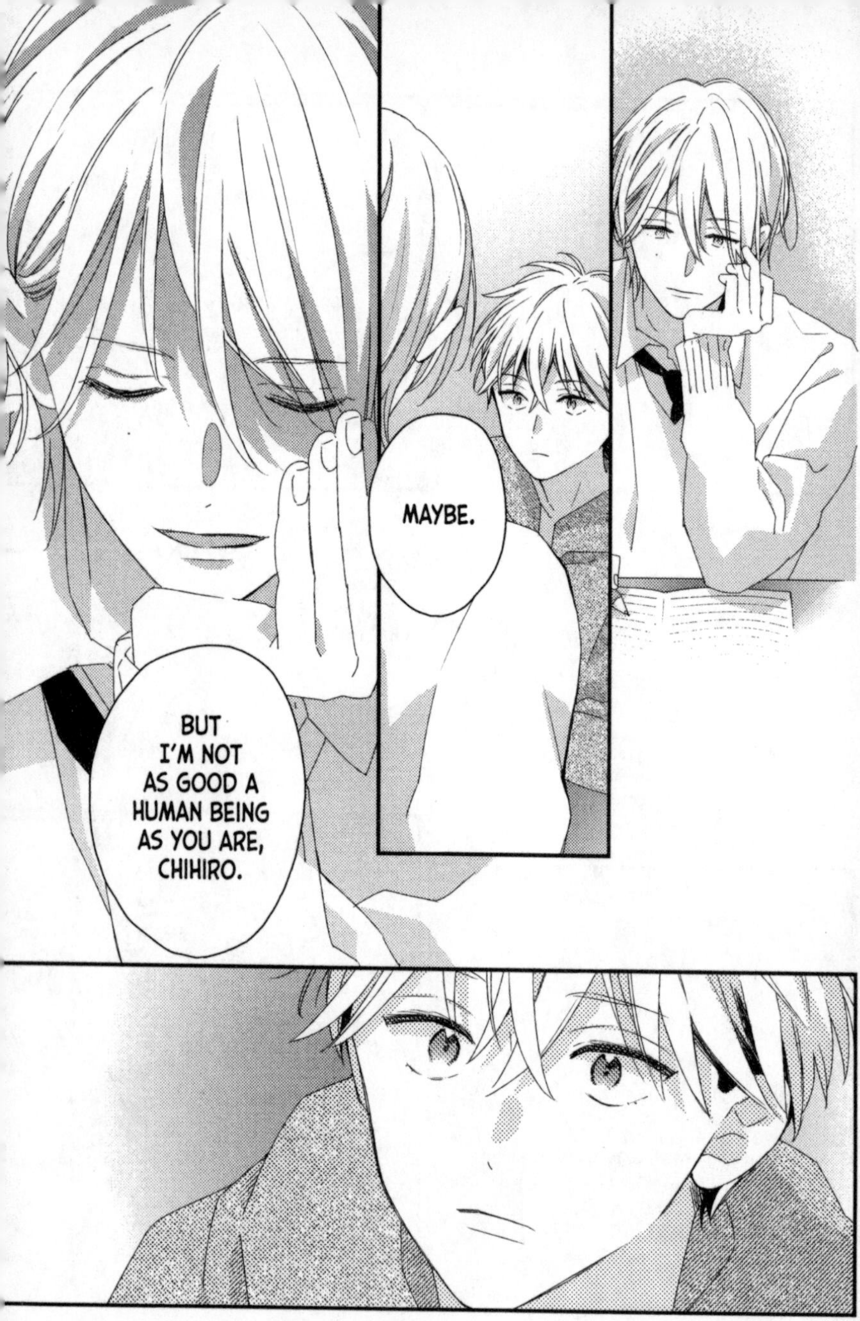
MAYBE.
BUT I'M NOT AS GOOD A HUMAN BEING AS YOU ARE, CHIHIRO.

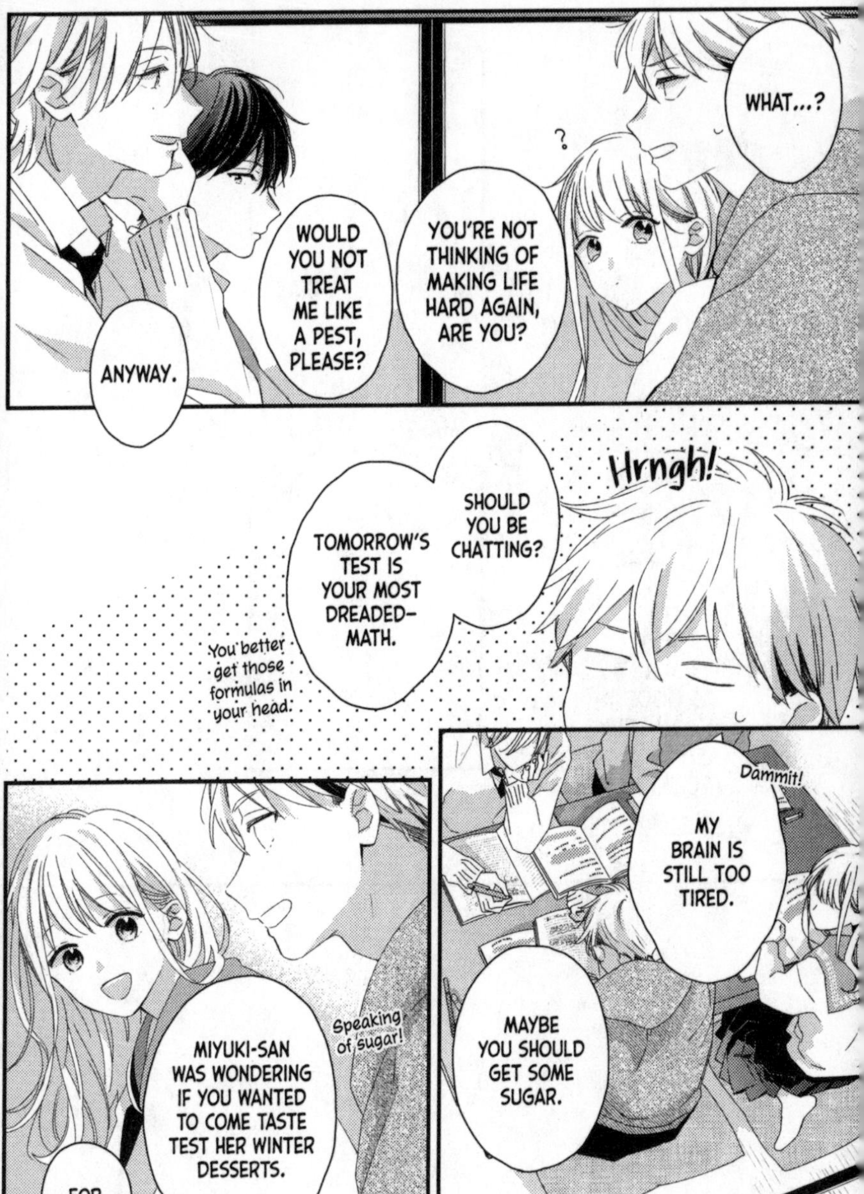
WHAT...?
?
YOU'RE NOT THINKING OF MAKING LIFE HARD AGAIN, ARE YOU?
WOULD YOU NOT TREAT ME LIKE A PEST, PLEASE?
ANYWAY.
Hrngh!
SHOULD YOU BE CHATTING?
TOMORROW'S TEST IS YOUR MOST DREADED—MATH.
You better get those formulas in your head.
Dammit!
MY BRAIN IS STILL TOO TIRED.
MAYBE YOU SHOULD GET SOME SUGAR.
Speaking of sugar!
MIYUKI-SAN WAS WONDERING IF YOU WANTED TO COME TASTE TEST HER WINTER DESSERTS.
FOR REAL?

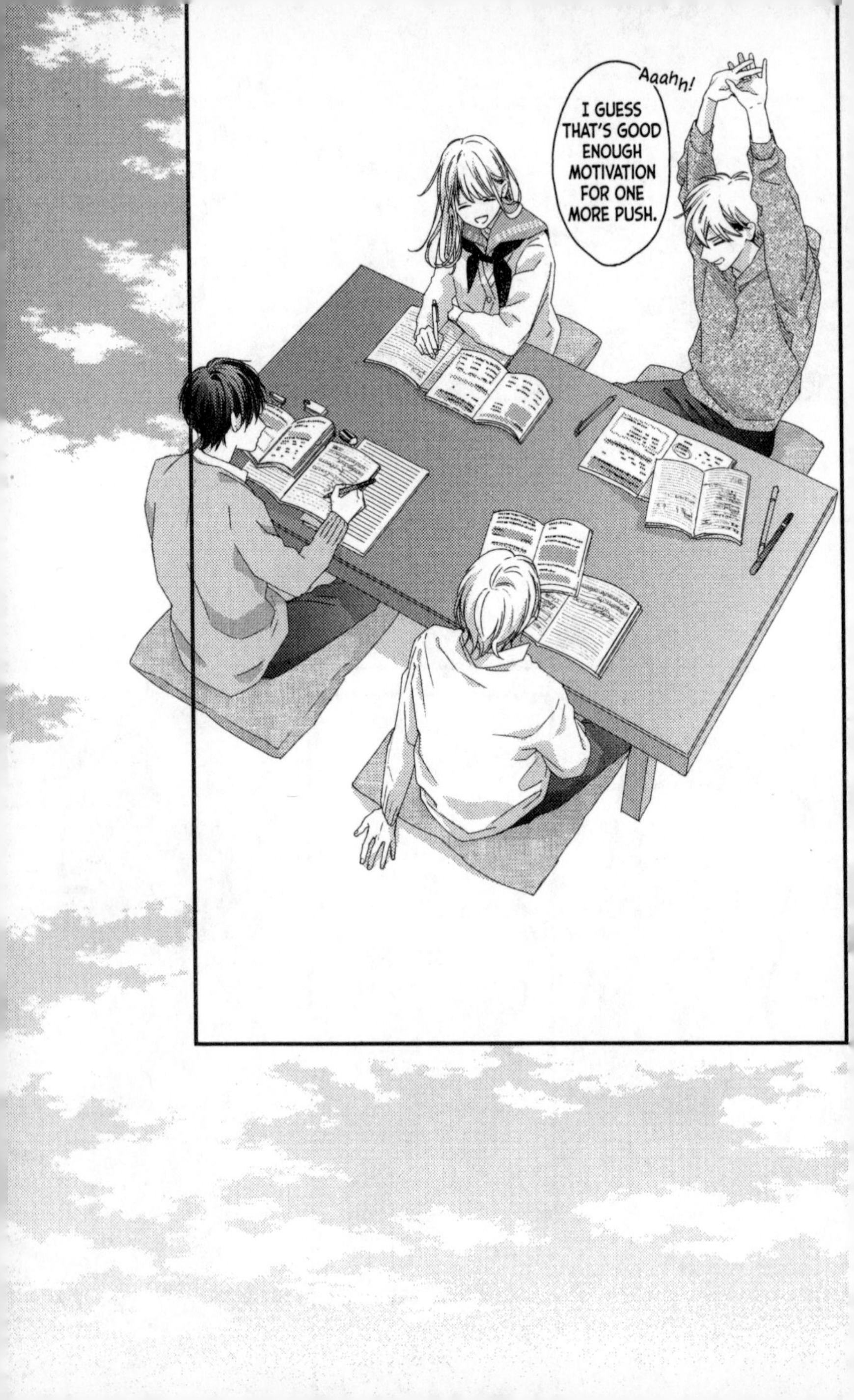
Aaahh!
I GUESS THAT'S GOOD ENOUGH MOTIVATION FOR ONE MORE PUSH.

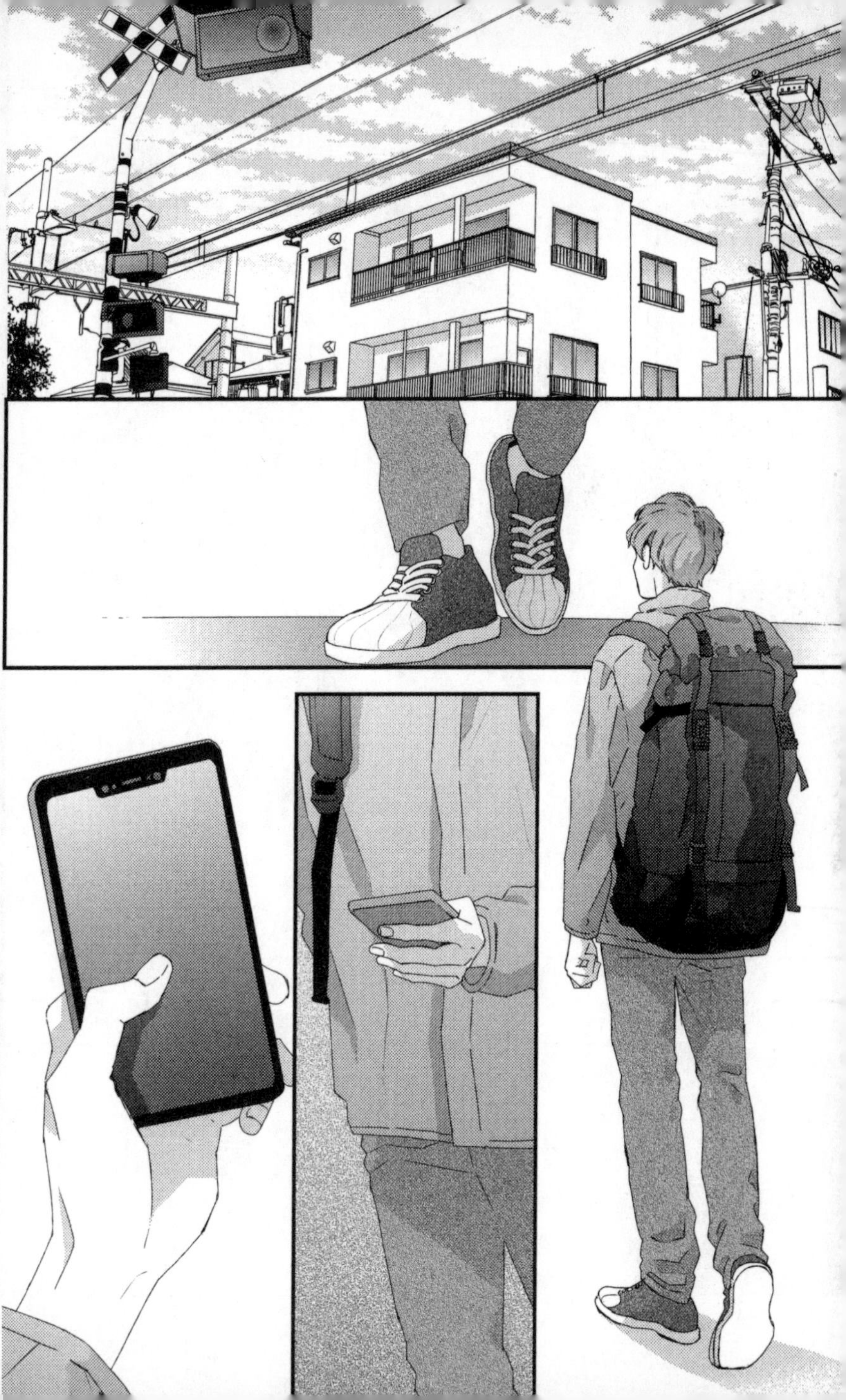

Just like last time...

Then, see here.

Right, right.

ヴーッ
ヴーッ

My phone...?

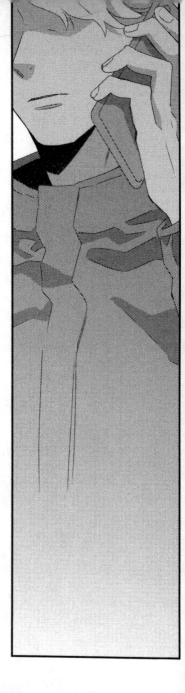

155

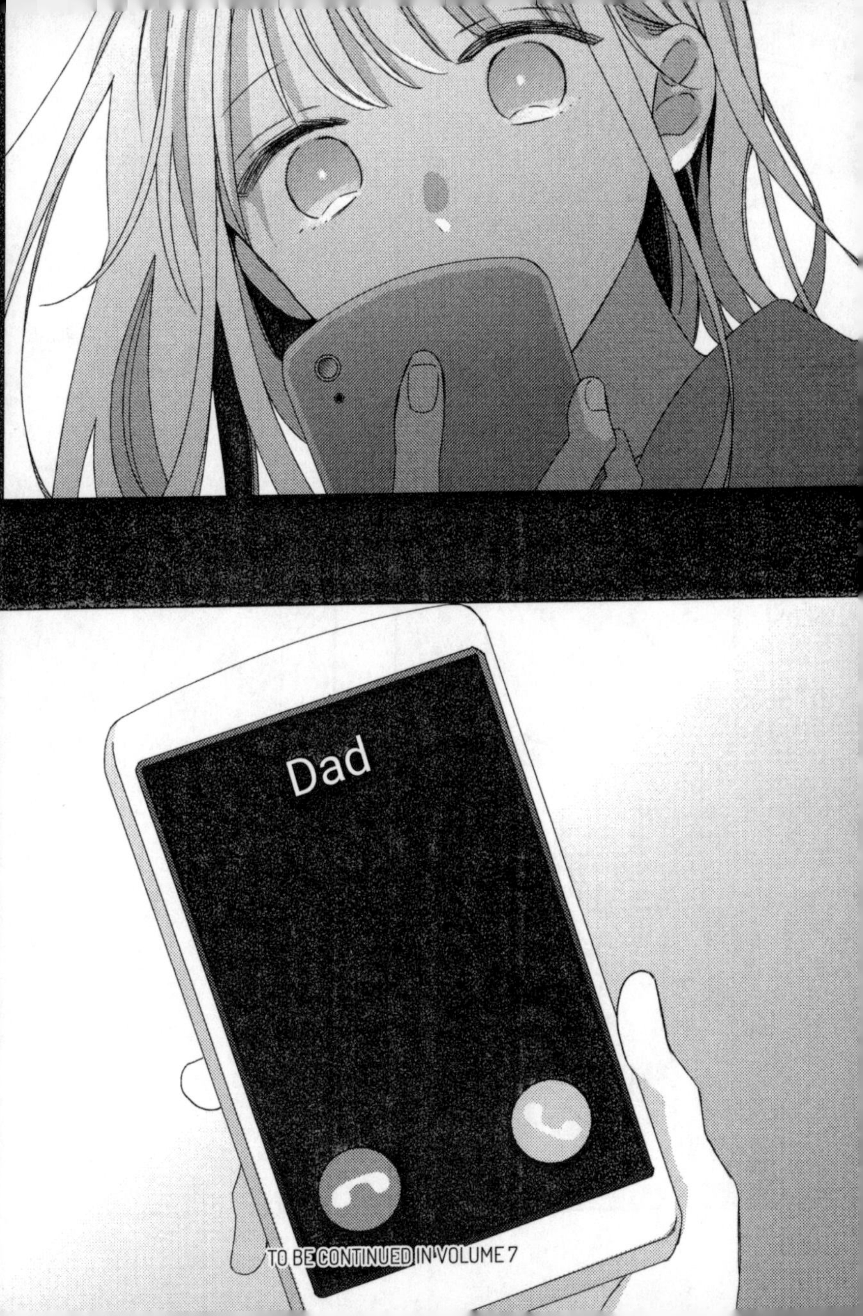
Dad
TO BE CONTINUED IN VOLUME 7

# Those Not-So-Sweet Boys

# THE TWINS AND KOTA

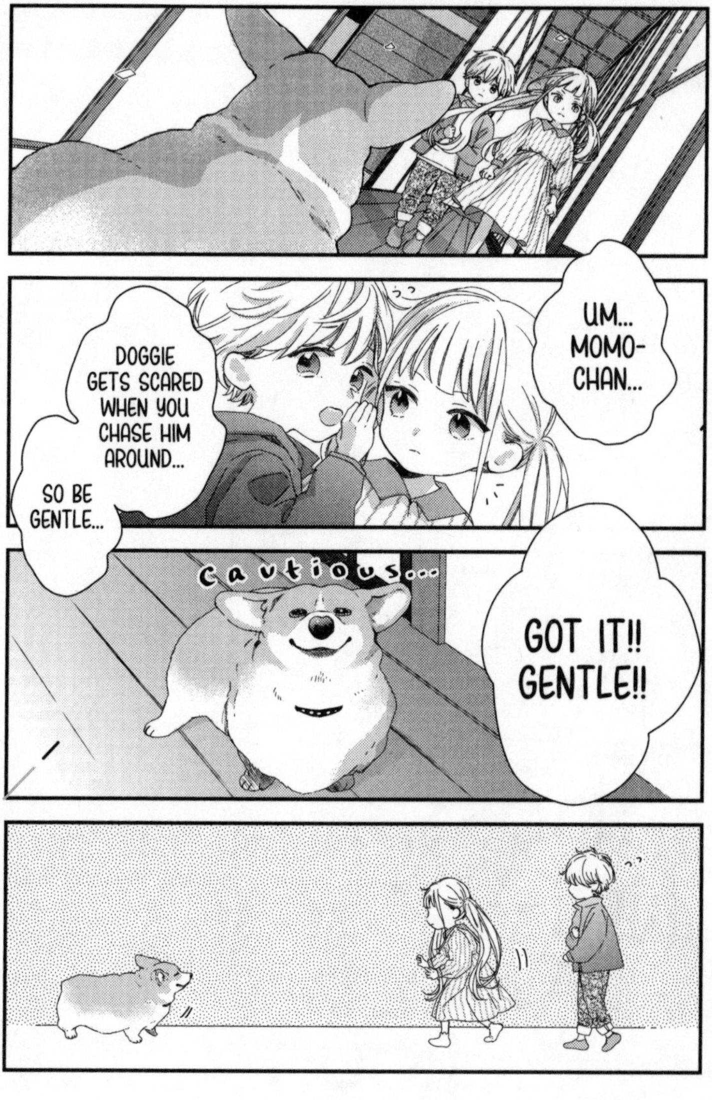
UM... MOMO-CHAN...
DOGGIE GETS SCARED WHEN YOU CHASE HIM AROUND...
SO BE GENTLE...
GOT IT!! GENTLE!!
cautious...

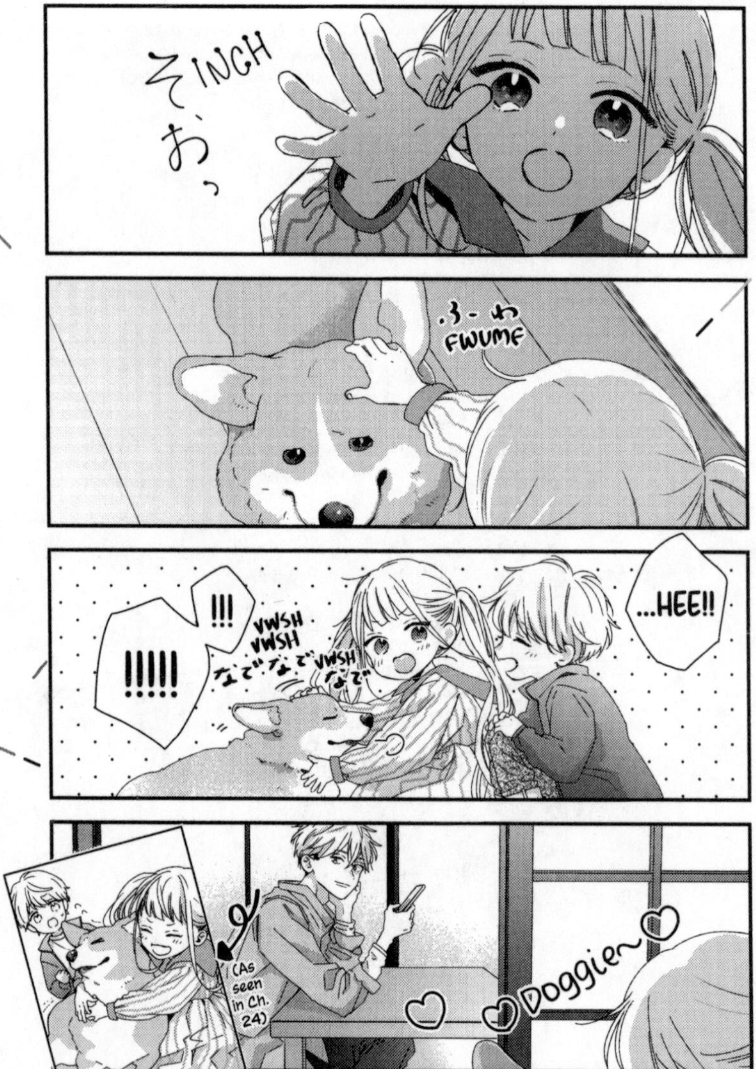
INCH
そおっ
ふーわ
FWUMF
...HEE!!
VWSH
VWSH
なでなで
VWSH
なで
!!!
!!!!!
Doggie~
(As seen in Ch. 24)

A Kodansha Comics Trade Paperback Original
*Those Not-So-Sweet Boys* 6 copyright © 2021 Yoko Nogiri
English translation copyright © 2022 Yoko Nogiri

Published in the United States by Kodansha Comics, an imprint of Kodansha USA Publishing, LLC, New York.

Publication rights for this English edition arranged through Kodansha Ltd., Tokyo.

First published in Japan in 2021 by Kodansha Ltd., Tokyo as *Amakunai Karera no Nichijo wa.*, volume 6.

ISBN 978-1-64651-362-8

Printed in the United States of America.

www.kodansha.us

1st Printing
Translation: Alethea Nibley & Athena Nibley
Lettering: Sara Linsley
Editing: Haruko Hashimoto
Kodansha Comics edition cover design by Phil Balsman

Publisher: Kiichiro Sugawara

Director of publishing services: Ben Applegate
Associate director, publishing operations: Stephen Pakula
Publishing services managing editors: Madison Salters, Alanna Ruse
Production managers: Emi Lotto, Angela Zurlo
Logo and character art ©Kodansha USA Publishing, LLC